The
EVERYTHING®

Personal Finance
in Your 20s & 30s Book

Dear Reader:

Are you on the road to financial freedom or do you need to take a U-turn? In four years of producing the Financial Planning Web site for About.com (*financialplan.about.com*), I've heard the same lament over and over from visitors to the site: "I don't know how to do a budget that works. I don't know how to get out of debt. I don't know how to save money." The feeling of helplessness that so many people experience when it comes to money makes it difficult for them to take control and turn their finances around.

In this book, you'll find solutions to these and other issues, written in plain English. You'll acquire a strong foundation for taking control of your finances, and you'll learn to use your money, whether it's a little or a lot, to reach the goals that matter most to you.

Deborah Fowles

The EVERYTHING® Series

Editorial

Publishing Director	Gary M. Krebs
Managing Editor	Kate McBride
Copy Chief	Laura MacLaughlin
Acquisitions Editor	Bethany Brown
Development Editor	Julie Gutin
Production Editor	Khrysti Nazzaro

Production

Production Director	Susan Beale
Production Manager	Michelle Roy Kelly
Series Designers	Daria Perreault
	Colleen Cunningham
Cover Design	Paul Beatrice
	Frank Rivera
Layout and Graphics	Colleen Cunningham
	Rachael Eiben
	Michelle Roy Kelly
	Daria Perreault
	Erin Ring
Series Cover Artist	Barry Littmann

Visit the entire Everything® Series at everything.com

THE
EVERYTHING®
PERSONAL FINANCE
IN YOUR 20s & 30s
BOOK

Erase your debt, personalize your budget,
and plan now to secure your future

Debby Fowles

Adams Media
Avon, Massachusetts

To Badger

—————

An Everything® Series Book.
Everything® and everything.com® are registered trademarks of F+W Publications, Inc.

Published by Adams Media, an F+W Publications Company
57 Littlefield Street, Avon, MA 02322 U.S.A.
www.adamsmedia.com

ISBN 13: 978-1-58062-970-6
ISBN 10: 1-58062-970-9
Printed in the United States of America.

J I H G F

Library of Congress Cataloging-in-Publication Data
Fowles, Debby.
The everything personal finance in your 20s & 30s book / Debby Fowles.
p.   cm.
(An everything series book)
ISBN 1-58062-970-9
1. Generation X—United States—Finance, Personal.
2. Finance, Personal—United States. 3. Investments—United States.
I. Title: Everything personal finance in your twenties and thirties book.
II. Title. III. Series: Everything series.
HG181.F713 2003
332.024'0562—dc21
2003011086

This book is available at quantity discounts for bulk purchases.
For information, call 1-800-289-0963.

Contents

11 Buying a Home / 143

12 Living with a Mortgage / 159

13 Getting Deals on Wheels / 173

14 Marriage and Family / 189

15 Unwed but Not Unwise / 205

Acknowledgments

I owe much to my parents, who taught me how to squeeze six cents out of every nickel, and my grandmother, who taught me to "save the pennies, and the dollars will save themselves."

I'd like to thank Barb Doyen for "finding" me and believing in me.

Top Ten
Personal Finance Tips

1. Make the effort to educate yourself about personal finance. Read financial magazines and good financial books and use well-known, reputable sites on the Internet.

2. Budget! Operating without a budget is like driving a car without a steering wheel. You don't have control over where you're headed.

3. Save the pennies, and the dollars will save themselves. Lots of small amounts add up to big savings.

4. Pay cash. If you can't afford to pay cash, maybe you can't afford to buy.

5. Always think about opportunity costs. You may not be paying for something directly, but giving up the opportunity to make money is a real cost.

6. If possible, take savings out of your paycheck before you see it. After a while you'll get used to planning your spending on the lower amount, while your savings grow.

7. Be a smart shopper. Don't buy cheap items that won't last and don't pay for bells and whistles that you don't need and won't use.

8. Know how to recognize the warning signs of too much debt and if you see yourself headed for trouble, act quickly, before you ruin your credit record.

9. Don't go without some type of medical insurance, even if you can only afford a policy with a very high deductible. If you become ill or are injured in an accident, the medical bills could ruin you financially.

10. Remember, most millionaires are just average people who practiced sound financial principles like those in this book. You could be one of them.

Introduction

▶ AVERAGE AMERICANS SPEND more time shopping each week than they spend playing with their kids. More Americans file for bankruptcy each year than graduate from college. We work longer, have less time for families, are deeper in debt, and are more stressed out.

It's so easy to spend all that you make, no matter how much that is. You naturally want all that your parents have, yet you may forget that it took them many years to get it. Like many people, you may also use money to satisfy emotional needs. Money may represent love, power, control, or security. Add the advertisers' messages that movies, television, magazines, and the Internet bombard you with to entice you into spending your hard-earned money on the "thing" of the moment, and it's no wonder you get caught up in having it all. Ironically, you could end up with little or nothing instead.

Studies show that the average high school graduate lacks fundamental money management skills and a basic understanding of earning, spending, and saving money. These concepts aren't being taught in our schools and young people aren't learning them from their parents, either because the parents don't understand them themselves or don't realize the importance of teaching them to their kids. That leaves it up to you to teach yourself sound personal-finance principles if you don't want to stumble through your life by trial and error.

How do you go about doing this? How do you learn how to save money and make it grow? How do you evaluate offers and deals and make wise choices? If you practice the basic personal-finance guidelines and concepts outlined in this book, you can become financially savvy and financially secure. You can learn to avoid the financial mistakes that can have such a negative impact on your future and your relationships. This book will show you how to live more simply, save more money, spend less, avoid impulse spending and credit card debt, stick to a realistic spending plan (budget), and plan for your retirement—without making huge sacrifices while you're doing it.

Your twenties are the best time to develop good personal-finance habits, before you get into debt that you'd have to struggle to pay off or make other financial mistakes that you'd spend years recovering from. In your thirties, it's still not too late to turn your financial life around if you're not on the right track.

There is little that's more rewarding than seeing your financial goals and dreams becoming a reality. Controlling your money instead of letting your money control you gives you a sense of empowerment and self-esteem. Watching your investments grow and knowing you have a nest egg to fall back on gives you a sense of security. In the end, you don't really give up anything of lasting importance. You gain everything that really matters to you.

If you're not too deeply in debt yet, your rapid progress will be its own reward. If you *are* deeply in debt, you'll have to work at it harder and longer, but it can be work that's empowering, stress relieving, and even fun. It all comes down to balance and making smart decisions about money. It gets easier with practice and is hugely rewarding, both financially and emotionally. Why not get started now?

Chapter 1

Setting Goals: Your Financial Road Map

All successful organizations have short- and long-term goals and a written plan for reaching them, and if you want to be financially successful, so should you. The first steps are to determine your financial status today and then decide what you want to achieve for your future and how you're going to accomplish it.

Why Financial Goals Are Important

You wouldn't start out on a long trip into unfamiliar territory without a road map, yet many people go through life without a concrete plan for their financial future. The road to financial freedom can lead directly to your destination or to a dead end. Specific financial goals and written plans for meeting them help you focus your efforts on the end result.

Goals are like the wheels on your car; they keep you moving in the direction you want to go, and you won't get very far without them. If you haven't already started planning for your future, now's the time to begin, no matter what your age. If you're in your twenties, however, you have a distinct advantage. Saving and investing in your twenties will give you the most powerful financial tool available: time. You'll have to work at it a lot harder if you start later in life. In fact, the smartest thing you can do in your twenties is save and invest. Ultimately, you'll have to save and invest a lot less money at a time and will still come out far ahead of the person who starts a decade or two later.

As the saying goes, "Most people don't plan to fail, they just fail to plan." Without planning, even the best of intentions lead nowhere. Start mapping out your route now. Your entire future depends on it.

Starting in your twenties is a huge advantage. If you invest $5,000 at the age of twenty, and it earns 7 percent per year, at retirement (age sixty-five) it will total over $115,000. The same amount invested at the age of forty would total less than $29,000.

Calculating Net Worth: Your Financial Snapshot

As with any road map, before you can determine how to get from here to there, you need to know where "here" is. Where do you stand financially? Answering this critical question is the job of the Net Worth Statement.

The Net Worth Statement is very simple in concept. Your net worth is the difference between all the things of value that you own and all the debts you owe, or in financial terms, your assets minus your liabilities. Your Net Worth Statement is a list of each of these items and their current value or balance.

Why You Need a Net Worth Statement

The Net Worth Statement gives you a snapshot of your financial condition at this moment in time. You need this information in order to effectively set the financial goals that you'll be working toward, assess your progress along the way, and make adjustments, using the important clues gleaned from updating your Net Worth Statement on a regular basis. It will also come in handy when applying for a mortgage, credit card, or car loan.

ALERT!

Learn about the magic of compounding (see Chapter 3). The longer you let your money earn interest, the more powerfully compounding works for you. That's why it's so important to start saving and investing in your twenties and thirties.

Sometimes people avoid making a list of their debts because they're afraid they won't like what they find or they believe they already have a good "gut feel" for their overall financial picture. However, burying your head in the sand like the proverbial ostrich won't get you far, and gut feelings can be way off the mark. Not having a handle on your financial condition can seriously hurt you in a time of crisis, like a job loss or disability, and it's difficult if not impossible to plan for the future if you don't know where you are today.

How to Prepare a Net Worth Statement

Start by listing all the things of value that you own, even if you owe money on them, like your house and cars. Use their full value as of today. The balances of the loans related to these assets will be included in the liabilities section, so your equity in the assets you list won't be overstated. For bonds, stock options, and retirement accounts, use the current value, not the value at maturity or the value on the date you're fully vested. You should receive statements showing the current value of your accounts from your employer for retirement accounts and from your broker for bonds. The human resources department where you work can help you determine the current value of your company stock options if you're lucky enough to have them.

List only those life insurance policies that have a cash value. Most life insurance policies are provided by employers and are term policies good only for the time you're employed by that company. These are not considered assets. If you've purchased cash value life insurance from an agent and you're unsure of the current cash value, he or she should be able to help you determine the amount you would get if you cashed it in today. Use that amount for your Net Worth Statement.

For cars and other vehicles, use the Kelley Blue Book value, which is the estimated price the car would sell for if sold privately to another consumer or to a car dealer. You can look up Kelley Blue Book values at the library or online at ✍ *www.kbb.com*. For all other assets, use your best estimate of the fair market value.

Assets			
Cash Equivalents	**Investments**	**Retirement Funds**	**Real Estate**
Bank and money market accounts	Stocks, bonds, mutual funds	401(k)/pension funds	House
CDs	Savings bonds	IRAs	Land
Cash on hand	Stock options	Keoghs	Rental property
Personal Property	**Household Goods**	**Money Owed You**	**Other Assets**
Vehicles	Furnishings	Rents due you	Life insurance
Campers and RVs	Jewelry and furs	Rental deposits	Privately owned business
Boats	Electronic equipment	Utility deposits	

Now you've listed everything you own that has a monetary value, but the total is not a true representation of your financial worth. It doesn't take into account the money you may owe banks or finance companies before you really own some of your assets—like your house or car, for example. It also doesn't yet take into account the money that you owe to other creditors. These are called your liabilities.

Liabilities			
Loans	**Credit Card Balances**	**Taxes Owed**	**Other Debts**
Mortgages	Visa/MasterCard	Real estate taxes	Unpaid bills due
Home equity loans	Discover	Unpaid income taxes	Alimony
Vehicle loans	American Express	Quarterly estimated taxes	Child support
401(k) loans	Department store credit		Miscellaneous
Student loans	Gas credit cards		

When you've listed everything you can think of, total the assets, then total the liabilities. Now, subtract your liabilities from your assets. If the number is positive (assets are greater than liabilities), you have a positive net worth. Congratulations! Now you can start working on building that net worth. If the number is negative (liabilities are greater than assets), you have a negative net worth, but don't let it discourage you. Now that you know exactly where you stand, you can map out your route to a positive net worth.

QUESTION?

What is "fair market value"?
The price a willing, rational, and knowledgeable buyer would pay. Fair market value may be more or less than you paid for the item and is the most meaningful measure of its current worth.

Decide What You Want to Achieve

Setting goals is as simple as deciding what you want and mapping out a plan on how to get it. Many people focus on paying their monthly bills at the expense of their short- and long-term goals. Monthly bills have a way of expanding to use all your available money, making planning for the future a moot point. How can you save for your future when today uses all the money that you generate? If you live beyond your means by using credit, or if you live paycheck to paycheck with nothing left over to save or invest, you'll never get ahead.

Go for the Goal

Think seriously about what you want to achieve. Do you envision retiring while you're still young enough to enjoy travel or an active lifestyle? Would you like to buy your first home or move up to a larger home in a better neighborhood? Is having a vacation home in the mountains or on the beach your dream? In the shorter term, maybe a new car or a boat is on your wish list. What's important to you?

Your goals should be just that: *your* goals, not your parents' or your friends'. Don't choose goals just because they sound like what you should want. The question is, do you really want them? Do you want them badly enough to give up the instant gratification of spending all your money now for the future enjoyment of having what is really meaningful to you later?

ALERT!

Don't let fear of failure cause you to set goals that aren't ambitious enough. You want to stretch yourself a little to reach your goal, but you have to believe that it's possible or you won't stay motivated for long. Try to strike a balance.

Put It in Writing

Whatever your goal, simply dreaming about it won't make it happen. A goal should be written down and reviewed often. Written goals give you something to work toward and make your efforts to save more meaningful, but figuring out how to achieve your goals is just as important as stating them.

Include a description of the goal, the time frame for achieving it, the amount of money needed, the amount already saved, and your plan for achieving the goal (for example, putting aside $100 a month, working ten hours of overtime a week, cutting entertainment costs in half, or getting a second job). Having a deadline for achieving your goal creates a sense of urgency that makes it easier to stay focused.

It's easy to get off track or drift along without making any real progress if all you have is a few vague dreams, so when writing down your goals, do it in enough detail to give yourself a visual each time you read it. If you're saving to buy a house, don't just write down "buy our own house." Write so you can almost see it: "I want to buy a cozy cape with a water view on two or more wooded acres on the coast of Maine." Each time you think of this goal, picture this cozy cape in your mind in as much detail as possible. The more you can imagine what meeting your goal will look like, feel like, and smell like, the better chance you have of achieving it.

FACT

One of the hardest adjustments for married couples is reconciling the differences about what's important to them and developing common goals. Daily financial tension can be high if the couple doesn't resolve the differences in their goals and come to a compromise that they both can live with.

A Few Ideas to Get You Started

Your financial goals may include saving for a down payment on a house, making home improvements, buying a new vehicle, paying off a loan, saving for graduate school or for your kids' college education, putting away some money for a dream vacation, or saving for a large purchase like a computer or new furniture. You may have the goal of being able to afford for you or your spouse to stay home to raise your kids without putting them in day care. In short, your goals should reflect your own values and dreams.

Your Net Worth Statement can be a valuable tool for finding clues about what your goals should be. If your short-term liabilities (due in a year or less) are greater than your current assets (cash and cash equivalents), paying down credit card debt may be your first priority.

Break It Down

At first, what you may have are long-term goals (goals you expect to meet in five years or more). You can break these goals down into short-term goals (one year or less), making it easier to stay focused on the future and giving you a sense of accomplishment and satisfaction along the way. In some cases, you may also want to identify a medium-term goal (one to three years).

Remember to make the goals specific. Ask yourself how you'll know when you've reached each of your goals. If you can come up with a concrete, measurable answer, you're on the right track.

After you've written down as many goals as you can think of, choose two or three short-term and two or three long-term goals to work on this year. Let's say you choose building a retirement fund as one of your most important long-term goals. To break it down into short-term goals, set a monthly goal to contribute a set dollar amount to your employer's 401(k) or other retirement plan.

ALERT!

Make goals specific. Instead of saying "I want to save for retirement," say "I want to contribute $100 monthly to my 401(k)." Instead of saying "I want to have less debt," say "I want to pay $100 extra a month toward my credit card with the highest interest rate."

Most of us struggle with the question of whether to use available funds to pay off long-term debt, such as paying down the balance on a mortgage, or to use them for short-term goals, such as building an emergency fund. The answer is to find a balance between the two. This takes thoughtful consideration of your short- and long-term goals, careful planning, and making adjustments in your plans as your goals and your financial situation change.

Evaluating Your Progress

You've prepared a Net Worth Statement, thought about what you want to achieve in life, identified some goals, and broken them down into short- and long-term goals. You're well on your way. Now you need to determine how you'll evaluate your progress.

You probably have a sense of whether you're making progress on your goals from month to month, but take the time to sit down at least monthly after you've updated your budget for the month and review how you're doing. Long-term goals can be reviewed less frequently than short-term goals because your time frame for achieving them is longer, but more frequent reviews allow you to spot problems earlier and take corrective action if you're falling short of where you want to be.

Tips for Recalculating and Reviewing

You should recalculate your Net Worth Statement at least annually, but more frequently is even better. For most people, it only takes a few minutes to update the information once you've generated your first statement. There's a real benefit to doing it monthly, if possible.

Go over your updated Net Worth Statement, and if you're married, talk with your spouse about how much you've accomplished and where you've fallen short. If you're single you'll have to do this on your own, unless you want to involve a close friend or family member. If you're not making satisfactory progress on a particular goal, re-evaluate your approach and discuss what would help you get on track. If you're making steady progress, seeing it in black and white can be motivating and rewarding. Give yourself credit for what you've achieved so far.

From time to time you may find your goals have changed, and that's okay. A good financial plan is flexible and changes with your needs. If you lose interest in a goal, don't consider it a failure. There's no reward in working for something you don't really want. Make the necessary changes in your goals and move on.

Sometimes it can be a tremendous help to engage the assistance of others. Talk to friends and acquaintances that have achieved a goal similar to one you're working on. You can gain from their experience and insight, and seeing their success can help keep you motivated.

If you find yourself falling short of your goals because you just don't feel motivated enough to stick with your plan, try making a list of all the benefits of succeeding in your goal, and review them often. Don't underestimate the power of your subconscious to help you stay motivated. Put positive thoughts in your mind about your goals and they'll be easier to attain.

Educating Yourself about Money Matters

Unfortunately, we don't always learn the basics of personal finance from our parents, and our education system doesn't adequately teach them to us. In fact, the Jumpstart Coalition for Personal Financial Literacy, whose mission is to improve the financial literacy of young adults, says that the average high school graduate lacks fundamental money management skills and a basic understanding of earning, spending, and saving money. It's no wonder that most people make financial mistakes in their twenties and thirties that they pay for over the next decade or longer. You can avoid these mistakes by educating yourself about basic money matters and practicing good money management.

FACT

A study conducted by the National Council on Economic Education a few years ago showed that the average American adult has a dismal understanding of basic economics, on which personal-finance concepts are based.

Where to Go for Help

Where do you start? Books like this one are one source. Check your local bookstore or surf an online bookstore like Amazon.com, searching for keywords like "personal finance" or "money management."

Magazines are another source. The bookstands are filled with financial magazines like *SmartMoney, Bloomberg's Personal Finance, Money,* and *Kiplinger's Personal Finance.* Some of them are definitely for people who are avid investors or interested in business financial news, but thumb through a few and see if any of them seem readable and interesting without being overwhelming or terribly boring. If you find one, consider subscribing to it.

The Internet is a source of nearly limitless information, some of it excellent. Try to stick with well-known sites rather than the folksy "this is how I did it" personal sites. Although the latter can have useful information on them, you could be steered in the wrong direction with some questionable advice or information. On the other hand, the personal sites about frugal living, downsizing, and cutting costs can be great for giving you ideas on how to do the same. (See Appendix B for a list of recommended Web sites.)

ALERT!

The less financially savvy you are, the more vulnerable you are to being taken advantage of or falling victim to financial scams. Not everything you read is true, so it's important to use reputable sources of information and practice some healthy skepticism if something sounds too good to be true.

It's All in the Attitude

Personal finance doesn't deserve the bad rap of being boring or complicated, which it sometimes gets, so don't feel a sense of dread about it or be intimidated by the fact that it involves numbers or terms you don't understand. Develop a positive attitude and consider your time and effort as an investment. You can learn everything you need to know, and you'll find it empowering as you learn to take control of your money and your future.

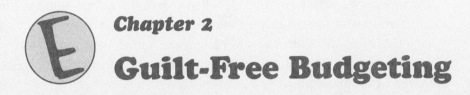

Chapter 2

Guilt-Free Budgeting

Part of meeting your goals is being able to create a budget and stick to it. Budgeting consists of setting up spending categories, tracking your expenditures, monitoring your progress, making adjustments, plugging spending leaks, and staying motivated. Your chances of being financially successful without budgeting are slim. It takes time and effort, but the rewards are tremendous.

It's All about Attitude

Budget. For some, the word conjures up images of sacrifice, penny pinching, and doing without. The most important ingredient in a successful budget is a positive attitude. At least 50 percent of budgeting is mental, so if the word makes you shudder, work on replacing this negative image with a positive one. If you've failed at budgeting in the past, ask yourself whether your budget was simply a review of how you spent your money after it was already gone, rather than a plan for spending and saving. The former is ineffective and frustrating. The latter is freeing and rewarding.

Attitude matters. Think of budgeting as eating right rather than being on a diet. You eat what you want in moderate amounts, you don't binge, you don't deprive yourself, and yet you end up better off.

Why Budget?

A budget is really a spending plan. You may struggle with an unrealistic plan to save thousands of dollars when what you really need to do is spend more wisely. If you think you can meet your financial goals without a spending plan, you will most likely be disappointed. Creating a spending plan is the first and most basic step you can take toward putting your money to work for you, regardless of whether you make thousands of dollars or hundreds of thousands of dollars a year.

Many people who spend more money than they make don't even realize they're spending too much until they're deeply in debt. Credit cards and loans are often the culprit, but spending without knowing how much money you have available can create the same problem. Decide in advance how to put your money to use instead of letting it happen accidentally. When you spend without a spending plan, you're not in control of your money; your money is in control of you. Budgeting works.

The Benefits of Budgeting

Budgeting and tracking your expenses shows you where your money goes and how seemingly inconsequential daily or weekly expenditures can add up over time. By tracking all of your expenditures, you can make conscious decisions about how to spend or invest your money instead of dribbling it away a dollar or two at a time. This can be the difference between never having enough money and being able to afford the things that are really important to you, like saving for a down payment on a house, buying a new car, paying off credit card debt, planning for retirement, or saving for that trip to Cancun.

Having a working budget can greatly reduce the stress in your life that revolves around money issues. You'll know what you can or can't afford. You'll feel confident that you'll be able to pay your bills when they're due, or you'll have advance warning that there's going to be a problem, giving you time to plan alternatives.

An unexpected side benefit of budgeting is that it can improve your relationship with your spouse or partner. Money matters are the single largest cause of marital discord and divorce, so getting a grip on spending by coming to an agreement about your financial goals and working together toward those goals can have a positive effect on your relationship.

FACT

The Millionaire Next Door by Thomas J. Stanley and William D. Danko shows that simple lifestyles, not big incomes, turn average people into millionaires. Many Americans buy a more expensive house than they can comfortably afford, drive the latest cars, spend large sums on their wardrobes, buy all the latest electronic gadgets, and live from paycheck to paycheck.

What Makes a Good Budget?

A good spending plan is flexible and realistic. It's a road map that offers alternative routes to your destination, depending on your personal road conditions. It should be dynamic, changing to fit your needs. If you have no kids, you wouldn't use the same budget as someone who does; if you live in rented housing, you wouldn't use the same budget as someone who owns their home. Life changes, and so should your budget.

The complexity level of a good budgeting system should match the level of your time and interest. Some people love recording the details. If you're not one of them, choose a simpler approach so it's not too much of a chore. The objective is to come up with a system you can live with for a long time.

Customizing Your Budget

It's a good idea to put together a budget worksheet to get started in setting up your budget. You'll get some help on doing it here, but make sure the categories you use fit your personal lifestyle. Use the basic common categories that apply to everyone, such as housing, utilities, insurance, and food, but customize the other categories to fit your personal situation.

Your categories should be detailed enough to provide you with useful information, but not so detailed that you become bogged down in trivia. First, list all your sources of income:

- Wages from your job(s)
- Bonuses
- Child support or alimony
- Rental income
- Interest income
- Dividend income
- Capital gains income
- Other income

Next, list the expense categories you want to track. Start out with a little more detail rather than a little less. You can always combine categories later if you find expenditures in one category are so small that they don't warrant being tracked separately.

Sample Expense Categories				
Savings	Mortgage or rent	Utilities	Auto expense	Other transportation
Credit card payments	Student loan payments	Other loan payments	Home maintenance	Child care
Child support or alimony	Insurance	Out-of-pocket medical expenses	Computer expenses	Entertainment/ recreation
Eating out	Clothing and shoes	Gifts and donations	Groceries	Household products
Dry cleaning	Hobbies	Interest expense	Magazines, books	Personal care products
Federal income tax	State income tax	Local income tax	Social security tax	Property tax
Retirement contributions	Investments	Pet expenses	Miscellaneous expenses	

Don't forget things that come up throughout the year but are not monthly expenses, such as subscriptions, holiday gifts, clothing, birthday gifts, insurance, maintenance agreements, adult education classes or seminars, car repairs, medical expenses, and so forth. To tweak your memory about the types of nonroutine expenses you're likely to encounter, look back through your records for the last year.

The first rule of personal finance is to pay yourself first. Make savings an expense category, with a set amount that you pay to yourself monthly when you pay your bills. Don't plan your savings around what's left over when you've paid everything else. Chances are, there won't be anything there.

Think about your own personal habits (smoking, drinking, buying lunch at work) or hobbies you engage in (woodworking, skiing, boating, golfing, gardening) to identify other spending categories. Some of your spending habits might make you uncomfortable when confronted in black and white. That's okay. It doesn't change the facts; it just brings them to light so you can make a conscious decision about your spending. It's not the purpose of budgeting to make you feel guilty about how you've spent your money in the past.

How Much Money Do You Have Available?

To curtail overspending, you need to set realistic spending goals in each category. First, figure out how much money you have available, and where that money goes now. To get started, collect as many of your pay stubs, bills, credit card statements, and receipts as possible for the last three months and complete the income section of your budget. Calculate your average monthly gross pay (before taxes) by adding the gross pay on a month's worth of pay stubs. If your pay varies substantially from one pay period to the next, try to calculate a realistic monthly average, but don't include uncertain amounts like year-end bonuses or overtime until you're actually paid for them. Estimate monthly averages for the other income categories as well.

Where Is Your Money Going?

In addition to bills, credit card statements, and receipts, your checkbook register will be important in completing the expense portion of the worksheet. Go through these documents and jot down your expenditures in each of the categories you've set up, then total the numbers in each category and transfer them to the worksheet. For the items you identified that aren't paid every month, calculate the yearly cost and divide it by twelve to get the monthly cost for your budget worksheet. Each month, set aside the monthly amount in a savings account so it's available when the bill becomes due.

To really get a fix on where your money goes, you'll need to keep track of your cash expenditures, too. Save receipts to record later, or jot the expenditure down on a notepad as you use cash. The more often you use an ATM, the more important it is to write down your cash expenditures, because this is where many people lose control of where their money goes. Tracking your cash expenditures is one of the more tedious aspects of budgeting, but it's where you have the most potential for budget leaks, and most people are surprised if not shocked when they see how much cash slips through their hands each month.

Tracking Small Expenditures

You may think you know where your money goes, but most people are more than a little surprised when they really start tracking their expenses. Small cash expenditures can add up to significant sums of money by month's end. That daily cup of coffee is probably costing you almost $400 per year. Three six-packs of beer a week adds up to at least $600. If you smoke two packs of cigarettes a day, it's probably costing you over $280 a month, $3,360 per year, or $33,600 in ten years—and that's if you discount the impact of inflation!

FACT

If you invested $280 every month instead of spending it on cigarettes, beer, or other common habits, and it earned a modest 5 percent return starting when you were thirty years old, by the time you reached retirement age you would have over $319,000! Think of what you could do with that money.

Finding Ways to Reduce Spending

After a month or two of tracking your actual spending, you'll begin to see a pattern, and will be better able to identify where you can comfortably make adjustments to start saving money. Consider this a process of self-discovery. You can start with an in-depth look at your largest spending categories if you prefer, but don't overlook the smaller categories. Sometimes these are the easiest to make cuts in because the spending may be more discretionary, and small amounts can add up quickly.

Identify areas where you can painlessly save money that you can use to build an emergency fund or save for an important goal. Brainstorm about ways to reduce spending in specific categories. Cutting costs becomes a challenge that can be very rewarding, especially as you see your savings grow.

Setting Spending Goals by Category

Once you feel comfortable that you know where your money is going and you've identified some ways to cut costs in a number of categories, establish a monthly spending target for each category.

Do your fixed expenses first, like your mortgage and car payment. In Chapter 3, you'll learn how to try and reduce your costs on seemingly fixed expenses, but for now let's assume that your mortgage, car payments, child care costs, and taxes are fixed. Look at each of your remaining budget categories and set a spending target, taking into consideration what you know about your own spending habits and where you can cut back without causing a hardship.

An important part of budgeting is coming up with concrete ways to cut costs. Setting a spending limit with no thought about how to reduce expenses will be an exercise in frustration as you review your failures monthly. Come up with innovative ways to put money in your own pocket.

Calculating Your Net Income

When you've set a tentative target for each category, subtotal the income and expense categories and subtract the total expenses from the total income to arrive at your net income. This will be the amount of money you have left over for building an emergency fund, making additional payments on your credit cards, and working on your other financial goals, assuming you've recorded all of your income and expenditures accurately. If the number is negative, your expenses are greater than your income. Don't be discouraged. Your situation can no doubt be greatly improved by tweaking your spending habits. If you have a positive net income, be sure to transfer most of it to a savings or investment account at the end of each month. Extra cash left in a regular checking account has a way of getting spent.

Monitor Your Progress Monthly

As soon as possible after the end of each month, update your budget with your expenditures for the month. You can do this manually—by going through your checkbook, statements, and receipts—but consider using personal-finance software (see "Personal-Finance Software" at the end of this chapter) and perhaps online banking (see Chapter 4).

Making Adjustments

If you find you've exceeded your budget for the month, don't despair. Use it as a learning experience to improve your budgeting for the future. Your budget will get more refined every month and you'll get better and better at managing your money and working toward your goals. If you find after a month or two that tracking your expenses is too much work, consider combining some categories, such as miscellaneous household expenses or utilities, to reduce the record keeping, rather than giving up.

As you readjust the categories, look for areas where you can save small amounts of money. Small savings are easier to find and easier to implement than large ones, and small victories will give you a positive feeling about budgeting before you get into the tough stuff. Remember, the idea is not to deprive yourself, but to funnel as much of your money as possible toward the goals that are most important to you.

As your personal situation changes, reflect those changes in your budget. Examples of changes that should prompt an overhaul of your budget include the following factors:

- Change in marital status
- Change in family size
- A new job
- Salary increase (or decrease)
- A new home
- Disability
- A major purchase that requires monthly payments

ALERT!

Be constantly vigilant about scams and schemes. New ones pop up almost daily and if you're not careful you'll end up losing some of your hard-earned money. Remember: If it sounds too good to be true, it probably is.

Plug Any Spending Leaks

Most spending leaks are the result of impulse buying and frittering away cash in small amounts, which add up by month's end. If you're an impulse shopper, buying things you don't realize you need until you see them, don't hang out at the mall or your favorite department store. Impulse spending is often the result of powerful advertising messages that are so appealing that we buy things we don't need and often end up not using. Why let advertisers influence your decision-making?

Plan all purchases and don't buy anything that wasn't part of your plan. If there's something you feel you really must have, think about it for at least two days and if you still feel compelled to buy it, do a little comparison-shopping first so you don't overpay. Then plan on how you're going to cover the cost by reducing another expense in your budget for the month.

The Small Leaks

Grocery shopping is one area ripe for cost cutting. Do you buy a lot of prepared foods instead of doing the cooking yourself? There's a tradeoff between the cost and the convenience of prepared foods when you're too busy to cook. Snacks are another expensive item, especially if you buy the serving-size packages to include in the kids' school lunches. Consider buying bulk and using baggies. Buy generic brands. Use coupons.

Do the workers at the fast-food restaurants in town know you by name? If eating out is a lifestyle instead of a treat, consider cutting back on fast food and enjoying a monthly dinner out with your spouse or a friend. You'll feel like you've treated yourself, and you'll probably end up spending less money than if you regularly buy fast food.

What's the deductible on your auto insurance? It should be at least $250, and if you have a good driving record, $500 is even better. The certain cost of paying higher insurance for a lower deductible weighed against the likelihood of having an accident may not be to your advantage. If the car is more than eight years old, consider dropping collision coverage altogether, and just keep liability coverage on that vehicle. The cost of collision coverage on a car that is worth only a few thousand dollars is out of proportion to the benefit you receive, especially if you have a good driving record.

Shop for long-distance telephone deals twice a year. Long-distance companies are constantly changing their plans, and you could save a chunk of change if you make a lot of long-distance calls. Be sure to read the fine print and ask specific questions.

These are just a few ideas to get you thinking about how you can cut costs. As you go through each item in your budget and on your Net Worth Statement, you'll find others. Question everything and look at things from a different perspective. You may save more by coming up with a number of ideas for small savings than you will by trying to reduce the large expenses.

The Bigger Picture

Once you've reviewed your spending and identified some small spending leaks that you can plug fairly painlessly, start looking for the larger leaks. Review items such as your mortgage, car payments, taxes, and insurance policies. The most painful cuts will be those related to your personal habits and hobbies, but these areas often yield the biggest savings. Chapter 3 includes a more detailed discussion of how you can make significant cuts in these and other areas.

Personal-Finance Software

If you're willing to invest the time, a personal-finance software program can bring your money management to a whole new level, but you don't need to do more than the basics if you don't have the time or interest. Unless you have very few expenses and they're relatively simple, a good software program will make the job of tracking everything easier and less time-consuming. Being able to print out graphs and reports from your PC with the click of a button can serve as a motivation for entering all that data. If you don't want to use a computer, that's okay too. It's entirely possible to budget successfully with paper and pencil.

FACT

Many banks now offer free or low-fee PC banking and free personal-finance software. You simply dial into the bank's computer (or your bank may use Internet-based banking), and download the checks that have cleared your account, directly into your personal-finance software. Then you indicate an expense category for each check and click a button for a report.

How Can Software Make Budgeting Easier?

You can balance your checkbook, pay bills, create budgets, do a basic comparison of budget versus actual expenses by category, or you can enter more detailed information such as investments, assets, liabilities, and so on, and print personal financial statements showing your net income and net worth.

Start out with the simplest steps. Detailed tracking of investments with personal-finance software can be time consuming and complex—not for the faint of heart. You can get the same results in your reports by setting up an account in the software for each investment and changing the balances each month to reflect the balance on the statement you receive from your brokerage, bank, or mutual fund.

Shop Around

Some of the most popular personal-finance software programs for automating your checkbook and tracking your expenses are Quicken, Microsoft Money, and Moneydance. These are available online or at big office supply stores like Staples.

Microsoft Money and Quicken are both user-friendly programs with many features you'll probably never use, but they're also great programs for the average person who just wants to do online banking, automatically reconcile their bank statement, track expenses, budget, prepare for tax time, and print reports. The budget versus actual report alone is worth the investment. Moneydance is a simpler program that is not as well known, but it provides the same basic features without all the fancy bells and whistles.

To purchase Quicken, visit ✍*www.intuit.com*; for MS Money, go to ✍*www.microsoft.com*; Moneydance may be purchased at ✍*www.moneydance.com*. All three software packages are also available for purchase at ✍*www.amazon.com*. The basic version of each software package costs between $30 and $40 after rebates.

Stay Motivated

Your budget won't work unless you stick with it. One of the keys to staying motivated is keeping the budgeting process from being too complex or time consuming. Make budgeting a family activity and involve each family member in some way. Reward yourself for reaching saving and spending goals and making progress on paying down debt.

One of the most rewarding things about budgeting is seeing results every month. This is easy if you use personal-finance software, because once you enter your expenditures and income for the month, a click of the mouse produces reports that show budgeted versus actual expenses by category, your new and improved net worth, balances in savings and investment accounts, and more. You can even print or view colorful graphs and pie charts for a visual look at how you're doing.

Don't forget to work on your attitude as well as your spending plan. Give yourself a pat on the back for the increases in your savings and decreases in your credit card debt. Remind yourself of the importance of your real goals. The budget is just a tool that increases your awareness of where your money goes and provides guidelines for spending so your money goes toward the things that are most meaningful to you. Ⓔ

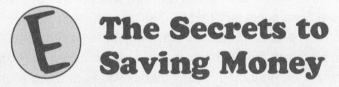 The Secrets to Saving Money

Without a savings plan, the chances of saving enough money to meet long-term financial goals are very slim. Like financial success, saving money doesn't happen by accident. It requires smart buying, cutting costs, planning, and understanding a few basic financial concepts like the magic of compounding, the Rule of 72, the time value of money, and the danger of inflation.

The Magic of Compounding

The magic of compounding is the biggest reason it's so important to start saving in your early twenties. People who wait until their forties to start saving will have to save much more than those who started in their twenties. What's worse, they will never be able to catch up with those who started in their twenties without saving and investing drastically higher amounts than would have been necessary had they started at a younger age.

There are two basic methods of calculating interest: simple interest and compound interest. Simple interest is calculated based only on your initial investment. Compounding means that as you earn interest on your investment, it is added to your original investment, and as a result you earn interest on your interest as well. The difference may not seem like much, but the effect that compounding can have over a long period of time is astounding, especially with larger initial investments and higher rates of return.

FACT

To illustrate how compounding works, assume you invest $1,000 at 10 percent interest compounded annually. At the end of the first year, you'll have earned $100, for a total of $1,100. At the end of year two, the interest is calculated on $1,100, so you'll earn $110, for a balance of $1,210.

Frequency of Compounding

Interest is usually compounded annually, monthly, or daily. The more frequently compounding takes place, the faster your money will grow. As the balance grows larger, the difference between simple interest and compound interest becomes greater. Let's say you put $5,000 in an account that earns 10 percent interest. Here's what your investment would be worth at the end of ten years if you didn't add another penny to it:

- Compounded annually: $12,968
- Compounded monthly: $13,535
- Compounded daily: $13,589

To illustrate the effect of a longer period of time on compounding, consider Bill, who contributed $2,000 at 6 percent interest to an IRA beginning at the age of twenty-two and continued doing so each year until he was thirty (nine years). By the time he was sixty-five, his $18,000 investment had grown to over $579,000. His friend Jim made a $2,000 contribution every year for thirty-five years, for a total of $70,000, but because he started at the age of thirty-one, his nest egg only totaled $470,000. Even though he contributed much more than Bill ($70,000 versus Bill's $18,000) he ended up with 23 percent less money.

The Rule of 72

The Rule of 72 is a nifty mathematical computation used to estimate how long it will take a certain sum of money to double at a certain interest rate (assuming the interest is compounded annually). You can use this simple rule to quickly determine how long it will take your savings or an investment to double, or how long it will take a debt to double. Try it out on some of your investments or debts.

The Calculation Is Simple

To calculate how quickly your investment will double, divide 72 by the interest rate or expected rate of return. The result is the number of years it will take your money to double at that interest rate, assuming you reinvest your earnings. So if your money is invested at 8 percent interest, you make the following quick calculation: $72 \div 8 = 9$. This means it will take approximately nine years.

It can be fun and interesting to keep track of the money you save by practicing frugality. Try keeping tabs on how much you save each time you make informed buying decisions or abstain from buying an item you would have bought before you came up with your spending plan.

You can also use the Rule of 72 to estimate what rate of return you'd need to earn in order for your money to double in a certain number of years, for example, ten years: 72 ÷ 10 = 7.2, so you'd need to earn 7.2 percent annually for your money to double in ten years.

How Many Times Will Your Money Double?

The power of the Rule of 72 doesn't stop there. It illustrates how important differences in interest rates are, because the lower the interest rate, the longer it takes to double your money, and the real key to growing your money is to double it as many times as possible. Look at this example of $100 doubling eight times:

$100	$3,200
$200	$6,400
$400	$12,800
$800	$25,600
$1,600	

As you can see, the real growth comes after the money has doubled several times, which is important when you're saving or investing for long-term goals like retirement. By using the Rule of 72, you can calculate how much you'll have by a certain time and you can compare the long-term effects of interest rates on various investments that you own.

Double Savings, Don't Double Debt

You can use the Rule of 72 to see how long it will take your credit card or other debt to double, too. If you have a $5,000 credit card balance with an interest rate of 10 percent, your debt will double in 7.2 years. If the interest rate is 19 percent, your debt will double in 3.8 years. You can see why it's so hard to pay off your credit card debt, especially if the interest rate is high. If you're only paying the minimum payment each month, it doesn't take long for your balance to double.

The Danger of Inflation

Inflation is the effect of rising prices on your buying power. Inflation is often left out of the equation when calculating how much money you'll have available at some point down the road, but it can make serious inroads into the buying power of your money. The average inflation rate since 1994 has been approximately 2.5 percent, but in the early 1980s, we experienced double-digit inflation. Since 1980, the price of goods and services has increased 80 percent, so an item that cost $100 in 1980 costs $180 in 2002. Since much of our financial planning is done for years into the future, it's important to consider the impact of inflation when determining how much money you'll need in retirement, for example.

You can use the Rule of 72 to estimate the real buying power of a sum of money at some point in the future, taking inflation into consideration. If the inflation rate is 4 percent, prices will double in eighteen years (72 ÷ 4 = 18), so if you plan to retire in eighteen years and you need $3,000 a month in today's money, you'd need $6,000 a month to retain the same buying power you have today.

ALERT!

The $30,000 salary you earn this year will be worth only $28,800 next year if inflation is 4 percent. If you're fortunate, you'll get a salary increase annually that at least keeps pace with the rate of inflation; otherwise you fall further behind each year.

The Time Value of Money

The time value of money is a basic financial concept based on the assumption that a dollar received today is worth more than a dollar received at some future date because a dollar received today can be invested and earn interest. If someone agreed to pay you $1,000 ten years from now, or some lesser amount today, you could calculate the amount you'd need to receive today to equal the value of $1,000 in ten years. You do this by discounting the amount using current interest rates. If the current interest rate is 6 percent, you might be willing to accept $558 today rather than waiting ten years for your $1,000 because you're confident that if you invest the $558 at 6 percent it will grow to $1,000 in ten years.

There's more to the concept of the time value of money, but the most important thing for you to remember is that receiving $1 today is better than receiving $1 tomorrow, and the entire amount in a lump sum is better than installment payments (assuming there's no interest involved). If you're paid in installments, you lose the opportunity to invest the lump sum for a longer period of time.

FACT

Opportunity costs are the benefits you lose by not choosing the best alternative for the use of your money. If you pay $100 in credit card interest each month, you've lost not just $100, but also the added value you could have received if you had invested that $100.

Building an Emergency Fund

More than ever, in these uncertain times, everyone should have an emergency fund. You won't know how much your fund should be unless you know what your basic monthly expenses are. Here's where a budget comes in handy. If you've already prepared a budget as outlined in Chapter 2, you have a good feel for how much you need in your emergency fund.

Financial advisors suggest having enough savings in an easily accessible account to cover your living expenses for three to six months. Having this financial safety net will give you peace of mind about how you'll meet your most basic financial obligations in the event of illness, job loss, or other serious emergency. The fund can also be used for unplanned expenses such as major house or car repairs, or medical costs not covered by insurance. In a volatile job market, an emergency fund is more critical than ever.

Now that you have a budget in place, you can easily calculate how much money you'd need to cover your basic, no-frills living expenses if you had a sudden loss of income. Write down your goal for your emergency fund and decide on an amount to contribute to it each month, using the "pay yourself first" rule. If possible, keep the fund in a separate account, such as a money market account, so you're less tempted to dip into it. Since emergency funds might be needed without notice, they should be kept in liquid accounts that are easy to cash in quickly.

The Fun of Frugality

Don't be discouraged if you currently have no extra money to put away. The secret to saving money is that there's no secret involved at all. By developing a realistic budget, setting spending and savings goals, and sticking to them, you can create money for savings.

Decide on a percentage of your income to designate as savings. Financial planners suggest 10 percent, but if 8 or 5 percent is all you can handle at this time, start with that. Don't make the mistake of thinking that if you can't save a large amount of money all at once, it's not worthwhile to try. This couldn't be further from the truth.

If you saved $25 a month at 6 percent interest, in five years you'd have $1,744. If you saved $100 a month at 6 percent interest, in five years you'd have $6,977; in ten years, you'd have $16,388. Even if you think you can't possibly save this much each month, you'll be surprised how much more money is available for savings as you continue to refine your budgeting and spending plans. It's okay to stretch to the point of discomfort, but saving shouldn't be painful to the point of making you do without things you truly need.

Strategies for Pumping Up Your Savings

Set up a separate savings account. If you mingle your day-to-day funds with your savings, it's almost inevitable that you'll end up using some or all of the savings, and you may never repay them. There's also a mental component. Seeing your savings balance grow from month to month and your financial goals becoming more of a reality is highly motivating.

If you have direct deposit at work and your employer allows you to split your deposit between two banks, consider having a set amount deducted from your paycheck each pay period and deposited in your savings account. It's much easier to save when the money doesn't have to take a detour to your checking account before reaching your savings account. Out of sight, out of mind. If you don't have this option at work, write yourself a check every month before you pay your bills, and deposit it into your savings account. After a while, as you adjust your budget and spending, you won't even miss the money you're putting into savings.

Use windfalls to pump up your savings instead of spending them. Bonuses, tax refunds, rebates, overtime pay, income from hobbies or yard sales, cash gifts from family, lottery winnings, and other sporadic cash receipts can make faster advances toward your goals without requiring additional spending cutbacks. When you receive a salary increase, put all or part of it into savings each pay period and continue living on your previous salary. When you pay off a loan, continue putting the payment amount aside each month, but pay it into your savings account instead of to the bank or finance company. Because you're already in the habit of doing without that money, you won't even miss it.

ALERT!

If you feel forced to dip into your savings in an emergency, consider it a loan. If you can't pay it all back at once, set up a repayment plan and pay yourself as though it were a regular bill. Otherwise you may never replenish your savings.

Don't Be a Victim of Advertising

When shopping, decide on how much you have available to spend before you actually shop, and don't give in to impulse spending. With a spending plan, you don't need to deprive yourself of things you really need, but you should question whether you really do need them. Experts recommend these strategies:

- Don't use shopping as a form of recreation.
- Don't shop on impulse.
- For items you really do need, look for sales and special offers.

- Shop at outlet or discount stores.
- Before buying appliances, electronics, computer equipment, and other expensive items, research them in *Consumer Reports* or other magazines that do consumer reviews.
- Do some of your shopping at a warehouse club, if there's one near you.

You can find product reviews and cost comparisons on the Internet—just be sure the source is reliable and impartial. One good site is ✍ *www.consumerworld.org,* with product reviews, price comparisons, best airfares and travel deals, and lots of other consumer resources.

Avoid the Holiday Hangover

If you're like most people you tend to go overboard on holiday spending, but you can avoid overspending on gifts by setting spending limits. Using your budget, figure out how much you can realistically afford to spend on gifts without going into debt. Make a list of all the people you'd like to buy gifts for, including the small gifts for babysitters, teachers, newspaper deliverers, and so on. Set a limit for each person on your list, then add up all the amounts and make sure they don't exceed your overall spending limit. Try to allow a cushion for unexpected items or price fluctuations. Don't get caught up in the commercialism that's rampant around the holidays, or you may have to deal with a depressing amount of debt when the holidays are over.

FACT

The Internet is a rich source of advice on being frugal, a word that sometimes has a bad connotation but that simply means economy in the use of resources. It's amazing how many different ways there are to cut costs and save money. Do a little Internet surfing and you'll find hundreds of ideas that have worked for others. Being frugal can be fun!

Finding the Fat

You may think there's no fat in your budget, but nearly everyone can find some if they look hard enough. Consider it a challenge to find ways to cut your expenses, or make a game of it. If you smoke, why not quit? Smoking is one of the most expensive habits you can have; many couples spend as much on cigarettes as they would on a new car payment each month.

Speaking of car payments, ask yourself if you really need the gas-guzzling SUV you drive. You could save considerable money on gas, repairs and maintenance, as well as insurance, not to mention your monthly car payment, if you bought a less expensive, more fuel-efficient vehicle.

Consider buying used instead of new. Check the classifieds for things like exercise equipment, vehicles, musical instruments, electronics, and more. There are always people who have made the mistake you're trying to avoid by buying something they ended up not wanting or needing. You can often get great bargains on items that may be as good as new.

The list of ways to save money is endless. As you get into the habit of questioning every expense and looking for ways to cut costs, you'll develop a saving mindset and you'll see the savings add up. You've discovered the "secret" to saving.

Saving for Large Purchases

There are a number of benefits to saving for a big purchase rather than buying it on credit. First of all, you have plenty of time to change your mind about whether it's something you really need or want. Have you noticed how many back yards have unused swimming pools or hot tubs? If you run right out and charge the item to your credit card or take out a loan, you'll be stuck paying for the item for a long time. Paying cash also gives you the satisfaction of really owning the item, and you'll pay much less for it because you won't be paying interest.

Luxury Items and Loss of Value

There are often significant costs beyond the purchase price associated with luxury items like boats, RVs, or certain cars. Be sure to evaluate all of these costs before making a buying decision, or you may find out after you've already made the purchase that although you can afford to *buy* the item, you can't afford to *own* it.

Take the purchase of a boat as an example. A new eighteen to twenty-one foot powerboat will probably cost between $15,000 and $20,000. You run all the numbers and decide that the payments fit into your budget. You commit to the sale and drive home with the goods, but during the next year you find you're sinking larger-than-planned quantities of money into owning the boat, starting with the day you register it. Besides registration fees for the boat and trailer, there's gas and oil, maintenance, repairs, insurance, safety courses, inspections, winter storage, personal-property taxes, dock and mooring fees, not to mention depreciation. These costs can add up to a substantial amount, so make sure you get estimates before you buy and make sure you can afford the costs of ownership.

Home appliances, electronics, cars, and other items are reviewed in *Consumer Reports* magazine, which accepts no advertising or sponsorships. Subscribe to their Web site for $24/year. Also visit Consumer World (✍*www.consumerworld.org*), which has links to over 2,000 of the best consumer resources.

The same principles apply to buying an RV, expensive car, furniture, appliances, or any luxury item. Buying cheaply made furniture or appliances may cost you more in the long run because you have to replace them more often. Try to buy quality products without overpaying unnecessarily for features you won't use or for a brand name that doesn't necessarily mean better quality. It makes sense to pay more for an item if that brand or model has a better record or costs less to maintain. Do your research, talk to others who have bought a similar item, talk to experts in the field, and read. Then try to balance cost and reward. Ⓔ

Chapter 4
Banking Basics

You probably have a checking account and maybe a savings account, but chances are you don't give much thought to the impact banking has on your finances. Being knowledgeable about how banks work can save you money. You might be surprised just how much your banking arrangements and habits are costing you.

Choosing a Bank

When it comes to choosing a bank, consider both convenience and cost. Find out what types of fees the bank charges. Some charge flat monthly fees; others charge a fee for each check written and each deposit made. Some charge if you go below the minimum balance, use a live teller, use another bank's automated teller machine (ATM), make an account balance inquiry, have your canceled checks returned to you each month, or close your account. Most charge for bouncing checks, placing a stop payment on a check, and using your overdraft protection.

ALERT!

Reconcile your checkbook monthly and review your credit card statements for errors. Scam artists are finding new ways to target these two areas and if you're not alert, you could get taken for a ride.

Review your banking habits, identify the services that are most important to you, compare fees for those services between several different banks, and then choose the bank that fits your needs for the best price. If you use ATM machines to withdraw cash from your account on a weekly basis, for example, you wouldn't want to choose a bank that offers free checking but charges a hefty fee for ATM transactions. You may decide to use a traditional brick-and-mortar bank in your neighborhood or an Internet bank in cyberspace.

How about a Credit Union?

In today's world, you've got a few options when it comes to banking. One such option is to pick a credit union over a traditional bank. Banks are owned by investors; credit unions are owned and controlled by customers, who are members. Credit unions are nonprofit organizations and return surplus earnings to members by lowering interest rates on loans, increasing interest rates on deposits, or offering free or low-cost services. The most basic requirement for any bank or credit union you choose is that it must be a member of the Federal Deposit Insurance

Corporation (FDIC), which is fully backed by the U.S. government. This ensures that your account will be protected for up to $100,000.

QUESTION?

How do I make sure a bank is FDIC-insured?
Go to the FDIC Web site at ✍ *www.fdic.gov*, click on "Is My Bank Insured?" and enter the official name, city, and state of the bank, then click the "Find My Institution" button.

Online Banking

Online banking allows you to view all your banking transactions, making it easy to update your checkbook register and ensure that you didn't forget to record any ATM withdrawals, deposits, or other transactions. Many people use this feature instead of actually reconciling their bank statement the old-fashioned way. If you're interested in trying online banking, contact your bank for information on how to begin.

There are two ways to bank online. Internet-based banking systems allow you to dial in to the bank's computer using any computer with a modem and use the bank's software to look at your account balance and transactions. Client-based systems require you to download information from the bank into personal-finance software that resides on your computer's hard drive. Internet banking is the way of the future, so if you're thinking of changing banks, you might save yourself time and trouble by choosing one with Internet-based banking.

Most large banks offer secure online banking free or for a fee of $4.00 to $6.50 per month for basic services, plus an additional $4.00 to $6.50 per month for online bill payment if you choose that option. Some smaller banks offer limited functions such as the ability to view your balance and history online. As online banking grows more popular, more banks will add full functionality.

Even if you don't bank online, you may use automatic debits to have payment for one or more of your bills automatically deducted from your checking account each month. To protect yourself from automatic debit scams, never give out your bank account number or other information printed on your check to anyone over the telephone. If you do, they may use it to fraudulently remove money from your account. If you believe you've been the victim of an automatic debit scam, contact your bank immediately.

With the Help of Software

The most popular software programs for taking advantage of online banking are Quicken and Microsoft Money. Both are robust personal-finance programs that allow you to download your banking transactions and help to manage your finances, budget, balance your checkbook, pay bills electronically, prepare and file your taxes, track investments, and build a financial plan for your future.

FACT

Online banking is definitely the way of the future. A study published in early 2002 indicated that 20 percent of U.S. house-holds use it, and this number is expected to grow significantly over the next several years as banks continue to make it more secure and easier to use.

Banking Costs

Sometimes you can gain as much by cutting seemingly insignificant costs that add up over time as you can by earning additional income. Banking costs are a good example. Banks charge so many different types of fees, some of them hidden, that you may not realize what your real costs are.

With minimum balance requirements, ATM fees, overdraft charges, and other fees, even your basic checking and savings accounts might be costing you more than they should. When your money could be earning more somewhere else, that's called opportunity costs. You may not be paying any fees directly, but you've lost an opportunity to make money elsewhere. For example, the balance that you maintain in your checking account to avoid a monthly fee could be earning more than the monthly fee if invested in a money market account or certificate of deposit (CD).

Service versus Cost

Be aware of your banking costs and make intelligent tradeoffs to get the services you use for the lowest overall cost. If keeping a minimum balance in your checking account costs you $5 a month in opportunity costs but saves you $7 in fees, it makes sense to go with that option. If you have savings and checking accounts at the same bank, keep only as much money in the checking account as you need to pay bills that are due immediately. Let the rest of your funds go to work for you by earning interest in your savings account. When interest rates are very low, the earnings may be minimal, but when rates are higher, the savings can be substantial over time.

Learn about the different banking features and then pay only for the ones that truly make sense for you. If you're keeping $5,000 in your checking account, maybe it doesn't make sense to pay a fee for overdraft protection.

Minimizing Fees

Bank fees may seem like small potatoes, but they are big business. Banks make billions of dollars annually on various fees, and the amounts are growing each year. You probably accept bank fees without question, but why pay more than you have to when it's relatively easy to minimize fees?

Banks use several methods to calculate your average daily balance and interest. This might seem like a minor concern, but if you usually keep a significant balance in an interest-bearing bank account, it's to your advantage to keep it in a bank that uses the average daily balance method for calculating your minimum balance and interest. This reduces the chances of incurring fees if you dip below the minimum balance during the month (as long as your average daily balance for the entire month is not below the minimum). You also earn interest on all your money.

When you borrow money, the costs are stated in terms of interest rates, so it seems fairly easy to choose the best deal, but it's not always as simple as it appears. A lower interest rate will not necessarily save you money if fees, points, closing costs, and other charges are added in. Be sure to read the small print.

FACT

Check printing is another area where it's easy to save a little money. Why pay the $25 to $50 or more that your bank charges for printing 200 checks when you can use a discounter and pay between $6 and $8?

Overdraft Protection

Overdraft protection is a checking account feature that allows you to write checks for more than the balance in your account. It provides a safety net to protect you from accidentally overdrawing your account. Some banks allow you to cover overdrafts automatically from your savings account, money market account, or credit card account.

The most common method of covering overdrafts involves establishing a line of credit, which typically has an interest rate that can be as much as two times higher than the going rates on credit cards or loans. The cost to you could be substantial if you don't repay it right away. There can also be a fee each time funds are drawn from another source to cover your overdraft.

If your overdraft protection is linked to your credit card, the bank issues a cash advance to cover your overdraft and charges it to your credit card. You pay a cash advance fee of 2 to 3 percent plus the fee your bank charges for the transaction, plus whatever interest you incur before you pay the cash advance back.

Don't Get Trapped!

Overdraft fees are one of the costliest banking mistakes you can make, and you should avoid them like the plague. Even if you don't balance your checkbook, at least compare your check register to your bank statement to make sure you've recorded all checks and ATM withdrawals and that the bank has properly credited you with all deposits. This will help prevent bouncing checks.

Typical fees for insufficient funds range from $20 to $35. Often when you bounce one check, at least one more check will bounce before you're aware of the problem, and before you know it you can rack up over $100 in bounced check fees.

Automated Teller Machines

ATM fees are huge money generators for banks. Originally, ATMs were intended to reduce banks' expenses by automating tasks that previously involved a live teller. Now many banks charge fees for the use of ATMs.

There are several different types of ATM fees. Some banks charge you a fee just to have the use of an ATM card. Others charge ATM access fees, which are weekly, monthly, or yearly fees in addition to the regular account fees. When you use an ATM that is not owned by your bank, you'll incur a surcharge, which is a fee in addition to fees charged by your own bank, a practice called double dipping.

Call or visit these discount check printers online to order checks at discount prices: Checks Unlimited (formerly Current) at ✆1-800-204-2244 (✉*www.checksunlimited.com*); Checks in the Mail at ✆1-800-733-4443 (✉*www.checksinthemail.com*); or CheckWorks at ✆1-800-971-4223 (✉*www.checkworks.com*).

Out-of-Network Fees

Using an ATM that is not in your bank's network is a costly convenience. Here's how it works: You withdraw $20 from an ATM that doesn't belong to your bank and incur a $1.50 fee. Your bank then adds an out-of-network surcharge of $3. You've just paid 22.5 percent to the two banks to access $20 of your own money.

Most banks also charge a fee, commonly $1.50 to $2.00, if you use an ATM to get a cash advance on your credit card. In addition, the credit card company will probably charge a fee for the cash advance, usually around 3 percent of the total advanced, with a minimum fee of $5.

The ATM can be an expensive way to check your balance or recent transactions, at $1.00 or $1.50 a pop at some banks. The receipt you get when you make another type of ATM transaction, such as withdrawing cash or making a deposit, often shows your account balance, so why pay extra?

FACT

Based on data from the U.S. General Accounting Office, it's estimated that consumers will pay $2.2 billion this year in ATM surcharges alone (the fee charged by out-of-network banks when you use their ATMs). This doesn't include the income banks earn from regular ATM fees.

Minimizing ATM Fees

You probably don't keep track of what you pay in ATM fees over the course of a year, but you can see how these fees can add up quickly, so it could be a substantial amount. Simply being aware of how you use the ATM can help you plan ahead so you can avoid some of the costs. Here are a few other ideas for avoiding fees:

- Establish an account at a bank with a large ATM network so you don't get stuck using out-of-network ATMs.
- Plan cash withdrawals when you can access your own bank's ATMs, or look for ATMs that don't impose a surcharge (usually indicated on the ATM).
- Withdraw large amounts of cash less often rather than small amounts more often.
- If your bank doesn't charge to use a live teller, use a teller instead of the ATM.
- Use personal checks instead of paying cash.
- Double up transactions, like using your ATM card to get cash back when you make a purchase at a point-of-sale cash register.
- When traveling, use travelers' checks, personal checks, or credit cards.
- Avoid higher-cost ATMs found in convenience stores, hotels, casinos, restaurants, and airports.

ALERT!

Beware of skimming devices posing as ATMs. They record electronically stored information from the magnetic stripe of your card or your PIN as you enter it. The thieves then skim money from your bank account. Stick to bank ATMs instead of those in malls, airports, and other public places.

Debit Cards

Many banks have added a feature to ATM cards that allows you to use the card for purchases instead of using cash or a check. The money is taken from your account electronically. These cards are called debit cards, or check cards. You can only take out as much as you have in the account, or in your overdraft protection account. Debit cards are for people who are disciplined enough to keep all of their receipts and diligently record every transaction in their checkbooks to avoid overdrafts.

Two Types of Debit Card

There are two types of debit cards. The first is referred to as an online debit card, which removes money immediately from your account when you use your PIN. The second type, called a deferred debit card, bears a MasterCard or Visa logo and can be used anywhere Visa and MasterCard are accepted. Deferred credit cards require you to sign a sales receipt and the amount is removed from your account a few days later.

Some banks combine both functions on one card, so when you're ready to pay using these cards, you have the option of hitting debit or credit on the keypad. Don't be confused by the Visa or MasterCard logo on these cards. They are NOT credit cards. Both types remove money directly from your checking account.

Debit Card Safety

Debit cards that require a PIN are safer than those that require only a signature. If your card is lost or stolen, anyone can sign your name, but a thief can't use your PIN-based debit card unless he or she has your PIN.

If you have a card that allows both types of transactions, a thief could use your card even without your PIN.

Don't leave your receipts behind when you use your debit card or throw them away without shredding them. Thieves who "dumpster-dive" may find your receipt and use the personal information on it to rip you off. Never write your PIN on your debit card or share your PIN with somebody else. Don't use a PIN that is too obvious, such as your phone number or birth date.

If you notice a transaction on your statement that isn't legitimate, report it immediately. If you report it within sixty days, your liability is capped at $500, but if you wait more than sixty days, you're liable for everything the thief removes from your checking account and your overdraft account, if you have one. This is another reason to review your bank statement each month.

FACT

There are often fees related to your debit card. Some banks charge a monthly fee for the debit card. Other banks charge a fee for each transaction. There may also be a requirement to keep a minimum amount in your checking account at all times.

Visa and MasterCard have voluntarily extended the same protection to customers using deferred debit cards as they offer to credit card customers: Your liability is capped at $50 if you report the card missing within two days. However, this feature was instituted voluntarily by Visa/MasterCard and doesn't have the force of law, so it could change at any time.

Under the Fair Credit Billing Act, if you aren't happy with the quality of an item you purchased with a credit card, you can withhold payment for that item. This same protection is not true of a debit card. You'll have to try to work out an agreement with the merchant and may be stuck with a store credit instead of a refund, or you may not get satisfaction from the merchant at all. For this reason, it's a good idea not to use your debit card for big items or services, for online purchases, catalog purchases, or other purchases where you don't walk away immediately with the goods.

It's Time to Balance Your Checkbook

Balancing your checkbook is a method of verifying that your records (your checkbook register) match the bank's records, as shown on your monthly bank statement. The method of accomplishing this task is changing in the electronic age, with the use of online banking and personal-finance software, but the pencil and paper method still works. The best time to balance your checkbook is within a few days of receiving your monthly bank statement so there are fewer transactions to wade through.

You have sixty days to inform the bank of any errors on your statement (and banks DO make errors). If you don't balance your checkbook monthly, how will you find an error if it does occur? Of course, it's much more likely that you made an error when recording a check or deposit or when adding or subtracting amounts in your checkbook register. You're unlikely to find your own errors unless you balance your checkbook each month or start bouncing checks, an expensive way to find out you made a mistake.

Step One: Reconcile Your Checks and Deposits

First, determine if there are any checks that haven't cleared the bank yet by sorting your canceled checks in check number order or by using the listing of cleared checks that's printed in a separate section of your bank statement. In your checkbook register, check off each item that cleared the bank, making sure the amount you recorded in your check register agrees with the amount shown on your bank statement. Watch for transposed numbers in your check register, for example, $97 instead of $79.

Step Two: Reconcile Your Deposits

Make sure that each deposit shown on your bank statement is recorded in your check register, including direct deposits. Next, go through your deposit slips and paycheck stubs and make sure that all the deposits you made are included on the bank statement. As you verify each deposit, check it off in your check register.

Step Three: Reconcile ATM and Debit Card Transactions

Go through your ATM and debit card receipts and check off each transaction on the bank statement and in your check register. Record any transactions that are on the bank statement but not in your check register. If you're not sure what the item is for, call your bank immediately.

Step Four: Record Interest Earned and Bank Fees

Check your bank statement for fees you may have incurred on your account and interest you may have earned on your balance, and record them in your check register.

When you receive a salary increase, put all or part of it into savings each pay period and continue living on your previous salary. Another way of saving the increase is to add it to your 401(k) plan contributions.

Step Five: Complete the Balancing Form

Your bank statement may include a form that you can use to balance your checkbook. If not, use the Checkbook Balancing Form provided here, using the following directions:

1. Go through your checkbook register and list the deposits that you did not check off in your check register as having cleared the bank.
2. Total the column of outstanding deposits.
3. Go through your checkbook register and list the outstanding checks (as well as any outstanding debit purchases or ATM withdrawals) that have not yet cleared the bank.
4. Total the column of outstanding checks, debits, and ATM withdrawals.
5. On **LINE 1**, enter the ending balance shown on your bank statement.
6. On **LINE 2**, enter the total outstanding deposits.

CHECKBOOK BALANCING FORM			
Outstanding Deposits		Outstanding Credits	
Date	Amount	Check Number	Amount

1. Ending balance from your bank statement: $ _____

2. Total outstanding deposits: + _____

3. Total outstanding checks: − _____

4. Bank fees: − _____

5. Interest earned: + _____

6. New balance (should equal the balance in your checkbook): $ _____

7. On **LINE 3**, enter the total outstanding checks.

8. On **LINE 4**, enter the bank fees shown on your bank statement.

9. On **LINE 5**, enter interest earned as shown on your bank statement.

10. Calculate your balance by adding and subtracting the numbers on the bottom section of the form, as indicated by the plus and minus signs. Enter the total on **LINE 6** and make sure it matches the balance shown in your check register. If it doesn't, check your math on the form first, and if you still don't find the error, start from the beginning and check all your entries on the form. Common errors include reversing numbers, subtracting a deposit instead of adding it, adding a check instead of subtracting it, math errors, and omitting automatic payments from your check register.

Best Places to Stash Your Cash

What do you do with money that you want to be able to access quickly when needed, such as your emergency fund? Hide it in the cookie jar? Stuff it under the mattress? Sometimes it's difficult to decide.

If you put it in a certificate of deposit, you may incur penalties if you have to withdraw it early. If you mingle it with your checking account, you're more likely to dip into it. Your savings account may not earn a very good interest rate. Under your mattress or in your cookie jar are really not viable options. So where is the best place to stash your cash?

Checking and Savings Accounts

Savings often end up sitting in the checking account just because it's the easiest option. It's not a good idea, though. Savings should be segregated from your day-to-day spending money for several reasons, including the fact that it's much too easy to dip into your savings if they're mingled with your checking account. You'll also earn better interest in a nonchecking account.

Savings accounts, like checking accounts, are safe if the bank is FDIC-insured, and usually pay higher interest rates than checking accounts. Savings accounts are a good place to park some of your savings, but only as much as you would need in the short-term in an emergency. Because savings-account interest rates may not keep up with the rate of inflation, you actually lose money in the long run.

Money Market Deposit Accounts

Money market deposit accounts, offered by most banks, are also FDIC-insured. They usually require a minimum balance of $1,000 or more, but they pay slightly higher interest rates than traditional savings accounts.

ALERT!

Be aware of the difference between money market deposit accounts offered by your bank and money market funds offered by brokerages and mutual fund companies, which are not FDIC-insured. These funds are typically invested in safe securities like government bonds and CDs, but their value is not guaranteed.

Certificates of Deposit

CDs are actually loans you make to the bank for an agreed-upon term in return for a guaranteed interest rate on your principal. Some have adjustable rates tied to an index like Standard & Poor's 500 stock index. Most CDs charge a penalty if you withdraw all or part of your funds before the maturity date.

Like other bank accounts, CDs are insured up to $100,000 as long as the bank is FDIC-insured. The $100,000 refers to the total of your accounts with that particular bank, so if you have more than $100,000 in one bank, you're not fully protected.

CD terms range from one month to five years or more. The longer the term, the higher the interest rate and the greater the risk that your money will be locked up at a lower rate when interest rates rise. As with any investment, you have to balance the risk with the reward and make a decision within your comfort level.

Banks and brokers also offer callable CDs with rates that may seem too good to pass up, but be sure to read the fine print and ask plenty of questions before investing in a callable CD. Usually the issuer has the right to call the CD at any time after one year, but this doesn't mean it matures in one year. It may be a twenty-year CD, which means you can't cash it in without a penalty for twenty years, but the bank can call the CD at any time.

If interest rates have risen since the CD was issued, the bank will keep the CD in force because the rate will be below the current market rates. If interest rates have fallen, the bank will call the CD so it doesn't have to pay you above-market rates. This leaves you with money to invest at low rates when you may have thought you were locked in at a higher rate for a longer period.

Read the fine print very carefully when investing in a callable CD and be sure you know the difference between the maturity date and the callable date.

Visit ✍ *www.bankrate.com* for screening tools to help you quickly find the best CD rates available. Click on the CD/Savings link on the left side of the page. This will take you to the CD rate page, where you can find the latest rates by state or by best rate.

Laddering CDs

Once your long-term savings reach a substantial amount, you may want to leave some of it in a savings account and invest the rest of it in a CD ladder, a low-risk way to increase your return without losing short-term access to your cash. Initially you buy several CDs with different maturity dates. As they mature, you roll them over into new CDs with longer maturity rates. For example, assume you have $5,000 in a savings account and you want to earn a better return. You take out five CDs, as follows:

- CD #1 for $1,000 for a one-year term
- CD #2 for $1,000 for a two-year term
- CD #3 for $1,000 for a three-year term
- CD #4 for $1,000 for a four-year term
- CD #5 for $1,000 for a five-year term

Each CD is referred to as a rung on a ladder. As each CD matures, renew it for a five-year term. At the end of four years you'll have five CDs with one maturing every year. You'll never be faced with having the bulk of your CD investment renew at a time when interest rates are low, and you'll never be more than a year away from being able to access a portion of your money.

ALERT!

Be especially careful when investing broker-issued CDs. These guarantee the return of your principal at maturity, but maturity may be twenty years from the purchase date. If you cash it in before the maturity date, you may lose not only interest, but a large chunk of your principal as well.

You don't have to do five-year CDs. You can do a two-year ladder instead of a five-year ladder, for example, by initially buying a six-month CD, a twelve-month CD, an eighteen-month CD, and a twenty-four-month CD. As each CD matures, you roll it over into a twenty-four-month CD. This way you have a CD maturing every six months.

Choose your maturity dates based on the current interest rate environment. If rates are very low, use shorter terms, such as six or twelve months, so you'll have cash available to invest in higher yield CDs if rates go up. If rates are forecasted to fall, you might want to lock in the higher current rates for a longer term. Whatever term you choose, continue to follow your plan. Like dollar-cost averaging when investing in stocks, laddering CDs takes much of the angst and frustration out of decision-making.

Chapter 5

Credit Cards 101

There's no question about it: Credit cards are a wonderful convenience that can make your life easier. However, if you overuse them, they're also the biggest deterrent to reaching your financial goals. To avoid this you need to have an understanding of how credit cards really work and how they can work in your favor.

The Good, the Bad, and the Ugly

With credit cards, you don't have to carry cash or your checkbook around with you. You can make purchases over the telephone or the Internet. You can reserve cars and hotel rooms, or have recurring expenses automatically billed to your card. You can buy things you need that you once would have had to wait years to obtain while you saved your money. You can cover unexpected large expenses like major auto repairs that once may have thrown you into a tailspin.

But the same cards that provide great convenience may become the means by which you are enslaved to debt, as charges you make become grossly inflated by high interest rates. As your debt grows out of control, it may even outlast the purchases that created the debt in the first place.

The Appeal of Credit

Young people today are impatient to live the American Dream, but the very tool they attempt to use is the tool that most often keeps them from attaining the dream: credit cards. Their message is one of instant gratification—you can have it all now. Credit cards can make it seem like you're not spending real money. But once you get too deeply in debt it could take you years, or even decades, to get out. In the meantime, your real dreams will be on hold.

FACT

As of 2001, the average American household had $7,500 in credit card debt, a 250 percent increase in ten years, and bankruptcies nearly doubled, with credit card debt the largest reason.

On the Bright Side

Despite the risk of turning credit card use to abuse, it's possible to use credit cards wisely. A credit card will allow you to establish credit so when it's time to buy a house or a new car you qualify for the mortgage or car loan. Keeping your debt manageable is the most important thing you can do to get on the road to financial freedom.

What's out There

Before you accept one or more of those preapproved credit card offers you find in your mailbox, make sure you understand the distinction between the different types of credit cards and the terms and conditions that will affect your costs. There are several types of plastic cards that are loosely referred to as credit cards, but they don't all work alike. Bankcards include Visa, MasterCard, Discover, and Optima. These card companies allow you to make purchases up to a preset credit limit ranging from $500 to $10,000 or more, depending on your income and credit history. You can pay the balance in full each month, the minimum required by the card company (typically around 2 percent of the balance), or any amount in between.

Travel and entertainment cards, including American Express, Diners Club, and Carte Blanche, require you to pay the entire balance due each month. They have no preset credit limits but if you are late with your payment, you may be charged interest or have the use of your card blocked until you catch up.

QUESTION?

What are gold and platinum cards?
These are cards that include extra perks such as collision coverage when you rent a car, extended warranties beyond the manufact-urer's warranty on certain items, travel insurance, discounts, and other benefits. They sound appealing, but consider what exactly you get for the privilege of paying a much higher annual fee.

House cards allow you to make purchases at a particular chain of stores such as department stores and gas stations, and make monthly payments, including interest charges. These cards are becoming less popular, since many retailers allow you to use your major credit card. It's easier to use one major credit card, and make one payment a month, and it helps you keep a handle on just how much you owe in credit card debt.

Smart cards, the latest in plastic cards, look like a credit card but contain a computer chip with a preset dollar amount built in. Instead of charging to the card, you spend the value at places that accept smart cards, or chip cards.

The Cost of Credit

There are several types of costs associated with credit cards. The annual fee is a flat dollar amount the issuer charges each year for the use of the card. Many, but not all, issuers charge annual fees, so look for no-fee credit cards (but be sure to consider all the other factors such as grace period, interest rate, and so on).

Finance charges are calculated based on the interest rate your card issuer charges and are the main cost of using credit. These rates vary significantly from one card to another, so you can save a lot of money by shopping around for a card with a lower interest rate.

Other fees that you might incur on your credit card include application fees, processing fees, charges for exceeding your credit limit, late-payment fees, balance transfer fees, credit life insurance, and fees on cash advances.

The Internet is a great tool for finding the best credit card. Visit ✍ *www.bankrate.com* for an up-to-date list of the best credit card deals in the country. Another great site, ✍ *www.financenter.com*, offers calculators to help you choose the best card and manage your credit.

Grace Periods

The grace period, commonly twenty-five days, is the time between the date you're billed and the date your payment is due. If you pay your entire balance within the grace period, you may not incur any interest charges. If you carry a balance, there's often no grace period on new purchases, so interest starts accruing from the date of purchase. Some issuers charge interest from the day you make the purchase, even if you pay your balance in full, so in effect there is no grace period.

Choosing What's Best for You

Before you choose a credit card, think about how you intend to use it. Do you plan to pay off the balance every month or carry a balance from one month to the next? If you pay the balance every month, the annual fee and other charges may be more important than the annual percentage rate (APR), so you should look for a no-fee or low-fee card. Even if the issuer charges an annual fee, you may be able to get it waived by calling and asking them to remove it. If you carry a balance and pay for your purchases over time, the APR and the method of computing your balance are most important, so you'll want to look for the lowest interest rate and the best grace period. Getting a rebate or frequent flier miles is usually not a good reason to choose one card over another unless everything else is equal. You'd have to do a lot of flying to build up enough frequent flier miles to pay for the fee that often accompanies these cards.

Beware of teaser rates, which sound tempting because the introductory rate is much lower than the going rate on most cards. The downside is that if you have a balance on the card when the introductory rate ends, you could be in worse shape than you were with a higher rate, depending on how high the rate spikes at the end of the introductory offer.

ALERT!

Interest rates on cards that award frequent flier miles for certain purchases are usually several percentage points higher than regular credit cards, so don't carry a balance on them. If you pay even one day late, you're hit with finance charges and you may lose any miles earned that month.

Interest Rates

In general, if you have a good credit history and you're paying more than 7 or 8 percent above the current prime interest rate on your VISA or MasterCard, you're paying too much. Considering that the prime rate is in the single digits, lenders that charge 16 to 21 percent interest on credit card balances are gouging you. A few percentage points in the interest rate could save you thousands of dollars depending on your balance and how quickly (or slowly) you pay it off.

If you can obtain a lower-interest credit card, you can usually use cash advances to pay off the balance on your other credit cards and transfer this debt to the lower-rate card. Be sure to read the fine print, though. The interest rate on cash advances and transferred balances is usually much higher than the standard interest rate, so be sure you can pay off the cash advance before the introductory offer runs out.

If you have a questionable credit history, you'll pay higher interest rates. Lenders try to reduce their risk by increasing the interest charges on higher-risk debts. The higher the rate, the faster your debt will grow, and the harder it will be for you to pay it off.

If You Have Damaged Credit

Sometimes people make unwise choices or take on more credit than they can handle and end up with a bad credit history. Sometimes they acquire bad credit through divorce, loss of a spouse, or bankruptcy. If you have bad credit, or have no credit history, chances are you can still get a credit card, but it will cost you more, and the terms won't be as favorable as they are for those with good credit or a history of making timely payments. You may only be able to get a $500 credit limit, and you'll probably pay an exorbitant interest rate. Use the card wisely and make your payments on time, and eventually you'll qualify for better terms.

Research the best credit card deals, and apply only to one at a time. Applications for credit show up on your credit report and can make potential credit card issuers nervous, because they think you may be taking on more credit than you can handle. If you get turned down for a major credit card, try a department store card or gas card. These are often easier to get and making your payments on time for one of these cards can build a credit history that will help you qualify at some point for a major credit card.

Secured Cards

If all else fails, consider a secured card. You put your own money into a savings account and that amount, or some portion of it, becomes the security for your credit line. If you don't pay your bills, the card issuer will use the money from your savings account to cover your debt. It may be difficult to come up with the amount to deposit, but you can build a credit history using this method. Many people find that after twelve to eighteen months of making timely payments on a secured card, they can "graduate" to a regular credit card.

Since your goal with a secured card is to establish or re-establish good credit, make sure that the company issuing the card reports to a credit bureau. Otherwise, the card can't help you build or repair your credit history.

As with any credit card offer, beware of disreputable issuers. Secured cards are a favorite with unscrupulous marketers and you're a potential target because you can't easily obtain credit. Study the fine print before applying. Secured cards typically carry a higher interest rate and higher fees. Ask whether there are application or processing fees, which can total hundreds of dollars. The latest trend in secured cards is no application fees, so do your homework and save yourself some money.

Cosigned Credit Cards

If all else fails, you may be able to find someone to cosign on a credit card for you. Remember: If you do this and you don't make your payments, you can ruin the credit of the cosigner, who would have to pay off your debt. You wouldn't want to do this to someone who was willing to go out on a limb for you.

Questionable Credit Card Offers

If you have poor credit, you're more susceptible to questionable credit offers, so stay on your toes. Don't fall for offers of easy credit, ads that require you to call a 900 number (you'll pay a fee for the call and may never see the credit card), or offers to repair your credit. You have the legal right to correct any errors in your credit report by directly contacting the credit-reporting bureaus; don't pay someone to do this for you. Some credit repair companies make false claims about their ability to clean up your credit. Only the creditor or the credit-reporting bureau can remove a debt from your record, and the only way to clean up your credit history is by making payments on time for several years and paying off your debts.

ALERT!

Don't fall for advice given by some credit repair services or credit doctors telling you to obtain an employer identification number (EIN) and apply for credit using that instead of your social security number, so your credit history doesn't pop up when a credit check is performed. It's a felony.

Using Credit Cards Wisely

Most of what we hear from financial experts about credit cards is negative, but credit cards can be a great tool when used wisely. Unfortunately, many people get in over their heads when they're just out of school and may never recover from the financial decisions they make unless they get serious about getting out of debt.

Staying Out of Trouble

A large percentage of credit card debt is incurred around the holidays. If you use your credit cards to do holiday shopping, you may not pay off the charges until months later. Using credit cards often leads to impulse spending and overspending, and those items that seemed like such bargains end up costing you 10 to 20 percent more than you thought, due to credit card interest. If you can't afford to pay cash, can you really afford to buy the gift? There are times when incurring credit card debt makes sense, but holiday gift buying isn't one of them. Instead, try saving small amounts of money throughout the year in a special holiday gift fund. When the cash is gone, you're done shopping.

Some people use their credit card for nearly all of their expenses and pay off the balance in full at the end of the month. This gives them one document that includes most of their expenditures for the month and can help in budgeting and keeping track of where their money goes. This practice is only for the most disciplined credit card users. If you don't have the money or the discipline to pay off your balance every month, you should avoid using a credit card for things like clothing, food, gas, dining out, and similar expenses. Doing so can encourage you to spend more than you can really afford.

Cash Advances

Cash advances on a credit card come with a price tag—very high interest rates and fees. This feature is for the true emergency, not for buying nonessentials. If you're using cash advances for nonemergencies like eating out, paying your regular bills, or for entertainment or vacations, run to your nearest credit-counseling agency.

Grace periods don't apply to cash advances, so you pay interest from the day you get the cash. There's also usually a transaction fee of anywhere between 2 and 3 percent of the cash advance total. To add insult to injury, the interest rate on cash advances is significantly higher than the rate on purchases. All in all, your cash advance can end up costing you a bundle of money.

FACT

Visa cardholders take out a staggering $100 billion a year in cash advances. At an average up-front fee of 3 percent, cash advances are generating $3 billion a year to Visa in this type of fee alone.

Correcting Credit Card Billing Errors

Review your credit card statement carefully each month, and if you see anything that doesn't look right, like purchases you didn't make, incorrect payments or credits, or other errors, call the number on your statement for billing questions. Sometimes a phone call can clear up the problem quickly, but if not, you have sixty days to notify the credit card company in writing. The credit card company has thirty days to respond and ninety days to resolve the error. In the meantime, you're not required to pay the disputed amount, and you won't incur any finance charges on the disputed amount while it's being investigated.

Pay It Off!

In order to get out from under the burden of debt and get ahead financially, you need to face the uncomfortable truth that it could take you thirty years to pay off that credit card balance. It may sound obvious, but one of the most important things to realize about credit cards is that the credit card company's goal is to make money from your account. When they establish a low minimum monthly payment, they're not trying to do you a favor; they're trying to maximize their profits. When you pay the minimum payment, it's good for them, but not for you.

The minimum monthly payment for most credit card companies is around 2 percent of the balance, including interest. If you made a purchase of $2,500 at an annual interest rate of 18 percent, it would take you almost twenty-eight years to pay off the balance by making the minimum monthly payment. Initially, 2 percent of your balance would be a minimum payment of $50.00, with around 75 percent, or $37.50, going toward interest and only 15 percent, or $13.50, reducing the amount you borrowed. You can see why it would take so many years to pay off your balance.

ALERT!

By paying credit card interest of $50 a month you've lost the opportunity to invest that money: $50 a month invested at 8 percent would total over $62,000 in twenty-eight years, the time it would take you to pay off a $2,500 balance if you make the minimum payment.

By the time you paid off the $2,500, you'd end up paying interest of $5,896 in addition to the $2,500 principal you borrowed. Your $2,500 item will have cost you $8,396. How can you ever get ahead financially if you're paying such exorbitant prices? Next time you're tempted to use your credit card, think about the real cost of the item you're buying. You wouldn't pay $8,396 for an item that is clearly marked with a $2,500 price tag, would you? That's exactly the type of inflated price you're paying when you make only the minimum payment each month on a credit card with an interest rate in the teens.

You should be absolutely unwilling to pay only the minimum balance on your credit cards each month. If you can't afford to pay more than the minimum payment, can you really afford whatever it was you charged to the card in the first place? Instead of paying the credit card company each month, you could put the money in a savings account until you have enough to pay cash for the item. If you need to buy on credit, at least do it with your eyes wide open.

Warning Signs of Too Much Debt

When it comes to debt, it's tough to face the fact that you're in over your head, but it's much easier to turn things around when you know the signs of too much debt and act quickly once they appear. Don't allow yourself to be lulled into a false sense of security just because you pay the monthly minimums on your cards (or even a little more) and you're not late on any payments.

Ask yourself if any of these warning signs apply to you:

- You have little or no savings and you live from paycheck to paycheck.
- You have more than two major credit cards and you make minimum payments on them.
- You use increasing amounts of your total income to pay off debts.
- You shop compulsively, buying things you don't need or don't use.
- You consolidate debts with a high-interest loan.
- You're at or near your credit limit on your credit cards.
- Your debts or spending create friction between you and your family.
- You don't know the total of all of your outstanding debts, or the terms and balances of loans.
- You use cash advances on your credit card to pay your bills.

- Your credit card has been declined when you tried to make a purchase or your application for credit has been denied.

The sooner you realize and admit that you're in over your head, the easier it will be to get out from under the burden of debt. Beware of debt consolidation services or companies that promise to fix your credit. There's no easy fix, but it is possible to turn your finances around if you work at it and break the habits that got you into trouble in the first place.

Protecting Yourself Against Losses

It's getting more and more difficult to protect your credit cards from theft. Thieves and scam artists keep coming up with more clever ruses to obtain the information they need to use your cards fraudulently or obtain credit in your name. Even your identity can be stolen.

Keep Your Credit Cards Safe

Your best protection against credit card fraud is to know where your cards are at all times. Don't leave them lying around on your desk at work or in your car or anywhere else they could be accessible to others. Keep the PIN for your debit and ATM cards a secret. Don't use personal information such as address, phone number, or birth date as the basis for your PIN; they're too easy for a thief to guess.

Don't disclose your credit card number over the phone unless you're dealing with a reputable company and you're the one who placed the call to them. If someone calls and tells you that you've won a prize but they need your credit card number to verify, hang up. Never write your account number on the outside of a piece of mail. When you get a renewal credit card or you cancel a card, cut the card up into small pieces, being sure to cut through the number.

Don't carry credit cards with you unless you know you're going to need them. This protects you against impulse shopping as well as theft.

Keep a record of your credit cards, account numbers, and the telephone number to report a loss so that you can do so quickly if your card is lost or stolen.

ALERT!

Shred or cut up credit card offers you receive in the mail. Thieves have been known to go through trash to retrieve these offers, apply for credit cards in your name, and then charge large amounts before you're aware of the problem.

If Your Card Is Lost or Stolen

As soon as you realize your credit card, ATM card, or debit card has been lost or stolen, report it immediately to the bank or other issuer in order to limit your liability if the card is used fraudulently. Keep a list of your credit cards and telephone numbers in a safe place so you can access the phone number as quickly as possible.

Under federal law, if you report the loss before any unauthorized charges are made to your card, you can't be held responsible for any charges. If a thief uses your card before you report it missing, the most you will owe for unauthorized charges is $50 per card. If somebody uses your credit card number fraudulently without physically stealing the card itself, you are not liable for the charges.

Even though you called the issuer to report the loss, it's a good idea to follow up with a letter in case you need to prove that you did so. After the loss of your card, review your monthly statements carefully and report in writing any unauthorized charges. Be sure to send the letter to the billing error address and not to the payment address (unless they are the same). Lost credit cards should also be reported to each of the major credit-reporting agencies: Experian, TransUnion, and Equifax. Ask them to place a security alert on your account to intercept possibly fraudulent applications for credit.

Identity Theft

Identity theft occurs when someone uses your personal information (such as your name, social security number, or credit card number) without your knowledge, to commit fraud or theft. Thieves may apply for a credit card in your name, using your date of birth and social security number, and charge large amounts before you even know the account has been opened. When the bills aren't paid, the delinquency goes in *your* credit history. It can take months or even years to prove that the card was obtained fraudulently and to clean up your credit report. In the meantime, you may be denied credit.

Another tactic used by thieves is to call your credit card company and report a change of address on your account. Your bills get redirected somewhere else, so you may not realize there's a problem while the thief is running up charges on your account. Other popular scams include establishing cellular phone service in your name or setting up a bank account in your name and writing bad checks on the account.

You can see why it's so important to be careful about how and where you discard bank statements, credit card statements, credit card offers, or any paperwork that includes your date of birth or social security number. In these times, it's a good idea to own a personal shredder and shred all documents containing personal information before putting them in the trash. Paper shredders can be purchased at an office supply store for less than $25.

If you believe you're the victim of identity theft, report it to the three credit-reporting bureaus, all of your creditors, and your local police as soon as possible so steps can be taken to control the damage.

For more information on how to avoid being a victim of identity theft and how to recover if you do become a victim, visit these Web sites: ✍ *www.consumer.gov*, ✍ *www.ftc.gov*, and ✍ *www.privacyrights.org*.

Chapter 6

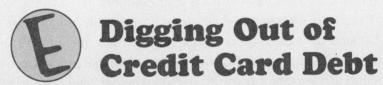 Digging Out of Credit Card Debt

Being in debt over your head can be an overwhelming, hopeless feeling. You may be embarrassed for others to know that you're struggling to pay your bills. You may toss and turn at night thinking about how to get out from under the burden. You're not alone, and with hard work and discipline, you *can* dig your way out.

Your Credit Report and How It Works

If you want to get out of credit card debt without falling victim to fraud and credit repair scams, you need to know what's on your credit report and why it's there, develop a plan to pay down debt, and change the way you use credit to avoid repeating the same problems.

The first step is finding out what your creditors are saying about you. A credit report is a record of your credit payment history as reported to credit bureaus by your bank, credit card companies, department stores, and other businesses you've borrowed from. Potential lenders use the information in your credit report to decide whether they want to take the risk of issuing you credit. If you understand how credit reports work, you can protect your rights and avoid being taken advantage of by unscrupulous credit repair clinics and so-called credit doctors.

Under the Fair Credit Reporting Act, you have specific rights related to your credit report. You can read about these rights on the Federal Trade Commission's Web site at *www.ftc.gov*.

If you're thinking about buying a house or applying for credit for any other big purchase, you'll need a good credit report. It's always best to know what's on it before your lender does, so you'll have an opportunity to clean up any discrepancies or errors. You should also cancel any unused credit cards so the lender won't include your credit limit in your total debt. Lenders consider how much *potential* debt you have, not just how much you have outstanding on your credit cards and other loans. If you have credit cards with no balance but with credit limits totaling $4,000, for example, the lender will consider it an additional $4,000 in debt, and will reduce the amount of the loan they're willing to give you.

What's in a Credit Report?

Your credit report includes the following basic personal information: name, current and previous addresses, telephone number, social security number, date of birth, and current and previous employers. The credit history section includes information about each credit account, including the date opened, credit limit or loan amount, balance, monthly payment, and your payment pattern during the past several years. Also included are bankruptcies, accounts sent to collection agencies, unpaid child support or alimony, tax liens, bounced checks, unpaid traffic or parking tickets, car repossessions, evictions from rental apartments, court records of tax liens and monetary judgments, and the names of businesses or individuals who have obtained a copy of your credit report. In addition, your report contains information obtained from public records, such as your job history, whether you own your home, and whether you've been sued, arrested, or have filed for bankruptcy.

FACT

Your credit report does NOT include information about your race or national origin, religion, personal lifestyle, political affiliation, medical history, criminal record, or other information unrelated to your credit history and ability to repay debt.

When issues between you and a creditor can't be resolved, the comments and explanations you're allowed to add to your credit report and the creditor's response to your statements become part of your credit report. If an account was turned over to a collection agency, your report will include it as a "collection account" until it's paid in full; then it will be noted as a "paid collection" and will stay on your credit report for seven years from the date of the first missed payment.

Review Your Credit Report

Financial advisors recommend that you obtain a copy of your credit report at least once a year and review it carefully. The Fair Credit Reporting Act limits how much credit bureaus can charge for your report. The fee is currently under $10 for a basic credit report (not including your credit score) and is increased by the Federal Trade Commission (FTC) in January of each year. If you've been turned down for credit, housing, or employment because of information in your report, you may be entitled to a free copy of your credit report. Some states require that credit bureaus provide free copies or charge a reduced price for residents of that state, so you may pay less than the maximum fee set by the FTC, depending on where you live.

There are three main credit bureaus: Equifax, Experian, and TransUnion. All other credit bureaus obtain their information from one of these three. Because some creditors report to only one of the bureaus, the information in your credit report may differ somewhat from one bureau to the other; experts recommend that you obtain a copy of your report from each of the three major credit bureaus once a year. You can also order a three-in-one report that includes the information from all three credit bureaus. It may cost more than obtaining the individual reports, so you'll have to decide if it's worth the convenience. If you can't afford to pay for all three reports, consider ordering your report from Equifax, the largest reporting bureau.

If you order online, the maximum legal cost for a basic report may not be clearly stated and you'll be encouraged to pay more for additional information, such as your credit score. You should be charged the correct amount as long as you don't order any of the extra features.

If you find an error in your credit report, call or write to the credit bureau explaining the error in as much detail as possible in 100 words or less. Provide any documents that help prove your statements.

The Lifespan of Credit Information

Your payment history will follow you around for a long time. Chapter 7 bankruptcies stay on your credit report for ten years from the filing date; Chapter 13 bankruptcies remain for seven years from the date fully paid or ten years if not paid as agreed. Unpaid tax liens stay on your credit report for fifteen years, and most other negative information stays on your report for seven years.

How Do Lenders Use the Credit Report?

Lenders use the information in your credit report to evaluate your character, your debt capacity, and your collateral or capital. Their evaluation of your character is based on the stability of your employment and residency history. How often have you changed jobs? How often have you moved and how long have you stayed at each address? This information gives lenders a feel for your personal stability.

To evaluate your debt capacity, lenders look at your living expenses, open credit limits, current debts, and other payments to get a sense of how much debt you can afford based on your spending habits, income, and credit burden. They're more likely to extend you credit that's secured by collateral or a down payment. For example, the car you purchase is the collateral for your car loan. If you default on the loan, the car can be repossessed, so there's less risk to the lender.

To get a copy of your credit report, call one of the credit-reporting bureaus or visit one of their Web sites:
Experian: ✆1-800-311-4769 (✍ *www.experian.com)*
TransUnion: ✆1-800-888-4213 (✍ *www.transunion.com)*
Equifax: ✆1-800-685-1111 (✍ *www.equifax.com)*

Lenders base their lending decisions on your credit score, which is a number indicating how likely you are to make payments on time and repay loans, based on information in your credit history. The score is computer-generated and factors in your income, education, job stability, how often you've moved, whether you own your own home, how often you take out cash advances, how close you are to your credit limits, what kinds of things you buy on credit, how many credit cards you have, and past payment history. A computer compares this information to patterns in thousands of other credit reports and predicts your level of credit risk.

For a fee, you can now obtain your credit score, or FICO score, named after the Fair Isaac Corporation, the company that developed credit scoring and the largest provider of credit scores to creditors and financial institutions. All three major credit bureaus offer this option with your credit report or as a separate option. If your credit score isn't exactly stellar, do your best to improve your score by concentrating on paying your bills on time, paying down your loan and credit card balances, and avoiding new debt. It can take considerable time to improve your credit score but is well worth the effort.

Paying Down Debt on Your Own

Once you realize and accept the fact that you have too much credit card debt, the question is, what are you willing to do about it? The first step is to put the credit cards away, or better yet, cut them up and cancel them. Then consider the following options to see which ones might work for you.

Use Your Savings or Sell Something of Value

If you have something of value, consider selling it. You may have some stocks or mutual funds you could cash in. How about those savings bonds Uncle Herbie gave you every year when you were a kid? Do you own a collection of some sort that has value?

If you're earning less than 3 to 4 percent interest on your savings account while paying 12 to 21 percent on credit cards, you may need to use your savings to pay off debt in order to prevent ruining your credit. Try to leave yourself a savings cushion even if you can't keep a full three months worth of basic, no frills living expenses.

Use the Equity in Your Home

Using the equity in your home may be another option. If interest rates are lower than your current mortgage rate, and you haven't yet damaged your credit, you may be able to refinance and roll your debts into the new mortgage. If that's not an option, you might be able to get a home equity loan or line of credit to pay off your other debts. Rates on mortgages and home equity loans are much lower than the rates on most credit cards, so besides the obvious slash in the interest rate, you reduce your interest costs even more by deducting the home equity loan interest from your taxes. Don't forget that although you can deduct 28 percent of mortgage interest if you're in the 28 percent tax bracket, the other 72 percent still comes out of your pocket.

Exercise extreme caution when you consider borrowing against the equity in your home. If you get into trouble financially due to job loss, illness, medical bills, or divorce, you may not be able to make your mortgage payments and the lender may foreclose on your house. Don't jeopardize your most valuable asset if you really can't afford the increased mortgage payments or if you haven't made changes in your spending habits and credit use. Using equity in your home to pay off consumer debt once may get you ahead, but you can't keep going back to the well.

Use the Credit Crunch Method

This method of paying down debt goes by a number of different names, but all the methods work the same way. They seriously reduce your interest expense, which could be 90 percent of your monthly payment if you've been paying the minimum, and they allow you to pay off your balances sooner.

ALERT!

If you drive an expensive car, consider getting a less expensive one. It's not just that the monthly payment is higher; it's the repairs and maintenance, special tires, gas, and insurance. Drive a reliable, inexpensive car for a few years and apply the savings to your credit card balances.

First, to really get a handle on your debt, develop a written plan. Prepare a schedule of your debts, listing the creditor, the balance due, the interest rate, and the current monthly payment. Rank the debts in descending order by interest rate (highest interest rate first, lowest interest rate last). Each month, pay the minimum balance on all credit cards except the one with the highest interest rate. Pay as much as you possibly can on this card each month until it's paid off. Use all available money for this payment including overtime pay, tax refunds, bonuses, money generated by reducing expenses, and your bottle deposit money.

When you've paid off the first debt, pause briefly to pat yourself on the back, and then start in on the next debt with the highest interest rate. Pay as much as you possibly can each month, including the amount you were previously applying to debt number one. Continue to pay the minimum balance on the others. Keep moving down the list of debts until they're all paid off. This is the only time you should ever pay the minimum balance on any credit card. The Credit Crunch method requires month after month of consistency and discipline, but it works.

Find out how long it will take to become debt-free and how much you'll pay in interest by making the minimum monthly payments by using the Debt Planner calculator in the personal-finance section of CNNMoney (*http://moneycnn.com*).

Getting Help from a Finance Company

If you don't think you're cut out for the Credit Crunch method, there are several options for consolidating your debt. Finance companies make your paperwork easier because they pay off all your debt so you make only one payment each month. The problem is that finance companies charge very high interest rates, so you end up paying a steep price for the convenience of writing fewer checks. Some experts believe that unless your debt problems were caused by job loss, disability, or other major life experience, a debt consolidation loan is just postponing the inevitable: bankruptcy. Many people continue to live beyond their means after paying off debt consolidation loans and end up in the same situation again. For debt consolidation to really make any sense, it's important to change the way you spend money and use credit.

Stay away from consolidation loans unless the interest rate will be significantly lower than what you're currently paying and you're committed to continuing to pay at least as much as you were before consolidating. Otherwise you won't be paying off your debt any sooner, it will cost you more in the long run, and you'll soon be back where you were.

Bill-Paying Services

If you use a bill-paying service, all your bills are sent directly to the bill-paying company, which makes payments for you and sends you a monthly transaction report. They also charge you a fee, typically around 10 percent of the total you owe. Bill-paying services don't actually lend you money, so you still have to cough up the cash yourself. At most, they offer the incentive for exercising a little discipline and the ease of writing one check instead of several each month. Evaluate the costs carefully. If you owe $5,000 and the bill-paying service charges 10 percent, that's $500 you'll be paying for the convenience of having them disburse the money you send them each month.

Transferring Credit Card Balances

Another popular method of reducing debt is transferring credit card balances to a card with a lower interest rate so more of your payment is applied to principal and less to interest each month. This only helps if you continue to pay at least as much as you were paying before, even though the minimum payment may be less.

ALERT!

The Internet makes researching and choosing a credit card easy, but read all the fine print. Make sure there's no fee for transferring a balance. If the transfer fee is 5 percent and you transfer $2,000, you'll pay $100 just to transfer your balance, unless there's a cap on the fee.

Beware the Introductory Rate

Shop around for cards with low interest rates, but beware of come-ons that offer a low introductory rate and then take a big jump a few months later. If you haven't paid off the transferred balance when the rate goes up, you could end up paying more than you bargained for. Determine how long the introductory rate will last. Most are only good for five to nine months, so be very sure you can pay off the balance before then. Also be sure you don't miss a payment or pay late, because most issuers jack up the introductory rate sharply as soon as you falter even slightly on your payments. Finally, make sure that you qualify for the rate advertised. The 1.9 percent rate in the big bold print may be more like 10 percent for you, depending on your credit history. If anything is unclear after you've read the fine print, call the credit card company and ask questions.

Borrowing from Your 401(k)

Most 401(k) plans include a loan feature that allows you to borrow money from your retirement account and repay it in five years or less at an interest rate determined by your plan administrator, usually a couple of points above the prime rate. Most plans with a loan feature allow you to borrow half of your balance, up to $50,000.

Paying Yourself Back

Since you pay the interest back into your own 401(k) account, you may think you can't go wrong with a 401(k) loan, but it's not quite that simple. Remember the discussion of opportunity costs in earlier chapters? Taking money out of your account could have a significant impact on your retirement income even though you pay the money back, because you have less money invested to earn interest and dividends or appreciate in value. There could be a double whammy if you reduce your contributions to the plan because you can't afford to make contributions in addition to the loan payments. Even if your loan is repaid in one year, going that long without new contributions will have a long-term impact on how much you accumulate by the time you reach retirement age. Still, there are times when using 401(k) funds to get out of a credit hole makes sense.

The Danger of Changing Jobs

Perhaps even worse than reducing the potential accumulation of earnings is the danger of being stuck with a loan balance if your employment terminates, whether it's because you've accepted a job elsewhere or you were fired or laid off. If you have an outstanding loan at the time your employment ends, you'll have to pay it back **immediately** *to avoid having Uncle Sam slap you with taxes and a 10 percent penalty.*

Let's say you borrowed $12,000 and repaid $2,000 before changing jobs. Your loan balance at termination is $10,000. If you can't come up with the money to repay it right away, *it will be considered a premature withdrawal.* If you're in the 28 percent tax bracket, you'll have to pay $2,800 in income taxes, plus another $1,000 (10 percent) early with-drawal penalty. All of a sudden your low-interest loan doesn't look so good. On top of that, if you have no other way to come up with the money to pay the taxes and you have to take them from your 401(k) plan too, that money will also be subject to taxes and penalties. The retirement fund that you've worked so hard to build could be decimated. In most cases, 401(k) loans should be used as one of the last options for debt consolidation.

FACT

Of all the employees who are eligible for 401(k) loans, 24.5 percent had one in 2001, with an average outstanding balance of $6,993, according to the Profit Sharing/401(k) Council of America's 45th Annual Survey of Profit Sharing and 401(k) Plans.

Credit-Counseling Service

Nonprofit consumer credit-counseling agencies may consolidate your debts into a single, manageable monthly bill. You pay the agency each month and they distribute the money to your creditors. This type of arrangement is not a consolidation loan, but it has its benefits because creditors will often accept lower payments if you're working with a reputable credit-counseling agency. Services may be free or provided for a very low fee of $10 to $15 a month.

Counselors are trained in helping consumers get out of debt and will work with you to get late fees waived and interest rates reduced. You may have to agree not to use credit and not to apply for new credit while you're participating in the debt repayment program.

QUESTION?

Won't credit counseling hurt my chances of getting credit?
It may, but don't let this keep you from getting help. Repayment programs through credit-counseling agencies show up on your credit history, but by the time you're in deeply enough to consider consolidation loans, your credit rating has probably already been affected.

Negotiating with Credit Card Companies

Credit card companies will often lower your interest rate if you simply ask. Call the company and tell them that you've received credit card offers with lower rates and ask if they can lower your rate so you don't have to switch. If you've been a good customer and have been with the company awhile, you stand a good chance of getting your rate reduced. This is one of the reasons it's important to work with your creditors before you start making late payments or missing payments altogether.

High Risk Equals High Rate

Once you start getting black marks on your account, your lender is likely to raise your rate sharply to offset the risk that you might not repay your balance. On the other hand, lenders want you to pay your debts and are sometimes willing to lower your interest rate or waive fees if they believe you're serious about getting caught up. It doesn't hurt to ask. If you get "no" for an answer, call back and ask again. Sometimes getting a different customer service representative can make a difference.

Prioritize Your Bills

If there's just not enough money to pay all your bills each month, you may throw up your hands in defeat instead of dealing logically with the situation. Some payments are more important than others. If your situation is so dire that you can't pay all your bills, prioritize your debts and expenses and pay the most important ones first, in this order:

- Mortgage or rent
- Car loan and auto insurance
- Other insurance (homeowners, health)
- Utilities
- Loans (banks, student loans, finance companies)
- Credit cards
- Miscellaneous

Talk to the creditors you can't pay fully and let them know you intend to meet your obligations but need some time. They may be willing to give you a month or two and tack the payments onto the end of your loan, reduce your interest rate, or reage your account so it's not reported as delinquent to the credit bureaus.

Avoiding Credit Repair Scams

Some companies claim they can "fix" bad credit histories for a large sum. This can sound very appealing if you're desperately in debt and are being hounded by bill collectors. You should know, however, that it's legally impossible to alter an accurate credit history. If you find yourself in credit trouble, develop a budget and work with your creditors to pay your debts and re-establish a good credit rating. There's no quick fix.

With so many people carrying too much debt, credit card repair scams are rampant. Don't fall for anything that sounds too good to be true, because it will end up costing you money and will not solve your debt problems. Ads that promise to fix your bad credit, create a new credit identity, or remove bad credit information from your credit report are scams.

If you find yourself a victim of a credit repair scam, contact your local consumer protection agency (click on "Agencies" at ✑ *www.consumerworld.org*), your state's attorney general (click on "The Attorneys General" at ✑ *www.naag.org*), or your local Better Business Bureau (information is available at ✑ *www.bbb.org*).

Errors in your credit report or outdated information can legally be removed, but you don't need to pay somebody to do it. You can do it yourself by writing a letter to the credit bureau. Negative information can't be removed if it's accurate. Credit repair clinics may use illegal tricks to get something temporarily removed from your credit report but it will show up again the next month when your lender updates the information provided to the credit-reporting bureau. Ⓔ

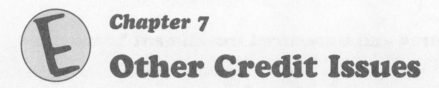

Chapter 7

Other Credit Issues

C redit card debt gets a lot of attention from financial advisers, and rightly so, but it's not the only debt in town. Understanding other types of debt can help you choose the kind of loan that makes the most sense for you. It can also make you less susceptible to being taken advantage of, and may help you avoid bankruptcy.

Installment, Secured, and Unsecured Loans

All loans are alike in some ways. You borrow an amount of money, called the *principal,* for a set amount of time, called the *term,* at a fixed interest rate or a variable rate. Some loans require the principal to be repaid all at once. Others, called *installment loans,* require regular payments of a specified amount at predetermined intervals, usually every month.

Secured and Unsecured Installment Loans

Loans can be secured or unsecured, which refers to whether they are backed up by collateral. For example, car loans and mortgages are secured loans. Your promise to repay the loan is secured by the car or house you're buying. If you fail to make your payments, the lender can seize the car or house to recoup the money it lent you. Unsecured loans are backed up only by your promise to repay.

FACT

Most people use installment loans when buying a car or boat. Sales contracts are a type of installment loan commonly used when purchasing appliances or furniture. The retailer provides financing or outsources it to a finance company and you make monthly payments, including interest, until the balance is paid.

Revolving Credit

Revolving credit is more flexible than an installment loan. There's a maximum you can borrow, and a minimum you must pay each month, but the rest is up to you. Personal lines of credit are a type of revolving credit account where you qualify for a certain amount and use it at your own discretion by writing special checks provided by the lender. Lines of credit are great if you're not sure when you're going to need the money and want to have funds available quickly. Many people use home equity lines of credit to make improvements to their home or pay down credit card debt.

Department stores often offer revolving credit loans with no interest and no payments due for three to six months on large purchases such as furniture or appliances. If you take advantage of these offers, be sure to pay the entire balance before the interest kicks in. Often these accounts are turned over to a finance company at the end of the interest-free period, and the interest rates are high. Although no payments are required for several months, it's a good idea to make them anyway, or put money aside each month to pay off the balance at the end of the interest-free period, so you'll be sure to have the money available. Otherwise, these are not such great deals, because your purchase ends up costing you considerably more when you factor in the interest.

Credit Insurance

Don't waste your money buying any of the various types of credit insurance from credit card or finance companies. Credit life insurance pays the balance on a loan if you die. Credit property insurance covers damage to the item that's being purchased with the loan proceeds. Credit disability insurance makes your loan payments if you're disabled, and involuntary loss of income insurance makes your loan payments if you're involuntarily unemployed.

ALERT!

Try to avoid using your home as collateral on any loan other than your mortgage. You could lose it if you're unable to make your payments, so unless you're financially disciplined, in control of your spending, and have income protection insurance, be very cautious.

You'll be offered one or more of these coverages when you buy a car. Some dealers add them in without telling you. They earn a commission from the insurance company for selling the insurance and they get the interest on the insurance premium when they fold it into your loan. Insurance that's tied to one particular debt is an expensive way to insure yourself against losses. If something does happen, only the payments for that particular item are covered. If you feel insurance is necessary, talk to your insurance agent about a broader policy, like disability insurance that would replace your income if you became disabled, or life insurance that would provide a lump sum to your beneficiary instead of to the lender.

Creditors and Debt Collectors

When you first go into debt, you will have to deal with your creditors. But keep in mind that your creditors want to work with you *before* you become delinquent on your bills. If there's a situation, like a job loss or medical expenses, that will make it difficult for you to meet your financial obligations, call your creditors before you miss a payment. Waiting until your account is already delinquent will hurt your credibility. The creditor may not be as willing to work with you and may turn your account over to a debt collector, which can be an unpleasant experience.

Creditors are also quicker than ever to report late payments to collection agencies because more and more people are filing for bankruptcy and walking away from their debts. If you make arrangements with the creditors ahead of time, they may agree not to report your delinquency to the credit bureau. Creditors will often try to work with you by allowing you to make interest-only payments for a while, deferring a payment or two to the end of the loan period, or reducing late charges. Sometimes these concessions are enough to help you get back on your feet.

When negotiating with creditors, don't agree to a plan that you're not sure you can stick to. If you make promises and then can't keep them, the chances of the creditor ever being willing to work with you again are slim. You'll need to do a budget and calculate how much money you can squeeze out of it each month to apply to the account in question before committing to a payment plan.

If you talk to a creditor over the phone, take good notes, including the name of the person you spoke to, the date and time you talked to her or him, and what arrangements were made. It's a good idea to then follow up with a letter outlining the key elements of your discussion. If you're not successful in getting the creditor to work with you, hang up and try calling again. Sometimes one customer service representative or credit manager will be more helpful or flexible than another.

Turned Over to a Debt Collector

Debt collectors are third parties hired by a lender to attempt to collect amounts you owe when you're late with your payments; they can be lawyers or companies in the business of collecting unpaid accounts. If your account gets turned over to a debt collector, you can save yourself a lot of grief if you're familiar with your rights under the Fair Debt Collection Practices Act, the federal law that specifies what third-party debt collectors can and cannot do in their attempts to get you to pay up.

Collectors are allowed to contact you in person, by mail, telephone, telegram, or fax, but they're not allowed to contact you at inconvenient times, such as before 8 A.M. or after 9 P.M., unless you agree to those times. Debt collectors can't threaten, harass, badger, or abuse you or use false or misleading information. The law includes a long list of specific restrictions governing third-party debt collectors. If you're being harassed by or experiencing other problems with a debt collector, report it to your state attorney general's office and the Federal Trade Commission.

The Fair Debt Collection Practices Act doesn't apply to employees of the creditor that you owe. They're governed by state laws, which vary from state to state. Consult the consumer information section of your state's Web site for information about your rights.

QUESTION?

Can debt collectors call me at work?
If you or your employer tells the debt collector that your employer doesn't want you to receive collection calls at work, the collector is prohibited under the Fair Debt Collection Practices Act from contacting you at your place of employment.

Filing for Bankruptcy

Bankruptcy is a federal court process that places you under the protection of the bankruptcy court while you try to repay your debts (Chapter 13 bankruptcy) or removes the debts altogether (Chapter 7 bankruptcy). When you file for bankruptcy, an automatic stay goes into effect; the stay prohibits your creditors from attempting to collect the debt without the approval of the court, even if the bank is in the process of foreclosing on your house. Filing for Chapter 13 in this situation could buy you the time you need to sell the house yourself and pay off the mortgage.

Bankruptcy should not be entered into lightly. It has far-reaching effects on your ability to obtain credit, buy a house, buy life insurance, and sometimes even get a job. There are other factors that might make one type of bankruptcy better for you than another. Consult a good bankruptcy lawyer and provide all the details of your financial situation so he or she can counsel you concerning the option that best suits your needs.

Chapter 13 Bankruptcy: Reorganization

Chapter 13 bankruptcy, which applies to most individuals, involves reorganization of your debts. You'll need to file a proposal with the bankruptcy court detailing your plan for repayment and include a detailed budget, which could be challenged by the court if the judge, the trustee, or a creditor feels you've padded it with nonessentials. Some debts can be erased altogether, others must be partially repaid, and others must be repaid in full. If your proposal is accepted, your wages will probably be garnished during the repayment period, which usually lasts three to five years. In Chapter 13 bankruptcy, you can prevent the loss of your home by immediately starting to make your regular mortgage payments and any catch-up payments required by your repayment plan.

ALERT!

If passed, Congress's overhaul of the bankruptcy laws will make it harder to qualify for bankruptcy if you earn more than your state's median salary, and may require you to sell your home. It will be easier for creditors to challenge your bankruptcy and more difficult to write off certain debts.

How Much Will You Have to Pay?

You must pay all of your missed payments on secured debt, like your house or car, if you want to keep the asset. The minimum amount you'll have to repay on your unsecured debt is the value of your nonexempt personal property. Each state has its own laws for determining nonexempt property, but in general, you'll be given an "allowance" that consists of several thousand dollars for a car, part of the equity in your home, necessary clothing, necessary household goods and furniture, appliances, and personal effects. You'll have to repay at least an amount equal to the rest. In other words, if you add up the equity in everything you own and deduct the amount of the exempt items, the difference is the least amount you'll owe. You'll have to pay more than this if you have nonexempt expenses like child support or back taxes.

The courts have discretion regarding how much of your debts you'll have to repay. Some courts don't require you to pay anything on debts that you aren't legally required to repay in full (keep reading to see the list of these debts); others will want you to pay as much as possible. You'll be responsible for paying a fee of 10 percent of your total to the trustee handling your case. You may also be required to pay several years of interest on the total value of your nonexempt property to compensate creditors for the fact that they have to wait several years to be fully paid.

Before you make the decision to file for bankruptcy, you should know which debts you may be able to walk away from and which you'll still be responsible for. Debts that can't be discharged or forgiven include:

- Child support and alimony
- Debts for personal injury or death caused by drunk driving
- Most student loans
- Traffic tickets and other fines or penalties imposed for breaking the law
- Certain types of taxes owed
- Debts you forget to list in your bankruptcy papers

Eligibility for Chapter 13

Because repayment of some of your debts is the basis for this type of bankruptcy, you have to have regular income in order to be eligible. Regular income can include social security benefits, child care or alimony, and rental income, and, of course, employment or self-employment wages. You also have to have enough disposable income after your basic needs like housing, utilities, and food, to use for debt repayment. In addition, your secured debts (those with collateral, like a car or house) cannot exceed $871,550 and your unsecured debts (those with no collateral, like credit card debt, student loans, and medical bills) can't exceed $269,250.

FACT

Bankruptcy is considered the debt management tool of last resort because it has serious consequences. Since it stays in your credit history for ten years, it can affect your ability to obtain credit, a job, insurance, or housing.

Chapter 7 Bankruptcy: Liquidation

Under Chapter 7, liquidation, you turn most of your personal property over to the court, which appoints a trustee to sell the property and use the proceeds to pay off all or some of your debts. As in Chapter 13 bankruptcy, you're allowed to keep certain exempt property, but to keep secured property such as your house, car, or furniture you're buying on credit, you have to sign a Reaffirmation Statement stating that you agree to be responsible for those debts.

Once you've signed the Reaffirmation Statement, these debts can't be discharged for at least six years. In other words, you can't change your mind in a few years and decide you don't want those assets and don't want to be responsible for paying for them. In order to reaffirm the debt, you have to make any payments necessary to bring your account up to date.

Is Chapter 7 Bankruptcy an Option for You?

Chapter 7 is typically the bankruptcy type of choice for people who have large credit card or other unsecured debt and few assets. If there's a risk that you might lose your home or car under Chapter 7, your lawyer may recommend that you file Chapter 13 instead. If you have more equity in your car or home than the exempt amount allowed by your state, the chance of being forced to relinquish these assets to be sold to pay your creditors is high.

Debts That Can't Be Forgiven or Discharged

Some debts may not be dischargeable in a Chapter 7 bankruptcy if a creditor challenges them. These include:

- Debts you incurred by fraud, like giving false information on a credit application
- Credit purchases over a certain amount in the sixty days prior to filing
- Loans or cash advances over a certain amount in the sixty days prior to filing
- Debts you owe under a divorce settlement or decree, with certain exceptions

A Chapter 7 bankruptcy stays in your credit history for ten years. During that period, you may be denied credit.

Bankruptcy as a Debt Management Tool

Filing for bankruptcy is not going to help you in the long run if you got there by irresponsible spending habits that you haven't changed. On the other hand, if job loss, high medical bills, disability, death, divorce, or other circumstances not entirely in your control have produced a financial burden you have no hope of getting out from under, bankruptcy may be the only way you can get a fresh start. The court will place restrictions on how you can spend money and will not allow you to buy what it considers nonessentials.

ALERT!

Chapter 13 bankruptcy can actually help you learn financial discipline that may prevent you from ending up in the same situation again, because you'll live under a strict budget for the entire repayment period, which is typically between three and five years.

Preventing Bankruptcies

Many bankruptcies can be avoided by practicing good money management:

- Avoid impulse spending.
- Don't use a credit card unless you have the cash to pay it off.
- Tear up credit card offers you receive in the mail.
- Stick to a realistic budget.
- Don't buy more house or car than you can comfortably afford.
- Protect yourself against loss by having adequate medical, homeowner's, and auto insurance.
- Don't make speculative or high-risk investments.
- Don't incur joint debt with others who have questionable financial habits.

If you do find yourself falling behind on your bills, call your creditors immediately. Most will work with you if circumstances (job loss, divorce, illness, etc.) have made it temporarily difficult for you to meet your financial obligations. Suggest a temporary reduction in your payment, a waiver of late fees or penalties, skipping several payments now and increasing future payments to make up for it, or skipping several payments and adding them to the end of the loan.

Bankruptcy is not exactly a walk in the park. You won't automatically walk away debt-free. The ten-year period following the filing of bankruptcy may be difficult, as the bankruptcy follows you around whenever you apply for credit or even sometimes when you apply for a job. Before you resort to bankruptcy, there may be things you can do to improve your situation. If your debt isn't totally overwhelming, you may be able to cut back on nonessentials and find the money to apply to debt. You may even want to sell your car or house and buy a less expensive one. If you haven't taken advantage of the latest low mortgage rates, refinancing your mortgage (again) may net you a few hundred dollars a month that you could put towards your debt. As a last resort, you could apply for a hardship withdrawal from your 401(k) plan.

Consulting a Credit Counselor

You may feel hopelessly overwhelmed by your debt and see no way out from under the burden, but before you take a step as drastic as filing for bankruptcy, consider consulting with a reputable credit counselor. Debt Counselors of America and the National Foundation for Consumer Credit are the best known of these groups. Debt Counselors of America assists people over the Internet and by phone, while the NFCC has a national network of 1,450 offices called Consumer Credit Counseling Services. They provide counseling in person, as well as electronically. You don't have to be in dire straits to use this service. If you need help getting your financial affairs in order or setting financial priorities, give them a call.

For the name, address, and phone number of the closest member of the National Foundation for Credit Counseling (NFCC), visit ✍ *www.debtadvice.org* or call ☎1-800-388-2227. Most members of the NFCC are known as Consumer Credit Counseling Service (CCCS) and provide free or low-cost debt counseling.

Many creditors will accept reduced payments or give you time to catch up on late payments if you enter into a debt repayment plan with a reputable debt counseling organization. The counselor works with you to develop a payment schedule. You pay an agreed-upon amount to the organization monthly and they use it to pay your creditors. These services are free or very low cost. An important part of the plan is your agreement not to apply for any new credit or incur any additional debt while you're in the program.

Avoiding Financial Scams and Schemes

Nearly every month, several new scams and schemes that try to separate you from your money rear their ugly heads. Some are misleading or take advantage of your vulnerability to charge you outrageous fees. Others are downright dishonest and illegal. The latter can often be avoided if you remember that if it sounds too good to be true, it probably is.

FACT

There's been an estimated $100 billion lost in illegal scams in the United States, ranging from illegal work-from-home employment scams to multilevel marketing scams, sweepstakes scams, telemarketing scams, fake charitable fundraising scams, credit repair scams, and many others.

Credit Repair Scams

You're in debt up to your ears, the debt collectors are hounding you every time you turn around, you can't get any new credit, and along comes a credit repair clinic that promises to clean up your credit history in days. Why would you fall for this? Doesn't it sound too good to be true? Yet many people, desperate to resolve their credit and debt problems, pay these clinics large fees and walk away with nothing. It's always good to have a little healthy skepticism when evaluating any type of financial offer.

Payday Loans and Advance Fee Loan Scams

In the category of charging outrageous fees, consider payday loans. You need money now but payday is not for another week. You write a check for $375 to the payday loan company. They immediately write you a check for $300 and hold your check for $375 until your next payday. They keep the $75 difference as their fee, a whopping 25 percent interest rate for a two-week loan, which would be equivalent to an over 500 percent annual interest rate!

In the category of dishonest and illegal, consider advance fee loan scams. You see an ad from a company that guarantees approval for a loan or other type of credit but requires you to pay a fee before you apply. Most legitimate lenders won't guarantee that you'll get a loan until after they've thoroughly reviewed your application and checked out your credit history. Advance fee loans are illegal. You'll never see the loan. Similar scams exist for credit cards. You're promised a credit card, guaranteed, even though your credit history is so bad that no lender dares extend you credit. All you have to do is pay a fee upfront. Once again, you'll never see the credit card.

Don't Be a Victim

Some scams have been around for years, yet there are new victims every day. "Make money from home" scams, nonexistent charities, investment "opportunities" that promise you a high rate of return or a chance to buy in at a discount—any of these should make you very skeptical.

The Federal Trade Commission's Web site at ✑*www.ftc.gov* lists current scams and unscrupulous schemes. Before you get involved in anything that sounds too good to be true, check it out with the FTC or one of the consumer groups online that monitor fraud.

Don't ever give your social security number, bank account number, or other personal financial information over the phone to someone you didn't call. No reputable company will require your social security number in order for you to claim a prize you won. Nobody needs your bank account number for any legitimate purpose. In fact, all a thief needs to call your bank and have money electronically transferred to his account as a "phone check" is your name and bank account number. Ⓔ

Chapter 8

Living with
Student Loans

If you're one of the 60 to 67 percent of
college graduates with student loans,
there's a lot you need to know about repayment and how to keep your interest
costs as low as possible. If the thought of
paying off the large balances seems overwhelming, or if you're struggling to make
the payments, you have options available
to you to make it easier.

Stafford Loans

If you're one of the millions of Americans who were able to attend college thanks to the availability of federally insured student loans, you have a responsibility to be informed about the repayment process. You're liable for your student loans even if you don't graduate, or if you graduate but can't find employment.

The most common type of student loan is a Stafford Loan. These are either subsidized, meaning that the federal government pays the interest while you're in school and during grace and deferment periods, or unsubsidized, which means you're responsible for interest during these periods.

If you didn't pay the interest while you were in school, you'll have a larger loan balance to pay now that you've graduated or dropped out, because the interest was capitalized, or added to the balance of your loan. Your monthly payments will be higher and you'll pay more interest over the life of the loan. You can use the online calculator on the Sallie Mae Web site at *www.salliemae.com* to estimate the accrued interest on your loan and your new loan balance after deferment.

Grace Periods

The day after you graduate, withdraw, or drop to less than halftime status, your six-month grace period begins (some types of loans have different grace periods). You're allowed one grace period per loan, during which no principal payments are required. Your first loan payment will be due approximately thirty to forty-five days after the end of your grace period.

Be sure to notify your lender of your current address, so they can contact you during your grace period to let you know the amount of your monthly payment, the payment due dates, how long it will take you to repay your loans, and the current interest rate.

Deferments and Forbearances

Deferment is one option for relief during a period of financial difficulty. If you qualify for a loan deferment, you won't be required to make principal payments on your loan during that period. Interest payments are still due, but if you have a subsidized Stafford loan, the federal government will make the interest payments for you. If you have an unsubsidized Stafford loan, you'll be responsible for making the interest payments yourself during the deferment period, or the interest will be added to your loan balance. You can qualify for a deferment under the following circumstances:

- Unemployment
- Enrollment in school
- Graduate fellowship
- Financial hardship
- Rehabilitation program due to disability

If you don't qualify for a deferment, you may qualify for forbearance, a special arrangement with your lender that allows you to reduce or postpone principal payments temporarily. Interest continues to accrue during this period on both subsidized and unsubsidized Stafford loans, and if you don't pay it during the forbearance, it will be added to the balance of your loan. This costs you more in the long run because you'll be paying interest on the interest.

To request a deferment or forbearance, you have to complete an application available from your lender. Some lenders provide these online. Within thirty days of submitting your application, you'll be notified in writing whether or not your deferment or forbearance was approved.

FACT

Late student loan payments are reported to the credit-reporting bureaus just like late credit card, mortgage, or car payments. This information may stay on your credit history for up to ten years, unless you rehabilitate your loan.

You can automatically receive a forbearance if you participate in a qualifying program such as a medical or dental internship or residency, AmeriCorps, or if you're serving on active duty as a member of the U.S. armed forces. You may also qualify for debt-burden forbearance if your student loan payments are high compared to your income. Other forbearances are granted at the discretion of the lender based on your individual circumstances.

Repayment Options

If you're trying to minimize your monthly payment, try to balance your immediate need for lower payments with your long-term financial goals, which include paying off debt at the lowest reasonable cost. Review the status of your student loans annually to see if you're taking advantage of all the benefits offered by lenders and if the plan you're in still suits your changing financial situation. Just because the terms of your student loans include a particular repayment plan doesn't mean you're stuck with it; if it isn't working for you, you can apply for a change (you can even do it online). There are several options available:

1. **Standard repayment:** You pay the same amount each month over ten years or less, which results in lower interest costs than most other options, except prepayment.
2. **Graduated repayment:** You repay the loan over the same period but the payments are smaller in the early years and significantly larger in the later years. Because the lower payments include mostly interest and you don't pay the balance as quickly, you'll pay more interest.
3. **Income sensitive or income contingent repayment:** If you're eligible for these options, your payments can be based on a fixed percentage of your gross income each month. The percentage is between 4 and 25 percent and your payments are made over fifteen years with the income sensitive repayment plan and twenty-five years with the income contingent repayment plan. You have to reapply every year.
4. **Extended repayment:** This plan gives you lower monthly payments over a twelve- to thirty-year period using either the standard or

graduated repayment plans if you owe more than $30,000 in federal student loans.

5. **Loan consolidation:** This option allows you to combine all of your eligible student loans into one loan with one monthly payment.

6. **Prepayment:** No matter what plan you have, there's always the option of prepaying all or part of your student loans at any time without penalty, which can greatly reduce your interest costs.

Forgiveness of Loans

In limited circumstances, some student loans can be forgiven without requiring repayment. You may be eligible to have part of your Stafford loan canceled if you obtained it on or after October 1, 1998 and you've taught full-time for five years in a low-income school. You can obtain an application from your student loan lender.

For more information on the loan forgiveness program for child care providers, call ✆1-888-562-4639 or write to the ✉Child Care Provider Loan Forgiveness Program, P.O. Box 4639, Utica, NY 13504. For information on the nursing forgiveness program, call NELRP toll-free at ✆1-866-813-3753.

The federal government recently instituted a new program whose purpose is to bring more highly qualified child care providers into the profession and keep them longer. If you're eligible for this program, you may be able to wipe out part of your undergraduate Stafford loan. To be eligible you must have an associate or bachelor's degree in early childhood education, have worked for at least two years as a child care provider in an eligible facility serving a low-income community, and must have taken out your loan as a new borrower after October 7, 1998. A similar program, the Nursing Education Loan Repayment Program (NELRP), exists for registered nurses who serve in eligible facilities located in areas experiencing nursing shortages.

Federal Perkins Loans

Most students need a combination of several different types of financial aid to pay for their education. When Stafford loans and other financial sources aren't sufficient to cover costs, Perkins loans are sometimes available.

The college decides on the amount of the loan, up to $4,000 per year for undergraduate students, with a maximum of $20,000 if you've completed two years of undergraduate study, or $8,000 if you've completed less than two years of undergraduate study. Graduate students can borrow a maximum of $6,000 for each year of graduate or professional study, up to a maximum of $40,000, including any undergraduate Perkins loans. Although these are the maximum amounts allowed by law, actual awards are usually less because schools try to use their limited funds to assist as many eligible students as possible.

FACT

Colleges award federal Perkins loans as part of their financial aid programs, based on financial need. The federal government provides most of the funds and the college kicks in the rest. To be considered, you would have checked "yes" in the section of your Free Application for Federal Student Aid (FAFSA) that asks about interest in student loans.

Interest rates are fixed at 5 percent for the life of the loan, which cannot exceed ten years. No interest payments are required while you're a student, as long as you attend at least half time. There's a nine-month grace period after you graduate, drop below half-time status, or leave school. Repayment begins at the end of the grace period and is made directly to the college.

Terms of the Loan

You may be able to receive a deferment or forbearance on a Perkins loan by applying to your college. During a deferment, you can temporarily postpone payments without accruing interest. If you're not eligible for a deferment, you may qualify for a forbearance, which allows you to reduce or postpone payments for a limited period of time. Interest will accrue during this period and you'll be responsible for paying it.

Part of your Perkins loan may be forgiven or canceled if you work full-time in certain occupations. For example, you may be eligible for loan cancellation if you teach full-time at a low-income school or in certain subject areas where there's a teacher shortage. See the financial aid officer at your college for details about the occupations that may qualify you for loan cancellation.

Keep Track of the Interest Rates

Stafford loans first disbursed on or after July 1, 1995 have a variable interest rate, which changes on July 1 of each year based on Treasury bill rates, but can never exceed 8.25 percent. Rates as of July 2002 were the lowest in the history of the student loan program: 4.06 percent for Stafford Loans and 4.86 percent for PLUS loans (loans to parents).

Stafford loans obtained through lenders associated with Sallie Mae, the largest education finance company in the United States, may be eligible for decreased interest rates if the first forty-eight payments are made on time. Consider having payments automatically deducted from your checking account each month to ensure you're not late with a payment.

FACT

According to the Collegiate Funding Service, average monthly payments among those currently owing student loans were $222 per month for men, on an average remaining balance of $12,900, and $141 per month for women, on an average remaining balance of $10,300.

If you don't have a Sallie Mae loan, consider transferring your loan or refinancing it with a Sallie Mae lender to take advantage of Sallie Mae's incentives, like the interest reduction. Other lenders may offer similar rewards. When rates are low, you can take advantage of the opportunity to pay off your loans more quickly by continuing to make the higher payments even though your required payment is lower.

The sooner you start paying off your loans and the larger your monthly payment, the less your loans will cost you in the long run. It may be difficult for the first few years to pay more than the minimum, especially if your loans are very large or your income is very low. If you find yourself having difficulty making your loan payments, it's better to be proactive than to make late payments or default on your loans. Call your lender at the first indication that you may have trouble making payments.

Defaulting on Your Student Loan

Student loans are the first real debt many people incur. Late payments or defaults can seriously harm your credit record for many years, but if you pay on time you can build a positive credit history that will help you qualify for a home mortgage, new car loan, or other type of credit. The federal government has made it increasingly difficult to escape your student loan debt, and there is no statute of limitations, so you can be sure it will dog you forever if you don't pay.

ALERT!

Sometimes default information doesn't get removed from credit histories, even though the law requires it. Wait two or three months after you've made your twelfth on-time payment to rehabilitate your loan, then order a copy of your credit report to ensure that the negative information has been removed.

What Constitutes a Default?

If you're late with a payment for 270 days, you'll be considered in default of your student loan. Once you're in default, your lender will file a default claim with the guaranty agency, which buys your account from the lender and assigns the loan to a collection agency. The government also notifies all the credit bureaus.

Consequences of Default

If you don't pay your defaulted loan right away, you could have your federal income tax refunds withheld and applied to the loan balance, your wages garnished, collection costs of up to 40 percent of the loan levied against you, and face possible legal action. If you have a professional license or certificate of any kind (medical, law, accounting, and so on), it could be revoked. You may no longer be eligible for federal financial aid programs. You also lose your eligibility for federal loans like FHA and VA loans, which enable many people to buy a house that they wouldn't qualify for otherwise, and you may be denied credit cards or other forms of credit.

The default will show up on your credit report for seven years and could affect your ability to rent a house or apartment, buy a car, qualify for a mortgage, or even find a job. In the long run, it will cost you much less if you make your payments on time. Collection costs that are charged to you could total nearly half your balance, plus there's a 28 percent commission charged by the collection agency and that gets passed on to you. The government may even sue you and take your car, bank accounts, and other valuable property that you own and place a lien on your house, if you own one.

Preventing Default

If you're having trouble making your loan payments, you have several alternatives. You could change your repayment plan, apply for deferment or forbearance, or apply for a loan consolidation, which could reduce your monthly payments by nearly half. If you've tried everything and are still having problems with your loan, contact your borrower advocate, who can act as a liaison between you and your lender and may be able to help find solutions to your problem.

Besides removing your loan default from reports to the credit-reporting bureaus, rehabilitating your loan helps you regain your student loan benefits if you still need them and restores your eligibility for student financial aid.

Rehabilitating Your Defaulted Loan

Once you've defaulted on your student loans, any unpaid interest is computed and the entire balance of the loan becomes due and payable immediately. Once you reach this point, you have several options to avoid the negative consequences of default:

- You can pay off your entire student loan in one lump sum.
- You can establish monthly payment arrangements with your guaranty or collection agency (rehabilitation).
- You can consolidate your account into one new loan.

When you come to a repayment agreement with your lender, guaranty agency, or collection agency, a new loan is created that wipes out the old, defaulted loan.

The Process of Rehabilitation

Rehabilitation is a federal repayment program offered to student loan holders who have defaulted on their loans. To rehabilitate your loan, you have to make twelve on-time monthly payments in a row. Then the government agrees to once again insure your loan and your guaranty agency can sell it to a secondary market or lender, removing it from default status. After making twelve on-time payments, apply for rehabilitation. Once your loan has been rehabilitated, you have up to nine more years to repay it. You can only rehabilitate a defaulted student loan once.

Resolving Student Loan Disputes

Sometimes errors occur in student loan record keeping. If you believe there's an error in your student loan, such as an incorrect balance, payments not credited, incorrect interest rate, incorrect personal information, or other error, contact the agency that holds your loan. If you can't resolve the issue on your own, contact the Federal Student Aid Ombudsman of the Department of Education by calling ✆1-877-557-2575 or writing to ✉ U.S. Department of Education, FSA Ombudsman, 830 First Street NE, Fourth Floor, Washington, DC 20202-5144.

Consolidating Your Student Loans

Decisions about student loan repayments can significantly impact your finances long into the future, so before you jump into a consolidation loan, research your options and make sure you're going to achieve your purpose without any costly surprises.

Benefits of Consolidating

There are a number of potential benefits to consolidating your student loans. If you have several loans, you may want to consolidate them after you graduate just to simplify your record keeping and bill paying. You may want to take advantage of lower interest rates, or the longer repayment period you get from consolidating. Consolidating may be a good option for you if you have heavy education debt, want to lock in at a fixed rate, or want to reduce your monthly payments and are willing to pay more over the length of your loan in order to do so.

FACT

A survey conducted by Collegiate Funding Services found that more than half (54 percent) of the student loan holders surveyed had not heard of the Federal Consolidation Loan Program, a program enacted by Congress to make repaying federal student loans more affordable.

Under the Federal Consolidation Loan Program, if you owe $7,500 or more in eligible federal student loans and you're not in default on any of them, you can consolidate your loans at a fixed interest rate with only one payment a month. The interest rate on consolidation loans is an average of the interest rates on all your student loans, not to exceed 8.25 percent, so you may benefit from locking in when the current rate is very low. It could save you thousands of dollars over the life of your loans, depending on how much you owe.

The federal program also allows you to extend the term of the loan up to thirty years. Obviously a loan period this long would cost you much more in interest, but there are no prepayment penalties, so you can always pay more or pay the loan off early. Before you extend your loan repayment period, use an online calculator to calculate the true cost over time.

You May Not Need to Consolidate

You can consolidate all your loans with one lender at any time without a consolidation loan if you just want to simplify your payments. If a lower interest rate is your goal, remember that after making forty-eight consecutive on-time payments, you may qualify for an interest rate reduction of 2 percentage points. This may put you at a lower rate than you could get by consolidating, depending on your current interest rate. To figure out what makes the most sense for you, try Sallie Mae's online loan consolidation calculator in the tools and calculators section of SallieMae.com (✍ *www.salliemae.com*).

You can manage your student loans online at ✍ *www.manage yourloans.com*, where you can make payments, view the status of your loan and payment history, update your contact information, reduce or postpone payments, and change your payment plan.

A Tax Break

Up to $2,500 a year in interest on some student loans (Stafford, PLUS, Perkins, consolidation, and private) may be tax-deductible, if certain criteria like income limits are met. The proceeds of the loan must have been used for qualified higher education expenses (tuition, fees, room and board, supplies, and other related expenses), and you must have been enrolled at least half-time in a qualified program at an eligible institution.

As of 2002, the rule that you could only deduct interest for the first sixty months of your loan has been eliminated. You can now deduct interest no matter how long you've had the loan. Also beginning in 2002, the income limits have been increased. Deductibility phases out if your income is between $50,000 and $65,000 for single taxpayers and $100,000 and $130,000 for couples filing jointly.

If you paid more than $600 in interest on your student loans during the year, your lender will send you a Form 1098-E showing the amount paid. To claim the amount on your income taxes, you must file Form 1040 or 1040A, but unlike the mortgage interest deduction, you don't have to itemize in order to get the deduction. If you're married, you have to file jointly.

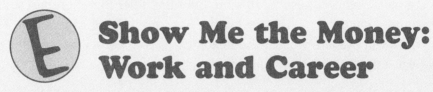

Chapter 9

Show Me the Money:
Work and Career

Salary is not always the most important indicator of job potential. Knowing how to evaluate a prospective employer, determine your worth in the job market, negotiate the best salary and benefits, and request a raise will help you optimize job potential. In today's volatile market, it's equally important to know how to protect yourself financially if you lose your job.

Choosing a Job with Potential

Salary is a very important factor in choosing a job, but it's not always the most important one. Evaluate the total compensation package: salary, insurance, paid leave, stock options, retirement plan, and other benefits. Once you've placed a dollar value on the employer-provided benefits, evaluate other aspects of the job, but remember that there are some things you can't put a price tag on, like training and experience. The best jobs will prepare you for the next step in your career by teaching you valuable skills and providing on-the-job training.

FACT

Education is important in qualifying for many good jobs. Sometimes just having a degree will get you the job—even if the degree is not in a related field. That's because successfully completing a degree program says a lot about you to a prospective employer. That's not to say that there aren't good jobs that don't require a degree, but they usually require some type of skill.

Large Company or Small?

Large companies are often considered the best employers, but small companies have their advantages, too. In a large company, your duties are more likely to be focused in one specific area, whereas in a small company you can often acquire a wide variety of skills more quickly because there are fewer people to do the work. For example, an accounting graduate may start out in a large company doing accounts payable or billing. The same individual in a small company may start out doing accounts payable, accounts receivable, bank reconciliation, and payroll, because the volume of work in each of these areas is much smaller than in a large company.

The person doing a variety of tasks will gain wider experience more quickly. However, opportunities to move within the company may be more limited. Start-up companies can be exciting and offer a great opportunity to learn but are also riskier. Because of the lack of security, jobs in these companies may be more suited to individuals who don't have a family to support.

Evaluating a Potential Employer

How can you choose a job that has potential and doesn't end up being a dead end? When evaluating a potential employer, find out as much as you can about the industry. What's the history of growth in the industry and what's the anticipated future need for goods and services produced or provided by that industry? Is the industry trendy? Is it subject to government regulation? If so, what's the possible impact on the company?

Also find out as much as you can about the company or organization. Check for newspaper and magazine articles. Detailed information, including current financial information, is easily available at your local library or online if the company is publicly traded. Is the company financially stable? What are its size, reputation, and growth potential? How do the company's products or services compare to those of the competition? If you know anybody who has worked for the organization, find out what you can about the company culture and atmosphere and the quality of management.

Evaluating the Job

What can you find out about the job itself? Is there a training program or opportunity to obtain additional education? What are the day-to-day tasks and duties? What is the level of responsibility? Who will you report to and what is that person's leadership style? What are your potential coworkers like? Does the job require travel, weekend work, or working long hours? What are the salary and benefits package? If the salary seems low, are there benefits that compensate for it?

ALERT!

There may be times when you need a job—any job—and you don't have the luxury of being selective, but you don't have to stay in one that's a dead end. Continue your search even after you find employment if the job doesn't provide you with what you need.

Choosing a good organization and a good job can make a vital difference in your job satisfaction, opportunities for advancement, and salary potential. Do your homework in advance; it can pay off in both the short- and long-term.

Your Worth to an Employer

When you get a job offer, how will you know if the salary is reasonable? Before you enter the job market, whether it's your first job out of college or a new step on your career path, you need to know what the going salary is in your geographical area for someone with your education, training, and skills.

The Bureau of Labor Statistics (BLS) Occupational Outlook Handbook is an invaluable source of information on salaries in hundreds of different occupations. It also provides descriptions of what workers do on the job, working conditions, training and education needed, and expected job prospects in a wide range of occupations. In addition, the BLS provides information on wages, earnings, and benefits for many occupations by region, state, and metropolitan area. Visit BLS online at *www.bls.gov*.

Negotiating Your Salary and Benefits Package

Much has been written about negotiating salary and benefits, but most of it boils down to knowing what you're worth in the marketplace, identifying which benefits are important to you, and putting a price tag on the benefits offered by your prospective employer so you can evaluate the real value of an offer. Total compensation encompasses much more than just salary.

When meeting with prospective employers, find out what benefits and perks the company gives employees in the position you're applying for, what an average pay increase is, and what benefits might be added to sweeten the pot if they're not able or willing to offer the salary you'd like.

Experts caution job seekers to delay discussing salary until well into the interview process and to avoid telling interviewers your current salary. You shouldn't be pegged into a salary range that's lower than the going rate just because you're underpaid in your current job, and discussing salary too early in the process can stick you with a lower than acceptable offer or, conversely, take you out of the running if your current salary is too high. The goal is to have enough interaction with the interviewer to have a chance to sell yourself and convince her or him that you're the right person for the job before salary is discussed in any detail. The objective of asking your current salary or the salary you're looking for is usually to pay you as little as possible.

To find out how much you'd need to earn in a new city to equate to your current salary, use the cost of living calculator at ✍*www.homefair.com*. Enter the city and state you're moving from and to, your current salary, and whether you'd prefer to own or rent.

Evaluating Your Employee Benefits

Employer-provided benefits are a significant part of any compensation package and can have a profound effect on your finances. Employers often provide a wide range of benefits, including the following:

- Retirement plans, such as the 401(k)
- Section 125 cafeteria plans
- Group health, life, dental, and disability insurance plans
- Tuition reimbursement
- Flexible-spending accounts
- Stock option plans
- Bonus plans
- Vacation, holiday, and sick leave benefits

All of these benefits, as well as others not mentioned, have a monetary value that you should consider when evaluating your salary or comparing job offers. Some benefits, like 401(k) and cafeteria plans (which have nothing to do with food—read on!), also have tax benefits that can save you additional money by reducing your taxes.

Insurance Coverage

Most people with health insurance are covered under a group plan offered by their employer or their spouse's employer. Although employers are charging employees more as prices continue to increase dramatically each year, employer-provided health insurance is still a bargain. If you aren't offered coverage through your employer you can purchase an individual policy, but these are becoming prohibitively expensive. Whether you're married or single, you need health insurance to protect yourself against financial disaster in the event of a serious illness or accident.

If you're fortunate enough to have employer-provided coverage, calculate its monetary value by first finding out what the company pays for your medical, dental, life, and long- and short-term disability on a monthly or yearly basis. If you contribute to the cost, subtract your contribution from the total. If your contribution is pretax (as in a cafeteria, or section 125, plan), factor in your tax savings by adding your social security tax rate of 7.65 percent (up to $84,900 in earnings, after which it's only 1.45 percent), your federal tax rate, and your state tax rate. Multiply the total percentage times the amount you pay toward your insurance coverage to calculate your tax savings.

For example, if you're in the 28 percent federal tax bracket and a 7 percent state tax bracket, add these two percentages plus the 7.65 percent social security tax. Your total tax rate is 42.65 percent. If you contribute $100.00 per month toward your insurance, your real cost is $57.35 ($100.00 × 42.65 percent = $42.65 in savings; $100.00 – $42.65 = $57.35).

Being young is no guarantee of health. If you don't have full insurance coverage, purchase a high-deductible policy to protect yourself against major medical expenses. The higher the deductible, the less expensive the policy, so consider one with a $1,000 to $5,000 deductible until you find a job with insurance.

Flexible-Spending Accounts (FSAs)

FSAs, or reimbursement accounts, are an employer-provided benefit that allows you to set aside pretax contributions to pay for eligible medical expenses that aren't covered by your health insurance, including premiums (unless they're paid with pretax money), deductibles, copays, and any other health cost considered an allowable medical expense by the IRS. For a complete list of allowable medical deductions, see Publication 502, "Medical and Dental Expenses" in the Forms and Publications section of the IRS Web site at ✍*www.irs.gov*, or request a printed copy of this publication from the IRS by calling ✆1-800-829-3676.

You benefit from an FSA because your contributions are deducted before taxes are calculated, thus reducing your taxes. Using the same tax brackets as the health insurance example, if your total tax percentage (federal, state, and social security) is 42.65 percent, every dollar you put into an FSA will cost you only fifty-seven cents. Don't contribute more than you think you'll use, because under IRS regulations, you forfeit any unused funds at the end of the year. If you have significant medical expenses you can save a lot of money, so don't overlook this great benefit.

401(k) and Other Retirement Plans

If your employer provides a 401(k) plan, you'd do well to participate—remember, your contributions are tax-deferred (except for social security taxes). If your employer matches a percentage of your contribution, add this to your compensation total when calculating the value of your benefits. Most employers match between fifty cents and $1 for every dollar you contribute, for up to 3 to 6 percent of your salary. If you earn $40,000 a year and contribute $200 a month and your employer match is 75 percent for up to 6 percent of your salary, your employer will kick in another $150 a month up to a maximum of $2,400 a year. Under this example, your employer is actually paying you an additional $1,800 a year ($150 × 12 = $1,800).

Employee Ownership Plans

The world of employee stock ownership plans (ESOPs), stock option plans, employee stock purchase plans, and incentive option plans is confusing at best, and it's difficult if not impossible to evaluate the potential worth of stock and stock options offered by your employer.

Stock options are a popular method of attracting employees in high-tech companies and are becoming more common in other industries as part of total compensation plans. Most closely held companies giving out options are eventually sold and the options are exchanged for cash or for stock in the acquiring company.

If you're offered stock options, be sure you understand which type they are and how they work. You can find detailed information about the various types of plans at the National Center for Employee Ownership Web site at *www.nceo.org*.

Stock Options

Stock option plans are a way for companies to share ownership with employees, reward them for performance, and attract staff. The days of average employees getting rich on stock options may be over, but stock options can still be a worthwhile benefit. We've all heard lots of talk about stock options during the heyday of high-tech growth in the late 1990s, but few people really understand what they are and how they work.

A stock option gives an employee the right to buy company stock at a specified price during a specified period after the option has vested. Companies use the vesting period to motivate employees to stick around. Let's say you receive an option on 500 shares at $10 per share and the stock price goes up to $20. You can exercise the option and buy the 500 shares at $10 each, sell them for $20 each, and pocket the $5,000 difference. If the stock price never rises above the option price, you don't lose money but you don't make any, either. You simply don't exercise the option.

Employee Stock Purchase Plans

Employee stock purchase plans (ESPPs) offer employees the chance to buy stock, usually through payroll deductions during an "offering period" at a discounted price. The employee can then sell it right away and take the profit created by the discount, or hold on to it in expectation that its value will increase.

Employee Stock Ownership Plans

Employee stock ownership plans (ESOPs) are a type of benefit plan that are regulated by the federal government in which a trust is set up to acquire some or all of the stock of the company and sell the stock to employees. Because ESOPs receive tax advantages, they're not allowed to discriminate in favor of key or highly compensated employees, so most employees get to participate. ESOPs are typically used as a type of retirement plan. Be cautious about investing the bulk of your retirement funds in company stock no matter how well established the company is. Take advantage of employee ownership but spread out your risk by putting most of your retirement money in other investment options.

FACT

An estimated 15 to 20 percent of publicly traded companies offer stock option plans to employees, and many privately owned companies do the same. These plans are not limited to high-tech companies.

Incentive Stock Options

ISOs allow employees to purchase shares of stock at some time in the future at a specified price. The employee pays tax on the gain upon sale or disposition of the stock, not upon receipt or exercise of the option. Nonqualified stock options don't have the restrictions of other options and don't receive any special tax consideration. When employees exercise nonqualified options, they pay ordinary income tax on the difference between the grant price and exercise price.

Asking for a Raise

If you already have a job but feel underpaid, you may be thinking about asking your boss for a raise. If this is the case, you need to be prepared to convince the powers that be that you not only deserve one, but that you're worth it. Don't make the common mistake of basing your request on your need for more money or your inability to meet your financial obligations. Businesses do not base salary increases on employees' personal needs; they base it on employees' worth to the company, the quality of their work, company pay scales, and budgetary concerns. Need has nothing to do with it, so it's best not to talk about need when asking for a raise.

QUESTION?

What's the number one rule for requesting a raise?
Don't give ultimatums. They'll put your boss on the defensive, and may force you to quit your job or eat crow. Your goal is to convince your boss that you're worth more money because you do an exceptional job or you've accepted additional responsibility that warrants an increase or promotion.

Evaluate Yourself

First, perform an evaluation of your skills, productivity, job tasks, and contribution to the company. Look at your job duties and performance from the company's perspective and base your approach on the company's needs. If you have a written job description, dig it out, along with copies of your last two or three written performance reviews. On your job description, jot down the major tasks you perform that may not be part of your formal job description. The goal is to show or remind your boss of your tangible contributions to the company, so make a list of your accomplishments, and if possible, the dollar value of each to the company. For example: "I saved the company $20,000 this year by researching and negotiating contracts with new vendors."

Determine the Going Rate for Your Job

Next, you need to determine the going rate, both inside and outside the company, for what you do. Ask your company's human resources department if there are company salary ranges for your position and several related positions above yours. Review these, along with the salary information and compensation surveys you obtained from the Bureau of Labor Statistics' Web site. National information can give you an idea of what jobs similar to yours typically pay, but salaries vary from one region to another, so be sure to consult some local information as well, by reading help-wanted ads, talking to friends and associates, or making a call to your local human resources organization, such as the Society for Human Resources Management (SHRM).

The Internet is the easiest way to obtain information about jobs and wages. JobStar at ✐ *www.jobsmart.org* offers more than 300 salary surveys by profession. You can also view the Bureau of Labor Statistics' Occupational Outlook Handbook and wage information online at ✐ *www.bls.gov*.

Know Your Company's Policies and Financial Status

To increase your chances of getting the raise you want, you need to know several things about your company. What is the policy on salary increases? Are all employees reviewed at the same time each year? Does your department have a budget for salaries that they're required to stay within? If so, you're in direct competition with the other employees in your department for limited funds, and you should work on making yourself stand out above the crowd.

What is the company's financial condition? Are they struggling to stay afloat? Are they in a budget crisis? Perhaps it's been a good year and there's bonus money to be awarded to deserving employees, but no salary increases. The more you know about the company's financial situation regarding compensation, the better prepared you'll be for your salary negotiation.

Pick Your Time Carefully

Timing is everything. If you've only been at your job for a few months, asking for a raise probably won't go over very well. However, if you find after a few months that you were hired at a salary well below that of others in your position and with your experience, it may pay to discuss this with your supervisor. If you've been formally or informally disciplined or chastised recently, wait at least a few months before asking for more money.

The time of month, week, and day are also important. Don't ask to meet with your boss during the busiest time of the month or busiest days of the week, which for most people are Mondays and Fridays. It's to your advantage to arrange an appointment at a time that's convenient with your manager.

Consider Benefits in Lieu of Salary

Not all companies are in a position to raise salaries. However, they may be able to offer you additional benefits instead, such as extra paid leave, tuition assistance, stock options, overtime, or a promotion, if one is warranted. When comparing salaries, it's important to consider the financial value of these and other benefits and perks. If your company pays for all or part of your health insurance, this is as good as money in your pocket. The same is true of a 401(k) match.

FACT

The average employer spends 42 percent of salary costs on employee fringe benefits like insurance, vacation and other paid leave, retirement contributions, and tuition assistance, including mandatory benefits such as state and federal unemployment insurance and workers' compensation insurance. The average employee making $40,000 per year receives $16,800 in benefits.

If at First You Don't Succeed . . .

If, after all your preparation, you don't get the raise you've requested, don't respond with sour grapes. Ask your boss what you'd have to do to qualify for an increase or a promotion, accompanied by a pay adjustment, and then renew your efforts to improve your performance. Make sure your boss is aware of what you do and how well you do it, and document your accomplishments in preparation for your next opportunity to discuss your salary.

Losing Your Job Without Losing Your Shirt

The days of working for the same employer from graduation to retirement are history. The average worker changes jobs at least half a dozen times. In this era of corporate takeovers, downsizing, mergers, layoffs, and most recently, stunning corporate corruption, nobody is immune from sudden job loss.

You can be plunged unexpectedly into financial disaster, especially if you live from paycheck to paycheck. If you don't have an emergency fund or other resources to fall back on, you can quickly take on unmanageable debt, or you may feel forced to accept a low-paying job or a job you hate, which can take a toll on your emotional state and on your family.

Prepare for the Possibility of Job Loss

You may feel that your job is very secure and then walk in one day to be greeted by a pink slip. You don't need to be paranoid, but being prepared for the possibility of job loss will make it easier to deal with if it does happen. To be prepared, you need to know your net worth, set up a budget, save, and keep your debt low.

You should also have a feel for the stability of your job. How are your employer's competitors doing? Are they experiencing layoffs? Layoffs in your industry can be a good indication of the instability of your job, even if your employer has not yet made any cuts. If job layoffs have already occurred where you work, you should have your resume updated and be looking around for possible opportunities that fit your skills.

Next, acquaint yourself with your employer's severance policy. Do laid-off employees receive severance pay? If so, is it based on years of service or other criteria? Will you be paid your accrued vacation balance upon termination? Knowing how much you could expect if you're laid off helps you calculate how much you need in your emergency fund for living expenses and can reduce the stress associated with waiting for the axe to fall if your company is reducing staff.

What will happen to your benefits if you lose your job? Will you be able to continue your health insurance benefits under COBRA? How much will it cost? It's foolhardy to go without at least catastrophic health insurance, so know what your other alternatives are if you can't afford to elect COBRA coverage. An illness or accident while you're uninsured could leave you no alternative but bankruptcy.

Update your resume and make sure it looks professional, polished, and free from typos. Compile a list of references, with job titles, telephone numbers, and addresses, and line up letters of recommendation, if possible. It's also a good idea to get contact information from coworkers, vendors, and customers so you can use it for networking purposes when you're looking for a job.

FACT

According to the U.S. Department of Labor, Bureau of Labor Statistics, during the first nine months of 2002 there were 14,150 mass layoff events in the United States resulting in 1,567,505 new unemployment claims. Mass layoffs involve at least fifty people at a time.

If the Worst Happens

If you get the pink slip, apply for unemployment on the first day of your layoff so you'll receive the maximum benefits for which you're eligible. Some people are reluctant to file for unemployment because they feel it's a type of welfare, but it isn't. Your employer contributes to your state's unemployment insurance fund as well as a federal unemployment fund. You earned those benefits by working. If you need them, use them.

Unemployment benefits are typically about half of your regular earnings, up to your state's cap, paid for a maximum of twenty-six weeks. Your state's cap is based on the average wages in your state. For instance, Massachusetts' cap is $512 a week, while Michigan's is $300 a week. You'll be required to prove that you're actively seeking work while receiving unemployment benefits, and you must be ready, willing, available, and ready to work. Unemployment benefits are subject to federal income tax, so you'll need to claim them at the end of the year. Be prepared for the additional taxes you may owe as a result.

During a period of unemployment, resist the urge to use your credit cards unless absolutely necessary for critically important expenses. If you can't make ends meet, contact your creditors, tell them you've lost your job but are actively seeking employment, and request an arrangement that allows you to make reduced payments for a limited time. If you have a good credit history, they will probably be willing to work with you.

ALERT!

If you lose your job, unemployment benefits won't be enough to live on, so if you receive severance pay, use it as a bridge to get you through your period of unemployment. Spend carefully, paying the most important things first: rent or mortgage, car payment, electricity, groceries, and so on.

So You Want to Be Your Own Boss?

At some point in your career, you may decide that you'd like to start your own business instead of working for someone else. Let's assume you've already thoroughly researched the viability of your idea for a business, prepared a business plan, and are confident that you have the skills, discipline, and work ethic necessary to be successful on your own. Here is what else you need to consider:

- Can you live without a steady income for an undetermined period of time? Before you give up your day job, you should have a healthy savings account to fall back on while you build a customer base, especially if the business is seasonal or cyclical.
- Will there be start-up costs? Do you have a solid, detailed estimate of what they'll be? Have you prepared a budget detailing projected monthly costs and estimated sales? Talk to your banker and find out what financing options are available, if any, and what's required in order to qualify for them.
- Have you thought about the legal form your business will take? Read up on the subject or talk to an accountant about the pros and cons of being a sole proprietorship versus a partnership or corporation.
- Have you familiarized yourself with the laws regulating your business and made a plan to comply with local ordinances and laws regarding

business licensing, safety, workers' compensation, and sales tax?

- Have you talked to your insurance agent? If you're running a business out of your home, you may need a rider to your homeowner's insurance policy. If you have employees, you'll need workers' compensation and liability insurance. If you have inventory, you'll want property insurance.

- What about the tax issues? You'll be required to file quarterly federal and state estimated taxes for yourself or, if you have employees, you'll need to register to withhold and submit income and other taxes to the state and federal government and file quarterly and annual payroll tax returns. Who will do your payroll and prepare and file these reports? Do you need to hire an accountant or payroll service or will you do this yourself?

Owning your own business can be challenging and demanding and will probably require that you work long hours. It's not for everyone, but it can be very rewarding for those who are cut out for it.

You will likely have to set up a double-entry bookkeeping system. Talk to an accountant if you don't know how. The easiest way to do your accounting is to buy an inexpensive but robust program like QuickBooks or Peachtree, which can more than adequately handle the accounting for most small or midsize businesses.

Chapter 10

Ⓔ Moving On: Finding New Living Space

Whether you're looking for a new place to live in the same town or moving to a new city for a job opportunity or change of scenery, there are financial issues to consider before you take the plunge. The more you know about the costs associated with your move, the better you can plan for the financial impact.

Your Housing Options

Whether you're looking for your first apartment or you're already in your own place but searching for new digs, there's a lot to consider before you take the plunge. Take a few minutes to think about what's important to you in your living space before you start pounding the pavement looking for the perfect apartment. Make a list of the most important features:

- Access to public transportation
- Being able to own pets
- Laundry facilities
- A parking spot or availability of on-street parking
- Safety of the neighborhood

Identify the things you won't compromise on and those that would be nice but aren't absolute requirements. This will help you quickly rule out places that don't meet your minimum standards. If you can't find a suitable apartment in your price range, consider sharing a house or apartment with a roommate, or renting a studio or efficiency apartment.

FACT

You'll need to have two months' rent saved up before you rent an apartment: one month's worth for the security deposit, plus the first month's rent. Some landlords require that you also pay the last months' rent up-front, for a total of three months' worth of rent.

How Much Rent You Can Afford

Before you start seriously shopping around for an apartment or rental house, you need to know how much you can afford to pay. As a general rule of thumb, allow no more than 30 percent of your gross income for housing. If you're making $35,000 a year, you shouldn't pay more than $875 a month for rent. You'd be more comfortable at 25 percent, or $729 a month. If some or all of the utilities are included, you could pay higher rent. You don't want to be strapped for cash all the time because of expensive housing, so it's best not to go with the maximum you can afford.

Moving Back in with Your Parents

There's a growing trend for young people to return to their parents' home for a few years after college graduation so they can save money before striking out on their own. If this option is acceptable to you and your parents, with discipline you could save a significant amount of money over the course of a year.

Let's say rentals in your area are $600 a month, and your parents will let you live at home rent-free as long as you contribute to household expenses like groceries and utilities. If you socked away what you'd be paying in rent living on your own, you could save $7,200 plus interest in a year—not exactly small potatoes. You'd have to earn as much as $10,000 in order to net $7,200 after taxes.

Once you've experienced the freedom of being on your own in college you may find it difficult to move back in with your parents, so it's understandable if you just want to strike out on your own.

Finding an Apartment

How do you find out what's available? If you're looking in your own town, you probably know about some of the apartment complexes in your area. It's more difficult if you're moving to a new city, especially if you don't have the luxury of being able to go there to find housing before you move. A number of methods can make it easier.

Word of Mouth

If you know people in the area, ask around for recommendations. Word of mouth is invaluable. You'll learn important information that might not be readily apparent when you walk through the place, like noise levels, the safety of the neighborhood, and whether management is good about maintenance and repairs.

Classified Ads

The local newspapers in most towns and cities advertise apartments for rent. Make a list of the ones that sound interesting and drive by to see if you want to look more closely at any of them. If you're familiar with the area, you'll be able to rule out some places up-front just by their address. If you're new to the area, be prepared to spend some time looking around.

Using a Real-Estate Agent

Call a few Realtors located in the Yellow Pages and ask if they deal with apartments. The benefit of using a real-estate agent is that they're familiar with where the apartment complexes are and with the neighborhoods they're in. Using a Realtor is a good idea if you're moving to a city that's unfamiliar to you. Another way to find Realtors with rentals is the Internet. Go to a good search engine and type in "real-estate agents" or "Realtors" and the name of the city and state. It may not be obvious from the description whether the Realtor does rentals, but a quick visit to the Web site will tell you. While you're searching, keep an eye out for real-estate agents who offer relocation packages with information about the city you're going to be living in. This could be helpful once you move.

Apartment-Finder Services

Apartment finders or locators are companies that specialize in knowing all the apartment complexes in a given area. They work with apartment property managers to keep up to date on apartment availability, and save you the time and hassle of making phone calls to each individual complex to get information. Try to avoid using an apartment-finder service that costs money. Some of them charge an entire month's rent. There are many free apartment- and roommate-finder services on the Internet, especially for larger cities, so you shouldn't have to pay for this service unless there's a severe rental shortage.

The better services will have a real-estate agent contact you when you fill out an online form indicating your housing requirements. Some will even have your utilities hooked up for you without charge once you find an apartment you want.

Two of the larger online apartment-finder services are Apartments.com (☞ *www.apartments.com*), and ApartmentGuide.com (☞ *www.apartmentguide.com*). Each of these guides has millions of listings nationwide, many with photos and floor plans, plus helpful articles on moving and settling in.

Signing the Lease

Four little words: Read the small print. Yes, it's boring, and it may not be the clearest writing you've ever read, but you have a lot at stake and you need to protect yourself by knowing all the rules and regulations of living in your new space and of leaving it. You don't want to end up trying to explain to Judge Judy that you signed a legally binding contract without even reading it.

If there are provisions in the lease that you object to, see if you can work out a compromise with the landlord. Cross out the unwanted language for any changes the two of you agree to, initial and date the change, and have the landlord do the same. Don't rely on oral agreements. They're difficult if not impossible to prove.

If there's something you don't understand, ask the landlord or property manager to explain it. Don't make any assumptions. A few things you might want to ask up-front are:

- Is there an on-site manager?
- What kind of routine maintenance is performed and what am I personally responsible for?
- How much notice do I need to give when leaving?
- What kind of security is provided?
- Is smoking allowed? Are pets allowed?
- Are there laundry facilities?
- What are the parking arrangements?
- What utilities and other services are included in the rent?
- How is trash handled?
- Are there provisions in the lease that allow the rent to be raised during the lease term?

You can come up with a list of other questions you should ask before signing on the dotted line. Don't be embarrassed if you have a lot of them. Landlords expect questions, and once you sign the lease, it's too late.

FACT

Most landlords check your credit report and rental history, and charge you the fee of $10 to $35. Most will also verify your income to ensure that it's at least three times your monthly rent, so if rent is $800 a month, your monthly income would have to be at least $2,400.

Breaking Your Lease

Getting out of your lease before the end of the lease term, which is usually twelve months, can be difficult and expensive. You can be held responsible for paying the rent for the remainder of the lease. Find out if there are circumstances that would release you from your obligation. What if you got a job transfer? Got divorced? Had a baby? Some landlords will allow you to break the lease for a fee. Others may allow you to sublet to another tenant.

Month-to-Month Leases

If you sign a month-to-month lease, be aware that the landlord can terminate the lease or raise the rent on short notice. Usually you're still obligated to give written notice of your intention to move out sixty days in advance. If you're not sure where you're going to be working or you intend to buy your own home after having a few months to get settled in a new town, a month-to-month lease might make sense for you.

Deposits and Other Charges

When you rent a house or apartment, you're usually required to pay a security deposit equal to one month's rent, which the landlord will hold until you move out. At that time, any expenses for cleaning or repairs beyond normal wear and tear and any unpaid rent will be deducted from your deposit and the balance will be returned to you. Most states have laws about how landlords have to treat security deposits. Usually they have to place them in an escrow account or an account separate from their normal operating account. The landlord may be required to pay you interest on the deposit, and is required to return it to you within a specified time after you vacate the apartment.

Getting Your Security Deposit Back

Security deposits are the cause of many disputes between landlords and tenants, but you can improve your chances of getting yours back without a hassle. Get a detailed receipt for any security or other deposits you pay. The receipt should show the date and amount paid, the name of the person you paid it to, the name of the landlord (if different), the address and apartment number the deposit is for, and a statement that it's a security deposit. Save the canceled check for the security deposit when your bank returns it in your monthly statement. This and your receipt are the best proof that you actually paid the deposit.

During the first week or so that you live in rented housing, go through every room and make a detailed list of everything that's broken, dirty, or damaged in any way, including chips in cabinets or tubs, holes in walls, broken windows, missing or broken knobs, tears in or stains on carpets, chips or rips in linoleum, burns, and so on. If possible, take pictures of the damage. Send a copy of the list to your landlord and keep a copy with your pictures to use if needed when you leave.

ALERT!

Don't give your landlord an excuse to make a deduction from your security deposit when you move. If the apartment isn't clean or you leave things behind for the landlord to get rid of, he or she will charge you for the cost of cleaning or removal and deduct it from your deposit.

Clean the apartment thoroughly before you move out (including carpets), and repair any damage you caused. Remove all of your belongings and any trash. Ask your landlord to walk through the apartment with you and give you a signed statement about the condition you left it in. This will be easier if you've already moved out your furniture. You may even want to take pictures of the condition of the apartment before you leave, in case you have to go to small claims court to get your security deposit back. Give the keys directly to the landlord (don't just leave them in the apartment) and leave your forwarding address so he or she can mail your deposit.

Pet Deposits

If you have a pet, plan to have a bit more difficulty finding an apartment and to pay a bit more. Many places simply don't allow pets. Others allow cats only, and still others allow small dogs under a certain weight and height. If you find an apartment that does allow pets, you may be required to pay a pet deposit in addition to your security deposit, to protect the property owner against any damages your pet may cause. Pet deposits can range from $100 to a full month's rent, and are often nonrefundable or only partially refundable.

Some states prohibit landlords from charging extra deposits for kids or pets or charging for credit checks. This doesn't mean your landlord won't try to charge you. It's important that you know your rights and the associated laws in your state or city.

Utility Deposits and Hookup Charges

You may be required to pay a refundable deposit and nonrefundable hookup charges to one or more utility companies, including electric, gas, water, sewer, and cable TV. Many electric companies require a deposit of several hundred dollars. If you can prove you had electric service recently in your name in another location and you had a good payment record, the utility company may waive this requirement. To prevent paying for utilities used by the previous tenant, if possible take utility readings as soon as you move in. (Ask your landlord how you can do this.) When you move out, be sure to request your deposit back from the utility company. Millions of dollars in unclaimed utility deposits sit in the coffers of state governments because residents moved without leaving a forwarding address.

Renting with Roommates

If you plan to rent an apartment with one or more roommates, your landlord may require separate deposits from each one of you. You have several choices. All of you can sign the lease, which will make you all jointly and severally liable for rent and damages. This means each one of you is fully responsible for all of the rent and all of the damages, if any. If one of you fails to pay the rent, the others will have to come up with his or her share or face eviction.

Another option is for one of you to sign the lease and "sublet" rooms to one or more roommates. You collect the rent from the others and pay it to the landlord. If one roommate fails to pay the rent, you evict him, deduct the rent from his security deposit, and find a replacement. Before you enter into this type of arrangement, make sure your complex allows subletting.

In any case, it's a good idea to design a written contract spelling out each person's responsibilities, including the amount of rent each will pay, sharing of responsibility for damages, how payment for utilities will be divided, the term of the rental agreement, and liability for rent if one person leaves.

Rentlaw.com (✍ *www.rentlaw.com*) has links to each state's laws governing rental housing, information about tenants' rights and landlords' obligations, and articles with advice and information about many aspects of moving. Check out the laws in your state before you sign a lease.

Renter's Insurance

Most renters have the mistaken belief that they don't need renter's insurance and that the property owner is responsible for any damages to the property. The owner's coverage doesn't protect you against damage that you or your guests cause to the property. If you overrun your bathtub and water leaks into the apartment below, you're liable for the costs, unless you have renter's insurance.

The building owner's coverage also doesn't protect you against personal injury lawsuits if someone is injured in your apartment. And it doesn't provide for replacement of your belongings if they're stolen or damaged by fire or water. Renter's insurance does all of this, and is well worth the cost.

How Much Coverage Do You Need?

Even if you don't have much furniture or large household appliances, you'd be surprised at how much your belongings would cost to replace. For starters, you probably have several thousand dollars' worth of clothing. Take a detailed room-by-room inventory of your belongings, write down a brief description of each item, and estimate what it would cost to replace it. Include clothes in your inventory.

Replacement Cost or Actual Cash Value?

When buying insurance, it's a good idea to buy coverage for replacement cost rather than actual cash value. Replacement cost coverage is just what it sounds like: if something you own is stolen or damaged by fire or water, the insurance company will pay you what it will cost to replace it with an item of similar quality. Actual cost value coverage assumes that your belongings lose value with time and usage, and pays you only the depreciated value of the items.

Note that you take big risks with actual cash value insurance. If you have stereo equipment that you paid $1,500 for and would now cost $2,000 to replace, you would be reimbursed $2,000 *minus* the insurance company's calculation for depreciation. If the item is considered 50 percent depreciated, you'd receive $1,000.

Deductibles

The deductible is the amount you agree to pay out of your pocket before the insurance company covers the rest of your loss. The higher the deductible, the less expensive the insurance. When choosing a deductible, you're deciding how much risk you're willing to take and balancing risk and cost. Most property deductibles are between $250 and $500 per year.

To obtain an estimate of what you would pay for renters' insurance, go to ✍ *www.insurancequote.com*, choose "Renters" and complete the online form to the best of your ability. You'll receive the best quote from licensed insurance agents in your area.

Cost of Living Differences

If you're planning a move to a new city, it's important to know the difference in the cost of living, especially if you already have a job offer and are trying to evaluate whether it's a good one. What sounds good in your hometown may not pay the bills in a new location, depending on the cost of living in that city.

Fortunately, help is available. Many sites on the Internet provide "cost of living" calculators. You enter the city you're moving from and the city you're moving to, and your current salary, and the calculator will tell you how much you'd have to earn in the new city to equal your buying power where you are now. We all know that cities like New York are outrageously expensive compared to many other parts of the country, but you may be surprised at the cost of living in some smaller or more remote cities. Take the time to find out this important information about the place you plan to call home.

Automotive Costs Related to Moving

Excise tax on automobiles is one of the biggest surprises people face when they register their car in a new city. This tax is based on the value of the vehicle and can amount to many hundreds of dollars on newer or more expensive models. Expenses this significant should be planned for, so when you're planning your move, call the city clerk's office and ask about the cost of registering your vehicle and whether excise taxes are charged. They'll be able to tell you how much you can expect to pay on your particular make, model, and year.

To add insult to injury, many cities collect excise taxes annually when you reregister your car. The only comfort is in knowing that the tax will decrease each year as the car depreciates. If you itemize deductions on your income tax return, you can deduct excise taxes.

Changes in Auto Insurance

Auto insurance costs can vary dramatically from one city to the next. Obviously you'd expect rates to be higher in large cities, but the size of the city is not the only thing that determines rates. If you're thinking of moving to a new city, call an insurance agent there (you can find agents on the Internet) and get a quote on coverage for the make and model of your vehicle so you don't have any unpleasant surprises when you arrive in your new location. (See Chapter 19 for a more detailed discussion of auto insurance.)

Tax Issues Related to Moving

You may be able to deduct some of the expenses of moving from your taxable income, even if you don't itemize expenses. There are two rules you must satisfy. The distance test requires the new job to be located at least fifty miles from your old residence. The time test requires you to work full-time in the new location (not necessarily at the same job the whole time) for at least thirty-nine weeks in the twelve months following your move.

If you're a new college graduate taking your first full-time job, the work location must be at least fifty miles from your former legal residence, which is the address you use when you file your income taxes, not your school address, so it's probably your parents' home. If you return home after college, you won't qualify for this deduction. If you're married, either you or your spouse can qualify, but you can't add your work times together to pass the thirty-nine week test.

Applicable Expenses

If you meet both of the tests, you can deduct the costs associated with physically moving your belongings from your former legal residence to your new home. This includes the amount paid to a moving company or the cost of a truck rental if you do it yourself. If you use your own car, you can deduct actual expenses for gas and oil or mileage at twelve cents a mile. Keep a mileage log and save it with your tax papers for the year. You can also deduct airfare, train, bus, and lodging expenses (but not meals) while en route for you and any dependents that you take with you. Keep receipts for everything.

FACT

If your former home was twenty miles from your job location, your new job location must be at least seventy miles (fifty plus twenty) from your old home in order to meet the distance test for deducting moving expenses from your income.

Employer-Sponsored Move

Employers use one of two methods of covering your moving costs. In the first method, your employer gives you a moving allowance for you to use as you see fit, and adds the amount to your taxable income when they issue your W-2 at the end of the year. You can offset some or all of this income by claiming your allowable expenses. In the second method, you pay the expenses yourself and submit a claim to your employer for reimbursement. Only expenses your employer reimburses you for that aren't IRS-allowable will be included on your W-2.

Not all moving related expenses are allowable. For instance, temporary housing at the new location, house-hunting trips, meals en route to your new home, and long-term storage of your household belongings are not allowable deductions. For details on the moving expense deduction, see IRS Publication 521, "Moving Expenses."

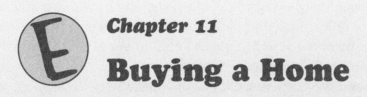

Chapter 11

Buying a Home

B uying a home is the most expensive decision you'll ever make. It's also an emotional and stressful experience for most people, combining excitement, anxiety, fear, and joy. There's a lot of information you have to absorb to make wise house buying and financing decisions, from deciding if owning is really for you, to understanding the nuances of home mortgages.

Owning Isn't for Everyone

You'd like to have the American Dream—owning your own home—but you're not sure if you can swing it financially. How much will you have to come up with for a down payment and closing costs? How do you know how high a mortgage you'll qualify for, how much you can really afford based on your lifestyle (regardless of whether the bank thinks you can afford more or less than that), and how much you'll save in taxes?

Maybe you're not sure if you really want to buy a house. Home ownership isn't for everyone, and that's okay. If you change jobs often or get transferred every few years, it may not make sense to buy right now. It usually takes at least five years to recoup the money you pay in up-front costs and the cost of selling.

You can search for homes online at Realtor.com (☞*www.realtor.com*), which has over two million homes listed from all over the country. Choose the town(s) you're interested in and see listing details and photos. The site also has mortgage information, links to Realtors, and articles on the home-buying process.

You may also be happier renting if you're not comfortable with performing repairs and maintenance and you can't afford to hire someone to do the work for you. Some people enjoy the amenities of apartment living, like swimming pools and other recreational features, or the flexibility of being able to move without too much hassle. Think about what's important to you. There's nothing wrong with renting if it suits you.

Getting Ready for Home Ownership

Before you start house hunting, there are some things you should do that will make the entire process easier. Establish a record of paying your bills on time. Avoid taking out any new loans or applying for any new credit cards in the months before you start looking for a house. Pay off as much debt as possible to help you qualify for the loan and to give you more expendable income after you move in.

Check your credit report. It's the first thing a lender will do when you apply for prequalification or a mortgage, so it's a good idea for you to do it first. Make sure there's nothing in it that's inaccurate or will raise a potential lender's eyebrow. Be prepared to explain any late or missed payments. For information on how to get a copy of your credit report, see Chapter 6.

Review your entire financial situation. If you haven't already prepared a Net Worth Statement, as discussed in Chapter 1, now's the time to do it. Ditto for a budget (see Chapter 2). Make sure you can really handle the mortgage payments on top of the other debt you owe, and that you have a realistic feel for what other expenses you'll incur from home ownership.

Avoid Becoming House Poor

You don't want to end up in a situation where you have such high house payments that you can't afford much of anything else. You may think buying your dream house is worth any sacrifice, but years of doing without the enjoyment of vacations, new cars, eating out, decorating, or a myriad of other simple pleasures can make your dream house feel like a jail. It can also put a strain on your relationship with your spouse or partner. A good rule of thumb is to buy a house that costs less than two and a half times your income. If your income is $50,000 a year, try to keep your home price under $125,000.

ALERT!

Don't let a Realtor who works on commission and makes more money on higher-priced homes pressure you into paying more than you can comfortably afford. Your first house probably won't be the house of your dreams. You may buy and sell several houses while in your twenties and thirties.

Prepare the Down Payment

A down payment is the amount of money you pay up-front when you buy property, and it reduces the amount of money you need to borrow. The larger the down payment, the smaller your loan and monthly payments will be, but it's difficult to save enough for a sizeable down payment and closing costs that require cash (real-estate transfer taxes, escrows for property taxes and insurance, title insurance, attorney fees, loan origination fees, and so on).

There are several options for coming up with more cash. One is to go on a crash budget for a few months by cutting your spending to the bare minimum and saving as much cash as possible. While you wouldn't want to stick to a budget this strict for long, you may be able to do it for a few months. Another method is to sock away all the extra money that comes your way: income tax refunds, overtime, bonuses, cash gifts, or—if you're lucky—lottery winnings. You may have a relative who's willing to lend you money, but it's not legal to borrow money for your down payment unless you identify the loan as a debt and can still qualify. Otherwise your lender will require a statement that the money is a gift.

If you're selling a house, use any equity you have in it to apply to the down payment on the new house. Borrowing from your 401(k) may be another option, but weigh the decision carefully. See Chapter 18 for the pros and cons of 401(k) loans.

How Mortgages Work

A mortgage is a legal contract that describes the terms of the loan obtained to buy a piece of property. It stipulates that if you don't meet the repayment terms of the loan, the lender can take your property and sell it to get his money back. This process is known as foreclosure.

Principal and Interest

Mortgage payments are divided between principal (the amount you borrowed), and interest (the cost of borrowing the money). Each month a little bit more gets applied to the principal balance (very little!). On a traditional thirty-year mortgage, the payments for the first twenty years or so will be more interest than principal. For example, on a thirty-year $100,000 mortgage at 7 percent interest, your payments the first year would total $7,983, of which $6,967 would be for interest and only $1,015 for principal. At the end of the year you would still owe a balance of $98,985. Over the life of the thirty-year mortgage, you'd repay the $100,000 you borrowed plus $139,509 in interest, for a total of $239,509. (The following chapter discusses ways you can cut tens of thousands of dollars from your interest costs.)

Private Mortgage Insurance

If it weren't for private mortgage insurance (PMI), which protects the lender in case you're unable to make the payments on your loan, you might not be able to buy a house for many years. Most lenders require a 20 percent down payment, so on a $100,000 loan, you'd be required to come up with approximately $25,000 for the down payment and closing costs. PMI, which ranges between $40 and $100 per month, helps you buy a house with as little as 5 to 10 percent down and is folded into your loan payments.

Under federal law, your lender is required to automatically terminate PMI when your equity reaches 22 percent of the original appraised value of your home. To calculate what percent equity you have in your home, divide your loan balance by the appraised value and deduct this number from 100.

If you bought your home after 1999, your lender must terminate your PMI when you reach 20 percent equity, if you request it. Some businesses offer a service to help you get your PMI dropped, but don't waste your money. Just call your lender and ask if you're paying PMI and if so, when it can be canceled. Then be sure to call again when that time arrives. If you have an FHA or VA loan, PMI isn't required because the federal government has already agreed to protect the lender if you default on your loan.

Types of Mortgages

You may think that all mortgages are alike, but they actually come in many shapes and sizes. There are several different terms (fifteen-year, twenty-year, or thirty-year), fixed interest rate and variable interest rate, balloon mortgages, government-backed mortgages, and more. To choose the best one for your personal situation, you should be familiar with at least these basic types.

Mortgage Terms

Most mortgages are for fifteen, twenty, or thirty years with an interest rate that's fixed over the life of the loan. Payments on fifteen- and twenty-year loans are somewhat higher than those on traditional thirty-year loans, so it requires higher income to qualify for the shorter terms. The benefit is that you build equity faster, pay your mortgage off years sooner, and save many tens of thousands of dollars.

QUESTION?

Should I choose a shorter or longer mortgage term?
If you can swing the payments comfortably, the shorter terms are definitely worthwhile. If you're a disciplined saver, you may be able to do just as well with a thirty-year loan if you invest the monthly savings in stocks or mutual funds.

To illustrate the difference between a thirty-year and a fifteen-year mortgage, take the example of a mortgage for $150,000 at 6 percent. The payment on a fifteen-year loan would be $1,266 per month, and the total interest paid over the life of the loan would be $77,841. The payment on a thirty-year mortgage for the same amount and the same interest rate would be $899 per month (a decrease of $367) and the total interest paid over the life of the loan would be $173,757 (an increase of $95,916). Moreover, interest rates on shorter-term mortgages are generally lower than those on longer-term mortgages, so the difference between the two loans in the example would actually be even greater.

Adjustable-Rate Mortgages

The interest rates on adjustable-rate mortgages (ARMs) vary. They often start out as much as 1.5 to 2 percentage points lower than the prevailing market rates and increase or decrease at predetermined intervals. The amount of increase or decrease depends on whether they're tied to Treasury bills, CD rates, or some other financial index. The rate is fixed for a certain period (between six months and five years) and then adjusted periodically, like every year or two. The amount the rate can increase at each interval is usually 2 percentage points, and there's often a lifetime cap of 6 percentage points.

In a time of rising interest rates, it can be disturbing to know that your rate can increase every year. Before taking out an ARM, be sure that you can afford the highest payment possible under the terms of the loan. ARMs might be a good option if you know you'll only be in the house for a few years, but if you use one because you can't qualify for a conventional mortgage, you're risking the possible loss of your house.

Balloon Mortgages

Balloon mortgages have lower interest rates than traditional mortgages, but the loan term is only for five to seven years. At the end of that time, the entire balance is due, and you have to either pay it off or refinance at the rates that are in effect then. If you plan to sell your house, pay it off, or refinance it within the time frame of the loan, this might be an option for you.

Government-Backed Mortgages

Government loans like FHA and VA loans make home ownership possible for people who might not otherwise qualify for a mortgage. The federal government insures the loan, which is issued by a regular lender. FHA loans require a smaller down payment than regular mortgages (5 percent rather than 10 or 20 percent), allow a higher debt percentage, and allow you to borrow the down payment and closing costs from a family member, which you can't do legally with a regular mortgage. VA loans are for veterans and don't require any down payment. They have even less stringent requirements on the income-to-debt ratio than FHA loans.

The more you borrow relative to the price of the home, the higher the interest rate, so when you make a small down payment, don't expect to get the best rates. Lenders charge higher rates because there's more risk that you'll default if you have little equity in your home.

Choosing the Best Mortgage for You

As you can see, there are many mortgage options (and we've barely touched the surface), so it's important to understand how each of the basic types would impact your payments. Read. Shop around. Ask questions.

Don't underestimate the impact of interest rates on your monthly payments. A $100,000 loan at 7 percent interest for thirty years would cost $665 per month. The same loan at 8 percent interest would cost $734 per month, a difference of $69 per month or $24,840 over the life of a thirty-year mortgage.

Federal Truth in Lending Act and the APR

The Federal Truth in Lending Act requires lenders to disclose the annual percentage rate (APR) and the total finance charges to borrowers in writing. The APR is the average annual finance charge. It's more meaningful than the interest rate alone because it includes costs such as loan origination fees, private mortgage insurance premium, points, and so on.

FACT

The Web site of HSH Associates (✍*www.hsh.com*), the largest publisher of mortgage rates and other financial information in the United States, can help you quickly track down the best mortgage rates offered by lenders located near you. Rates for borrowers with perfect credit are separated from rates for those with "bruised" credit.

You can't just assume that the loan with the lower interest rate is best. The APR levels the playing field by allowing you to quickly and painlessly compare loans that have different rates and fees. It's a much more accurate indicator of the cost of the loan. Be aware, however, that it can't be used as an accurate comparison of borrowing costs on adjustable-rate mortgages.

Paying Points

Points are a percentage of the loan amount that you pay up-front to "buy down" the interest rate on a mortgage. One point is 1 percent of the loan and usually lowers the interest rate by ¼ percent. One point on a $100,000 loan would be $1,000, two points would be $2,000, and so on. When comparing interest rates, you have to consider points. A 7 percent loan with one point is not necessarily better (or worse) than an 8 percent loan with no points. Remember, you have to look at the APR to compare rates and fees. Paying points in order to get a lower interest rate may be worthwhile if you're planning to stay in the house for five years or more. The lower interest rate saves you a lot of money over the long-term, but if you sell in less than five to ten years you won't have time to recoup your costs.

The Home-Buying Process

One of the first steps to take when you've decided you want to be a homeowner is to determine how much house you can afford. There are two parts to this. The first is to follow a budget for at least three to six months so you know your spending habits and how much money you have to work with. The second is to estimate how much money the bank is likely to lend you so you don't waste time and emotional energy looking at houses or neighborhoods you can't afford. Buying a house should be an exciting time, and you don't want to be discouraged at having to "settle" for a two-bedroom bungalow with a carport if you've been looking at four-bedroom colonials with a two-car garage.

Calculate Your PITI

To estimate how much you can expect to borrow, use the two basic guidelines that banks and mortgage companies follow. The first guideline is that principal, interest, taxes, and insurance (PITI) shouldn't exceed 28 percent of your gross income (your pay before taxes). Let's say that your gross income is $50,000 a year. Your principal, interest, property taxes, and insurance shouldn't exceed $14,000 per year, or $1,166 per month.

Property taxes can vary drastically between states and even between towns in the same state, so call the town or city tax assessor and ask what the typical taxes would be on a house that's in your approximate price range. You may be able to afford to buy the house but unable to afford the taxes.

We'll assume that the property taxes on a $100,000 house are $1,800 per year, or $150 per month, that homeowner's insurance is $400 per year, or $33 per month, and that PMI is $50 per month. You would qualify for $933 per month in principal and interest payments ($1,166 – $150 – $33 – $50 = $933). So how much house can you buy for $933 per month? Try plugging several different interest rates into one of the mortgage calculators found at Web sites like CNNMoney (✎ *http://money.cnn.com*) or Quicken.com (✎ *www.quicken.com*).

Consider Your Long-Term Debt

The second guideline is that PITI plus all your other long-term debt shouldn't exceed 36 percent of your gross income. Your long-term debt (car loans, credit cards you won't have paid off within the next ten months, furniture or equipment loans, student loans, child support and alimony, and so on) shouldn't exceed 8 percent of your income (36 percent – 28 percent for PITI = 8 percent for other debt). Again, using the example of $50,000 in gross income, your monthly payments toward long-term debt other than your PITI shouldn't exceed $333 per month ($50,000 × 8 percent = $4,000 ÷ 12 months = $333 per month). If your debt payments are more than this, you'll need to come up with a larger down payment so you don't have to borrow as much.

If you make a small down payment, your lender may only use the lower percentages for PITI and long-term debt to protect itself against the possibility that you might default on your loan. However, there's a growing trend for lenders to automatically use the 28 percent guideline for PITI.

Check the Mortgage Calculator

Just because you qualify for a certain amount doesn't mean you can afford it. That's why it's invaluable to have tracked your spending and income for several months. You'll have a better picture of your overall financial condition and how much you can realistically pay for housing.

Play around with an online mortgage calculator that will help you determine how much you can afford to pay for a house. Monstermoving.com (*www.monstermoving.com*) has an excellent calculator for this. Click on "Find a Place," then "Tools," then "Home Buying Calculators." Run a few different scenarios to get a feel for the numbers. There are also several helpful calculators related to the home-buying process at Mortgage101.com (*www.mortgage101.com*) under "Calculators."

Getting Preapproved or Prequalified

It's a good idea to apply for your mortgage early in the process instead of waiting until you find a house you like. Prequalification means the lender has looked at your credit report, income, and level of debt and determined that you appear to qualify for a loan. Preapproval means that the lender has actually approved you for a specific loan amount.

Preapproval gives you the most credibility with the seller, who may be deciding between two or more offers and doesn't want to accept an offer from someone who may not qualify for the financing. You'll need to provide a heap of paperwork to the mortgage company during the application process, including the following forms:

- W-2 forms for the prior two years
- Federal tax returns for the prior two years
- Documentation for any other income you're claiming, such as overtime, bonuses, child support, or alimony
- A list of all your debts, such as credit cards, student loans, car loans, child support, or alimony, and the name of the creditor, balance owed, and minimum monthly payment
- Copies of bank statements

- Proof of assets, such as stock or mutual fund statements and car and real-estate titles
- Proof of rent or mortgage payments (canceled checks)

FACT

Mortgage brokers bring lenders and borrowers together but do not lend money or service loans. Their fee is added to the cost of your loan. If you don't have great credit, you may get a better rate through a broker than through a bank, but watch out for the fees.

Making and Negotiating the Offer

Once you've found the house you want to buy, the next step is to make an offer, which is a legally binding contract. The offer will be in writing and will include the amount you're willing to pay for the house (it can be more or less than the asking price) and the time frame for the purchase. It will be contingent on a satisfactory house inspection and bank approval. You'll pay earnest money, usually $1,000, which will be credited to the sales price if the sale goes through. In most cases (but not always), you'll get your money back even if the deal falls through. Fees may be deducted, and the seller and buyer usually have to come to an agreement about how to handle the balance.

The sellers may accept or decline your offer or they may make a counteroffer. Sometimes this takes hours, sometimes days. If you come to an agreement, the buyer will accept your final written offer and the home inspections will take place as quickly as possible. Once you notify your mortgage company that your offer has been accepted, they'll perform an appraisal to make sure the house is worth what you offered. When all is in place, you and the seller will sign the Purchase and Sale Agreement.

Closing the Deal

After your bank gives the final approval for your loan, and you have proof of homeowner's insurance on the property, you'll be ready to close the deal. Just prior to the closing, you'll walk through the house, which should be empty and clean, and make sure there are no surprises. Then you'll meet with the seller or his representative, the closing attorney, and your Realtor to sign the mortgage papers and make the transfer of the property. Don't be surprised if you feel both excited and nervous. Buying a home is exciting but it's also a big financial commitment.

Understanding Closing Costs

Closing costs are all of the costs associated with the transfer of the property, the processing of your mortgage, and the fees charged by those who make it all happen. Closing costs include:

- Attorney's fees
- Property transfer fees charged by state and local governments
- Property taxes and homeowner's insurance placed in an escrow account (so that they're available to pay when due)
- Real-estate commissions
- Lender fees such as appraisal, processing fees, points, origination fees, land surveys, interest from the settlement date until your first payment is due, and title insurance

For lots of easy-to-read, helpful information on the ins and outs of mortgages, visit Bankrate.com (*www.bankrate.com*) and click on the "Mortgages" button on the left. You'll find rates, articles, and online tools and calculators that will help you make informed decisions about buying and financing your new home.

Closing costs vary by location but are typically 3 to 6 percent of your loan, so if you're buying a $100,000 house, you can expect closing costs to be between $3,000 and $6,000. Like the down payment, closing costs must be paid at the time of purchase. Federal law requires lenders to provide you with a Good Faith Estimate of your closing costs before you go to settlement.

Home Ownership Tax Savings

When you own a home, you can deduct the mortgage interest and a few related costs from your taxable income by itemizing your deductions on Schedule A of Form 1040.

By the end of January each year, your lender will send you a Form 1098 showing the amount of mortgage interest you paid during that year. Points you paid at closing are deductible the first year you own your home if they're considered a prepayment of interest and meet a number of other requirements. For a complete list of the requirements, see IRS Publication 936, "Home Mortgage Interest Deduction." If your points don't meet these requirements, you can deduct them over the life of the loan. Most of the other costs paid at closing are not tax-deductible.

Real-Estate Property Tax Deduction

You can also deduct real-estate property taxes from your taxable income. If property taxes are included in your mortgage payment and paid by your lender, claim the amount the lender actually paid out during the year, not the amounts included for taxes in your monthly mortgage payments. Your lender places these funds in an escrow account for safekeeping and uses the funds to pay your real estate and insurance.

FACT

According to a study by the Center for Housing Policy, many low- and moderate-income families are spending half their income on housing instead of the recommended 28 percent because wages haven't kept up with the increase in housing prices.

If your local real-estate taxes include charges for services like trash removal or water and sewer, this portion of your taxes is not deductible. Look carefully at your copy of the real-estate tax bill to determine how much you can deduct. The bill should identify services separately from taxes, which are based on the value of your property.

Calculating Your Tax Savings

To calculate how much you'll save by deducting mortgage interest and property taxes, you need to know your marginal tax rate for federal and state income taxes. You can get these rates from the tax rate schedules in your tax return packets or from the IRS Web site (✎*www.irs.gov*). In 2002, a married couple filing jointly with income between $46,701 and $112,850 had a marginal tax rate of 27 percent. We'll assume a state tax rate of 6 percent, for a total of 33 percent. Multiply this rate times the amount you can claim on your income tax return for mortgage interest and property taxes to get the amount you save in income taxes. If you were married with a 33 percent combined tax rate and $10,000 in deductions, you'd save $3,300 in taxes ($10,000 × 0.33 = $3,300), a monthly savings of $275. If your mortgage is $1,000 a month, your actual after-tax cost is $725 ($1,000 − $275 = $725). This is a significant tax savings, but remember that there are other costs associated with owning a home that you don't incur when renting.

Moreover, you may save more than this example if owning a home allows you to itemize for the first time. When you itemize, you can also deduct state income taxes, charitable gifts, and medical and dental expenses that exceed 7.5 percent of your income. You can file a new W-4 to claim more exemptions and have less tax taken out each week or leave your withholding as they are and get an income tax refund at the end of the year.

Be Prepared for Other Expenses

Mortgage payments aren't the only expense to consider when evaluating whether you can afford to buy a house and how much you can afford to spend. There are also property taxes, which can be substantial, homeowner's insurance, repairs and maintenance, utilities, sewer and water bills, major appliances, landscaping and yard maintenance costs, and more. Utilities can be very expensive if you live in a cold region of the country like the Northeast, where bone-chilling winters drive up heating costs, or in the South, where hot, humid summers run up air conditioning bills.

If you've been renting and are considering buying a house, try to think of all the things you'll need to buy that you didn't need when you had a landlord who took care of repairs and yard work. You may need a lawnmower, weed whacker, chipper/shredder, leaf blower, rototiller, or other lawn and garden equipment; a washer and dryer, a new stove or refrigerator, or other household appliances; a snow blower or snow plow. Then there are the items that aren't absolutely necessary but that you'll want to have as soon as possible, like window coverings (blinds, shades, or curtains), and new or additional furniture. If you're buying a fixer-upper, you'll need money for materials even if you intend to do most of the work yourself. Even a few of these things can add up to a lot of expenses.

Buy a less expensive house than you can afford. Then you'll have money for other things and won't be as likely to get in over your head with credit card and consumer debt. You'll even be able to make extra principal payments on your mortgage. Even small amounts can have a significant impact over the life of your loan.

Most people use all the cash they can scrape together for the down payment and closing costs, and then end up having to use credit to buy the things they need or want for the new house. Between the mortgage payments and the increased credit card payments, you may struggle to make ends meet. If you plan ahead and know how much house you can really afford, you can avoid being house poor—unable to afford anything but the house payment. Being house poor can propel you more deeply into debt because you use credit for purchases you'd pay cash for if you weren't so strapped.

Chapter 12

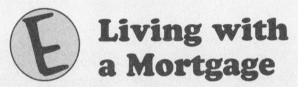

Living with a Mortgage

If you own a home, you may have questions about refinancing your mortgage to pay for home improvements, consolidate debt, or reduce payments. You may wonder when to refinance, what kind of loan to choose, how to prepay your mortgage, or how to go about selling your house. You may even be facing foreclosure and need urgent help.

Planning Home Improvements

Whether you've just bought a fixer-upper and need to do some renovations, you're trying to make room for a growing family, or you just want to increase the value of your home by remodeling, you have several options for financing the improvements. Before you approach a lender, make a detailed plan of the work you want done and get bids from several contractors.

Whenever you use your home as collateral, as in a mortgage or home equity loan, you risk losing it if you can't make the payments. That's why it's so important to get detailed, accurate cost estimates from reputable, experienced contractors. If the contractor's work is incomplete or shoddy and you have to hire someone else to finish or fix it, you still have to repay the loan.

Shop for financing at established financial institutions and compare rates and fees from several different lenders. Contractors sometimes offer to arrange financing with a particular lender, but it may be best to steer clear of these arrangements unless you have the time and inclination to research them thoroughly. The contractor usually receives a commission from the lender for the referral and you can end up paying for it in higher interest rates or fees you wouldn't incur at your local bank or credit union.

FACT

According to estimates from the U.S. Department of Commerce, in the year 2000 Americans spent $149 billion on repairs and improvements to their homes. Many big-ticket improvements don't pay for themselves when it comes time to sell, so choose them wisely.

The Best Way to Find a Contractor

Try word of mouth—ask friends, neighbors, and coworkers who have remodeled or made home improvements. Who did they use? Were they satisfied with the results and the costs? Once you've identified several possible candidates, check them out with the local Better Business Bureau or consumer protection agency to see if they've had complaints filed against them and, more importantly, whether they resolved any problems satisfactorily.

Get at least three detailed written estimates that spell out exactly what will be done, the type and quality of materials that will be used, and the cost, based on your written description of your project. Compare the bids carefully and make sure you understand any significant differences between them. Don't automatically choose the lowest bid without discussing each bid with the appropriate contractor so you can determine why they differ. If a bid is significantly lower than the others, you may want to toss it out. The contractor may be bidding inferior materials or planning to take laborsaving shortcuts that compromise the quality of the work.

Once you've chosen a contractor, ask for the name of his insurance agent and call to verify that he carries workers' compensation insurance and coverage for property damage and personal liability in case of accidents. You don't want to be held financially responsible if a worker is hurt on your property. It's also a good idea to call your state and local government and find out if contractors have to be licensed or bonded. If they do, check to make sure the contractor has complied.

Before hiring a contractor to build or renovate your home, educate yourself about contractor fraud so you know what to look out for. Visit ✍ *www.contractorfraud.net* for information on popular contractor scams and advice on finding and using reputable contractors.

The Payment Schedule

Never pay a contractor the entire cost of the project up-front. He'll probably request a down payment, the amount of which may be limited by state law. Try to keep the first payment to no more than 10 to 20 percent. Additional payments should be tied to completion of measurable milestones, so you're paying for the work that's actually been accomplished. Include these milestones in your contract to ensure that your contractor understands and agrees to them. You should be holding at least 15 percent of the contractor's money until the job is finished to your satisfaction and you have written proof that all subcontractors and suppliers have been paid.

Mechanic's Liens

One of the biggest concerns about hiring a contractor who uses subcontractors is the possibility of what's known as a "mechanic's lien." If the contractor doesn't pay his subcontractors or suppliers, they can demand payment from you directly even though you already paid the contractor for their services or supplies. If you don't pay, they can place a lien on your home and force you to sell it to pay them if you can't come up with the money any other way. Never settle for a contractor's promise that he'll pay everybody.

You can protect yourself by asking your contractor to provide lien waivers or lien releases from all his subcontractors and suppliers before beginning work. A lien waiver is a simple form that the subcontractor signs stating that he won't ask you for money you've already paid the contractor. If the subcontractor won't sign a lien waiver before performing the job, you could meet with the contractor and subcontractor together and write a check to each one separately. Then get the subcontractor to sign a lien release, which is similar to a lien waiver but states that the subcontractor has been paid.

Building a Home

It may be that you're not interested in improving your home, but in building it yourself. Don't kid yourself: This is a huge undertaking and will require a commitment of time and money.

If you've decided to buy a custom-built house, hiring a reputable builder who uses quality subcontractors is more important than finding the builder who will agree to build the house you want for the lowest price. Interview several builders. Ask for references from the ones you like and call several recent homebuyers who used the builder. If the project is still in progress, ask if you can see it. Try to look at a finished house as well. Call your local Better Business Bureau, consumer protection agency, and state attorney general's office to see if there have been complaints about the builder, and if so, the nature of the complaints and whether the builder rectified the problems. Before you sign a contract, verify that the builder has property, liability, workers' compensation, and builder's risk insurance.

There are special loans for building your own home. You may need to take out two separate loans: a construction loan and a regular mortgage. An interim construction loan provides money to the builder and subcontractors while your house is being built. During the building process, you pay only interest on the loan. When the house is completed, the construction loan is converted to a regular mortgage. You'll probably need a commitment letter from the permanent mortgage company in order to get the interim loan because the commitment letter pledges to pay off the construction loan when the home is finished. Some lenders now offer the two types of loans together with only one closing, so you save closing costs.

FACT

Debt consolidation is the number one reason people use home equity loans. According to the Consumer Bankers Association, 44 percent use them to pay off credit card and other consumer debt and 25 percent use them to make home improvements. Other uses include buying a car, education costs, or a major purchase.

Home Equity Loans and Lines of Credit

The two most common methods of financing home improvements are cashing out the equity in your home by refinancing, and taking out a second mortgage or home equity line of credit. Home equity loans, a type of second mortgage, have a fixed term, usually between five and fifteen years, at a fixed interest rate. You borrow one lump sum of money and make regular monthly payments over the life of the loan.

Home equity lines of credit are a type of revolving credit, like a credit card. You're allowed to borrow a certain amount over the life of the loan, and you don't have to borrow it all in a lump sum. Some lenders give you special checks; others provide a type of credit card that you use to access the money. As you pay off the principal, you can borrow more. For example, let's say you have a line of credit of $15,000. You borrow $6,000, leaving $9,000 of available credit. You pay off $3,000, making your available credit $12,000 ($15,000 − $6,000 + $3,000 = $12,000). The interest rate is variable so your payments change depending on the current rate and your outstanding balance. At the end of the loan term, any unpaid balance is due. If you sell your house, the balance is due at the time of sale.

Which Type of Loan Is Best for You?

Home equity loans are best suited for times when you need a lump sum amount. Lines of credit are best if you need the money at intervals, so you borrow only the amount you need, when you need it. Lines of credit can be dangerous if you have trouble controlling credit card debt because they work in much the same way as credit cards. But there's one very important difference: With a home equity line of credit your home is at stake. If you get in over your head, you could lose your home.

Home equity loans are attractive for a number of reasons. Their rates are higher than interest rates on first mortgages but much lower than credit card interest rates. Interest on home equity loans is also tax-deductible, another attractive feature. Closing costs for home equity loans are similar to those for first mortgages. Expect to pay 2 to 5 percent of the loan amount.

You can't use the APR to compare home equity lines of credit and home equity loans because the APR for a line of credit doesn't include points and fees, so it will be misleadingly low if you try to compare it to the APR of a home equity loan.

Should You Get Your Loan Online?

Even if you're not comfortable with the idea of handling the entire mortgage process online, don't hesitate to use the Internet to research rates and fees being offered by various lenders. Lenders who offer the most competitive rates tend to be online, so you can find the best rates much more quickly than you could by calling or visiting local lenders.

QUESTION?

Where can I find the best mortgage interest rates and costs?
Research or apply for mortgage loans online at E-Loans
(✐ *www.eloan.com*), LendingTree (✐ *www.lendingtree.com*),
Bankrate.com (✐ *www.bankrate.com*), or Realtor.com
(✐ *www.realtor.com*). All four sites also offer easy-to-read articles
about all aspects of the home-buying process and an assortment
of online calculators and tools related to refinancing.

You may not want to complete the lengthy loan application form
online, but you can call the lender and give the information over the
telephone. You may be able to track the progress of your loan online.
At the very least, you can use the Internet to educate yourself quickly
and painlessly about various mortgage products and current rates.

Escrow Accounts

An escrow account is a special account your lender sets up if your
mortgage payments will include amounts for property taxes and
homeowner's insurance and the lender or mortgage servicing company
will be disbursing the money when these bills become due. Homeowner's
insurance is typically at least several hundred dollars on the average
home, and property taxes can be several thousand dollars or more. If you
have trouble saving for large expenses, escrow accounts can make it
easier because each month you pay one-twelfth of the annual amounts
needed. However, you're paying the money before it's really due and in
most cases not earning any interest on it.

Lenders can easily make mistakes in escrow accounts, so it's
important to keep an eye on them and make sure all the money is
accounted for and that you're not paying more than is necessary. By law,
there has to be at least one month per year when the balance in your
account is no more than one-sixth of your annual expenses paid from
escrow. Once a year your lender will perform an escrow analysis to
determine how much money should be deposited into the account for
the coming year in order to cover the expenses that will be paid. If you
have more than $50 in excess of what's needed, you should receive a

refund. If you have a shortage, one-twelfth of the amount needed will be added to your monthly payments for the next year.

Refinancing Your Mortgage

When you refinance your mortgage, you take out a new loan at a lower rate or for a different term and use the proceeds to pay off the original mortgage. Most lenders require you to have at least 10 to 20 percent equity in your home before you can refinance.

When Does It Pay to Refinance?

How do you know if the difference in interest rates is enough to make refinancing worthwhile when you include the costs of closing on the new loan? The old rule of thumb was that interest rates should be at least 2 percentage points below your current rate, but the low-cost refinancing that many lenders now offer makes that guideline obsolete. Refinancing may make sense if you have a second mortgage or home equity loan with a higher rate. You can save money by rolling both your first and second mortgages into one new loan with an overall lower rate. Refinancing also makes sense if you want to take advantage of lower interest rates to shorten the term of your loan, from thirty years to fifteen years, for example, for around the same monthly payment. You'll pay off your mortgage many years sooner and slash total interest costs dramatically.

Sometimes refinancing doesn't make sense. If you've had your mortgage for more than ten years, for example, you could end up paying a lot more in interest by refinancing at a lower interest rate. That's because in the early years of a mortgage most of your payment goes toward interest and very little is applied to your principal balance. By the time you've been making payments for ten or more years, you've started to make some dents in the principal, and if you refinance with a new thirty-year loan, most of your payments will once again be interest. Evaluate your situation carefully and consider not just the monthly payment, but also the total interest costs over the life of the loan added to the total interest costs you've already paid. Online calculators can help you quickly determine the total interest under different scenarios.

FACT

Some lenders offer loans that allow you to roll the closing costs into your new loan so you don't have to come up with cash out of your pocket. If your loan balance goes above 80 percent of the value of your house, however, you'll be subject to private mortgage insurance even if you didn't have to pay it on your old loan.

The Time Frame Issue

The first question to ask yourself when you're thinking about refinancing is how long you expect to live in the house. If you plan to move within the next three years or so, you may not have enough time to recoup your closing costs. Assuming you'll be sticking around, the next thing you need to do is get a detailed written estimate of your closing costs from the lender.

To figure out how long it will take you to pay off the cost of refinancing and really start saving money, deduct the new, lower monthly payment from your current payment to find your monthly savings. Multiply your monthly savings by your combined effective state and federal tax rate to get your tax cost and subtract this from your monthly savings. The reason for this adjustment to your savings is that your new loan with the lower payment reduces the tax benefit you had under the old loan. Now divide the total of all the fees and closing costs on the new mortgage by your net monthly savings after the tax adjustment. This is how many months it will take you to pay off the cost of refinancing.

For example, let's say that your closing costs are going to be $3,000. Your current monthly payment is $875 and your new payment is $750, a monthly savings of $125. If your combined effective state and federal tax rate is 20 percent, decreasing your interest payments by $125 per month will increase your taxes $25 per month ($125 × 0.20), so your net savings are $100 ($125 – $25). Your closing costs of $3,000 divided by your monthly savings of $100 equals thirty months, the time it would take to repay your closing costs and start saving money. If you plan to be in your home for more than thirty months, it makes sense to refinance. Before you do, check with your lender and make sure there's not a prepayment penalty on your current mortgage. If there is, it may cost you more to refinance than it's worth.

ALERT!

Be aware that you may not qualify for the low interest rates you see advertised. When you apply for refinancing, the lender will do a credit check, and if your credit isn't what it should be, you'll pay a higher rate.

Look at the Big Picture

When it comes to mortgages and home equity loans, the bottom line is to look at the big picture whenever possible. If you're on a tight budget and can barely qualify for a thirty-year mortgage, you may not have any other options, but if possible, look beyond the monthly payments to your overall financial plan. What will benefit you the most in the long-term? Even if you'd love to have a fifteen-year loan to build equity quickly but can't quite swing it, you may be able to make extra principal payments on your thirty-year loan. You'd still come out ahead without the monthly commitment to higher payments. Whatever road you take, be sure to leave enough financial cushion so that you're able to contribute to your 401(k) and save for your other financial goals.

Cash-out Refinancing

Some people refinance for more than the value of their current mortgage if they have a lot of equity in their home. This is called cash-out refinancing. Let's say you paid $125,000 for your house and your mortgage is $100,000. Your house has appreciated in value and is now worth $175,000. You might refinance for $140,000, pay off the balance on your $100,000 mortgage and pocket the difference of $40,000 or more. You'd still have 20 percent equity in your home ($140,000 ÷ $175,000 = 80 percent). Don't forget that your monthly payments would be significantly higher, so make sure you can afford them. If you're planning to borrow anyway to make improvements to your home, this may be the way to go instead of taking out a second loan to pay for the renovations.

FACT

Cash-out refinancing loans are expected to hit a record $785 billion this year, with over $140 billion in cash, according to *USA Today*. Nearly two-thirds of those refinancing in 2002 took cash out.

Prepaying Your Mortgage

You can shave thousands or tens of thousands of dollars off the long-term costs of your mortgage by prepaying. There are several ways to do it. You can add a little extra to your regular monthly payment, make one extra payment a year, or pay half your regular payment every two weeks, which equates to paying an extra full payment each year.

If you had a thirty-year mortgage for $100,000 at 7 percent interest and you paid an extra $25 every month, you'd cut more than three years off the length of the mortgage and save over $18,000 in interest. However, please note that when mortgage rates are significantly lower than other consumer borrowing rates, it makes more sense to pay off your high-interest credit card debts first.

When you make extra payments, be sure to tell your lender to apply them to the principal. Don't pay a company that offers to set up a prepayment plan for you for a fee. It's totally unnecessary when you can achieve the same thing yourself as easily as including the extra amount in your check and writing, "apply extra payment to principal."

Before making prepayments, check with your lender and read the fine print of your loan documents to make sure your lender won't penalize you for prepaying part of your mortgage in the first three to five years of the loan. These prepayment penalties are rare in the primary mortgage market (lenders who directly negotiate mortgages with borrowers), but common in the subprime market (investors who buy and sell pools of mortgages from lenders, which makes mortgages more accessible to those with less than perfect credit). Even if your loan does have a prepayment penalty, you'll probably be allowed to prepay up to 20 percent of your mortgage in any twelve-month period without incurring a penalty.

Selling Your Home

Selling your home can be a difficult and emotional experience. It involves a lot of hard work to get everything shipshape, keep it clean for prospective buyers who come by on short notice with Realtors, and prepare to move. It may also involve sadness at leaving a house full of memories, or excitement about moving to a different area or buying a new house. If housing prices have gone down and you lose money on your house, you may feel stressed and depressed. Try not to let any of these emotions interfere with the many decisions you'll have to make during the selling process.

If you're selling your home yourself, get maximum exposure by listing it on the Internet's largest "for sale by owner" real-estate site, I Sold My House (✍*www.isoldmyhouse.com*). Listings are free.

Using a Realtor

Once you decide to sell, your next decision is whether to use a real-estate broker or sell your house yourself. Most brokers charge 6 to 7 percent, so if your house sells for $150,000, you'll be paying between $9,000 and $10,500 in real-estate fees. If your house hasn't appreciated that much in value, you could end up losing money on the deal. However, using a broker has major advantages:

- They know the market in your area.
- They have the power of the Multiple Listing Service, a computerized database that includes all properties for sale in your state.
- They screen potential buyers, bring them to your door, and show them your house.

- They have all of the necessary legal contracts and forms critical to the selling process.
- They take care of all the paperwork and coordinate the meeting with closing attorneys.

Selling It Yourself

The obvious benefit of selling your home yourself is saving money on the Realtor fees, which can be substantial. Some of the money you'll save by not using a Realtor will have to go toward marketing your home, hiring an attorney, and other expenses of selling. The biggest disadvantage of selling your house yourself is that you don't have access to the Multiple Listing Service, which exposes your house to the largest possible number of potential buyers. Selling your own home also takes a serious commitment of time and effort to get yourself up to speed on all of the legal issues and to be available to show your house to potential buyers or browsers.

Facing Foreclosure

The number of home foreclosures is at an all-time high. Unemployment rates rise as the economy worsens. Job loss, getting too deeply into debt, and buying a more expensive house than they can afford propel people into foreclosure. The rising popularity of loan products like interest-only loans allows borrowers to buy bigger, more expensive houses. An interest-only loan lowers your initial monthly payment for a set period of time, typically five years. During that time you make only interest payments and pay nothing on the principal, so at the end of the five years, you still owe the full amount borrowed. To pay off the balance in the remaining years of the mortgage, you have to pay a higher amount once the interest-only period is over. If you can't afford the higher payments, you may be headed for foreclosure.

If you fail to make your mortgage payments for ninety days, your lender will probably start foreclosure proceedings to take over your house and sell it to get back the money they lent you. If the house sells for less than you owe on it, they could sue you for the difference. Obviously foreclosure is a major black mark on your credit record and will affect your ability to obtain credit in the future.

Act Quickly to Prevent Foreclosure

If your financial situation is so critical that you're headed toward foreclosure, you're probably in an emotional state that includes feelings of anger, frustration, fear, and helplessness, but don't let these emotions keep you from taking action. There are things you can do to help prevent foreclosure. If you anticipate having trouble making payments, contact your lender immediately and explain your situation. Don't wait until you've already missed a payment. Your lender may be willing to come up with a new payment plan that takes your current situation into consideration. You may be able to refinance the loan, extend the term, or spread the missed payments out over several months. If you have an FHA mortgage, you may have other alternatives as well. Your lender doesn't want to foreclose, but the lender can't work with you unless you're willing. You may be embarrassed and ashamed and may even try to keep your spouse in the dark about the situation, but if you wait too long you'll have ruined your chances of resolving the problem.

ALERT!

You may find lower refinancing interest rates than your current lender advertises, but don't rule your lender out without talking to your loan officer. Sometimes banks and credit unions will waive certain fees or offer a slight rate discount for current customers.

You Do Have Alternatives

If worst comes to worst, you can protect your credit by holding a preforeclosure sale, during which you live in the house while you go through the process of selling it to pay back the lender. A second option is a deed in lieu of foreclosure, where you give the house to your lender and the lender sells it to get its money back. Ⓔ

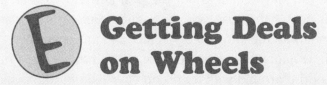

Chapter 13

Getting Deals on Wheels

Buying a car is a big deal that can cost you big money. Whether you pay cash, lease, or finance your new car, there are pitfalls to steer clear of and information to gather to avoid paying too much. And maybe you should consider buying a used one, anyway. The Internet has revolutionized how we buy cars and made it possible for you to educate yourself before you head to the dealer.

New or Used?

When you're in the market for a car, the first step is deciding whether to buy new or used. If money is no object, you'll probably go for new. If you want to minimize the costs, you may decide to buy used. If it's important to you to have a new car or you're concerned about the potential problems with a used car, you may decide to buy the best new car you can afford even if money is tight. Either way, you can reduce your costs substantially if you arm yourself with the information included in this chapter.

No matter how many times you do it, buying a new car is a heady experience. You drive around with a grin on your face for days, sniffing that special smell that permeates new cars. Will you still be smiling when you make your monthly payments? How about when it's time to trade the vehicle in for a newer model? Will you experience trade-in shock?

As gratifying as it is to buy new, you can save a lot of money by buying a car that's one to three years old. That's because cars depreciate dramatically in the first two years—as much as 30 to 40 percent. The car that you paid $20,000 for just two short years ago may be worth only $12,000 now. If you plan to keep it for eight or ten years, it's a moot point, but if you like to trade cars every few years, it could cost you a lot of money.

FACT

According to the National Automobile Dealers Association (NADA), in 2001 the average selling price of new cars was $25,797 and the average length of new car loans was fifty-one months.

If the cost is important to you, consider a vehicle that's one to three years old. Ask your dealer to notify you of models you're interested in that are coming off leases. Dealers are very picky about their leased cars and charge for anything over and above normal wear and tear. People who lease are more likely to take good care of the car to avoid these charges. Mileage on leased cars tends to be lower, too, because they have mileage restrictions. In contrast, former rental cars are not a good buy because they're ridden hard and usually have high mileage for their age. When you buy a used car from a dealer, be sure to haggle over the price. The dealer's profit margin on a used car is considerably greater.

The used cars of today are not the same as the used cars of yesterday. In general, today's cars are built better. Dealers and manufacturers now offer warranties on used cars that are in good condition, so you don't have to buy new to get quality. The deciding factor in choosing new versus used is how much money you want to pay or can afford.

Do a Background Check

There's always a chance with a used car that you're buying somebody else's problems. Once you've identified a used car you're interested in, play it safe and check out its history to make sure you're not buying a lemon. In just seconds, Carfax.com (*www.carfax.com*) will check its database of over two billion records and produce a report that reveals hidden problems that may affect the safety or resale value of the car. You may find that the car was turned in under the lemon law, salvaged after being totaled in an accident or flood, or used as a taxi. The report may reveal that the odometer was rolled back. To use this service, all you need is the vehicle identification number (VIN) of the car, usually found on a metal plate inside the windshield. The cost is $14.99 for a single report or $19.99 for unlimited reports for thirty days. The service is really worth the price—it could save you thousands of dollars and many headaches.

ALERT!

Treat the trade-in and purchase of new cars as two separate transactions. Otherwise the dealer will make you believe he's giving you a good deal on the new car but will low-ball your trade-in, or will give you a good trade-in price but up the price of the new car.

Trade In or Sell It Yourself?

You can really get fleeced when you trade your car in. You almost always come out ahead by selling your old car yourself. If you want to trade the car in, discuss the possibility only after you've already negotiated the best possible price for your new car. If you then decide to get a quote for a trade, you know there's no shuffling going on between the price of the new car and the trade-in amount.

Paying for a New Car

When you're ready to buy a new car, you have three basic methods of paying for it: cash, loan, or lease. Most people don't walk into a dealership and plunk down $15,000 to $25,000 in cash for a new car, but if you're one of the few who are able to do this, or if you're financing part of the car but making a very large down payment, there's only one important factor you need to consider.

Paying cash will save you several thousand dollars in interest charges. But before you use your cash to avoid paying 5 to 7 percent interest on a car loan, you should have all your credit card or revolving credit loans paid off. It doesn't make sense to use cash if you have credit cards with higher interest rates than those of new car loans.

Financing Through a Bank or Other Lender

Most people finance the car through the dealer or their own bank and make monthly payments. The car is collateral for the loan, meaning that if you miss a payment, the lender can repossess it. The typical car loan used to be three years, but five-year loans have become very common. This makes a new car more affordable because the payments are spread out over a longer period, but it also costs more in interest charges. This can make you "upside down" on your loan if you decide to trade the car in for a new one in a few years. Being upside down means you owe more on the loan than it's worth. If you try to sell it while you're upside down, you'll have to pay cash in addition to the balance on your loan. You can prevent this by using the shortest loan period possible, preferably three or four years.

FACT

Buying a new car is probably the largest financial transaction you'll make other than buying a house; so educate yourself. You can save a lot of money by boning up on a few car-buying tips.

Car manufacturers often promote special offers to entice potential buyers. Very low-rate financing or even 0 percent interest loans are sometimes offered, but dealers who offer these low rates won't always negotiate on the price of the car. You may find it's cheaper to negotiate a lower price and get your financing elsewhere even if the interest rates are higher. In fact, you're better off arranging your financing yourself through a local bank or credit union, especially if you don't have great credit. People with bad credit often get fleeced in the finance department of the dealership.

Don't take anything at face value when you're buying a new car, and don't make your decision based on the monthly payment alone. The payment is influenced by the price of the car, the length of the loan, and the annual percentage rate (APR). You could have what seems like an affordable monthly payment but end up paying far too much for the car by the time you pay it off. If the salesperson keeps pushing the monthly payment when you're trying to negotiate the price of the car, you might be better off walking away if you can't convince her or him that you're too savvy to fall for that ploy.

What about Leasing?

A lease is like borrowing a car rather than buying it. You make monthly payments for the period of the lease, usually three to five years. At the end of the lease term, you have the choice of returning the car to the dealer, buying it, or in some cases, renting it from month to month. Even though you don't own the leased car, you're responsible for insurance and regular maintenance and repairs not covered by the warranty. You'll be required to keep detailed records of service and repairs and will probably be required to have all services performed at the dealership where you bought the car or another dealership of the same manufacturer. If you lease only for the length of the warranty, you'll never have to pay for major repairs.

When you lease, you're paying only for a portion of the car's value, the part you "use up," known as depreciation. In a closed-end lease (a lease with a specific term), the price you'd pay to buy the car at the end of the lease is determined ahead of time. In an open-end lease, the car is priced at the end of the lease based on market value and the condition of the car.

FinanCenter.com (✐ *www.financenter.com*) offers eleven calculators to assist you in making good financial decisions when buying or leasing a new car, including whether to buy new or used, lease or purchase, choose between two loans, choose between a rebate or low-interest rate financing, and more.

The Benefits of Leasing

One of the major attractions of leases is the lower cost. They require relatively little cash up-front, usually $500 plus one month's payment as a security deposit and the first month's payment on the lease. Instead of the sales tax being paid up-front like it is in new-car loans, a portion of it is paid each month. If sales tax in your state is 5 percent, the sales tax on a $20,000 car is $1,000. If you lease, that's $1,000 you don't have to borrow or cough up all at once. Leasing may be a good option for you in two situations: you like to have a new car every few years and don't want to incur the costs of buying and selling, or you don't have the money to come up with a down payment on a new car.

On the Other Hand

Leases may not be a good option for you if you put more than 12,000 to 15,000 miles per year on your vehicles. All leases include a mileage allowance, usually between 12,000 and 15,000 miles per year. If you exceed the allowance, you'll have to pay a fee at the end of the lease (often between ten and twenty cents per mile), which can add up to a significant amount of money. If your lease allows 12,000 miles per year and you average 14,000 per year for four years, the 8,000 extra miles at twenty cents per mile would cost you $1,600 in addition to your lease payments.

Understanding Leases

Leases can be confusing and most people enter into them without understanding how they work. As a result, they may end up paying far more than they should. Read all the fine print and ask questions to be sure you understand what you're getting into.

Leases have three basic components:

- Capitalized cost
- Residual value
- Interest rate or money factor

The capitalized cost is the price of the car. It's important to negotiate the lowest possible capitalized cost in order to reduce the size of your payments. Tell the salesperson that you want to negotiate the price of the car just as you would if you were buying it outright.

You have no direct control over the second component, the residual value, but you can influence it by choosing certain makes over others. Cars that depreciate quickly will cost you more to lease than those that hold their value. Remember, you're paying for the depreciation on the vehicle, so if you choose a car that depreciates quickly, it comes out of your pocket. A Toyota, for example, which retains more value than most American cars, would result in a lower lease cost than a Ford, everything else being equal.

The third component of a lease is the interest rate, which dealers aren't obligated to reveal to you. If the dealer won't tell you the interest rate, you can calculate it yourself. You should do so anyway just to be sure the salesperson is giving you an accurate rate.

FACT

Visit Edmunds.com (✍ *www.edmunds.com*) or check your library for the printed version of Edmunds's auto guides to look up the makes and models you're interested in buying and see which retain their value better. Financially, these make the best cars for leasing and buying.

How to Calculate the Interest Rate

To calculate the lease's interest rate, or money factor, go through the following steps. Don't be intimidated—this is easy with a calculator and pencil and paper.

1. Subtract the residual value from the capitalized cost to calculate your depreciation.
2. Divide the depreciation in step 1 by the number of months in the lease to calculate your monthly depreciation charge.
3. Subtract the monthly depreciation in step 2 from the monthly payment quoted by your dealer. This is the monthly interest charge.
4. Add the residual value and the capitalized cost to get the total cap cost and residual.
5. Divide the monthly interest in step 3 by the total cap cost and residual in step 4 to get the money factor.
6. Multiply the money factor in step 5 times 24 to get the interest rate implicit in the lease (24 has nothing to do with the length of your lease—it's a mathematical constant).

Compare this interest rate to the going rates for new-car loans in your area to make sure it's in the ballpark.

The Bottom Line on Leasing

The most important thing to remember about leasing is that you should never judge a lease solely by its monthly cost. If you let the dealer know that you understand how leases work and the components that go into the lease price, you'll be able to walk out with a better deal.

LeaseGuide.com (☞ *www.leaseguide.com*) offers an online Lease Kit that rates cars for leasing purposes and helps you analyze any lease you're thinking of entering into. For $19.95 you have unlimited lifetime use of the program.

Don't enter into a lease lightly. They're very difficult and expensive to get out of if you terminate them early. Also be aware that you will have to pay for any damages or abnormal wear and tear on the car when you turn it in, as well as the charge for any excess mileage.

Negotiating the Price

It's surprising how many people walk into a dealership and pay the quoted price for a new car without attempting to negotiate. If you're one of those people, dealers will love to see you coming. They expect you to negotiate and will gladly pocket the profit when you don't.

There are two main keys to negotiating a price on a new car. The first is to keep the purchase, your trade-in, and the financing as three totally separate transactions. The second is to start with the invoice price (the dealer's cost) instead of trying to chip away at the manufacturer's suggested retail price (MSRP). Starting at the invoice price, subtract any manufacturer's rebates that you found on Edmunds.com to get the real dealer's cost (include rebates the dealer receives from the manufacturer but doesn't pass on to you). Make an offer of 5 percent above that and don't allow yourself to be pressured into paying more.

FACT

The dealer profit on options is higher than the profit on the base car, so there's more room to negotiate on options. You should go to the dealership armed with information on dealer cost not only for the car, but also for any options you're thinking of adding.

Manufacturer's Rebates

Manufacturers often offer rebates, sometimes to buyers and sometimes to dealers. If you don't know about a rebate to the dealer, you could end up paying more for the car than you should, even if you're paying only 5 percent over the invoice price. You may also be able to get good deals at the end of the model year, when dealers are trying to get the current year's models off the lot to make room for next year's models.

The Dealer's Real Cost

The manufacturer's suggested retail price (MSRP) is just that: a suggestion. Dealers don't expect you to pay it but will gladly take your money if you don't try to negotiate. The invoice price is the manufacturer's initial price to the dealer, not the final price. Dealers receive rebates, allowances, discounts, and incentive awards that reduce the cost of the cars they sell. If the salesperson shows you the actual invoice price and tells you he's not making any money on the deal, he's not being entirely up-front with you. You need to know the dealer's real cost, not what the salesperson tells you or shows you on an invoice fabricated in the back office.

Don't Pay for More Than What You Want

If you can't find a car with the options you want, try calling around to other dealerships. If you still can't find what you want without extra options that you don't really care about, consider ordering a car. You'll have to wait longer, but why pay for features you don't need or want just because the car is sitting on the lot? On the other hand, if the dealer is willing to negotiate a good deal because it wants to move cars off the lot, it may be worthwhile to buy a car with extra features. The only way you'll know whether or not it's a good deal is to know the dealer's cost on the car and each option.

QUESTION?

Where can I find more tips and information about car buying?
Check out Web sites such as ✎ *www.carbuyingtips.com*, ✎ *www.carinfo.com*, and ✎ *www.edmunds.com* for comprehensive advice on all aspects of buying, selling, and leasing cars. Read up on car dealer scams, too. You'll be amazed at how many ways an unscrupulous dealer can rip you off.

Check Prices

Once you've determined what car you want to buy, call around to several dealers and ask for their best price. Compare their estimates to information found on Web sites like Edmunds.com or Autobytel. Armed with this information and the true dealer's cost of the car and each option, you're ready to head to the dealership to begin your negotiations. The more information you're armed with and the more you appear to know about how new-car pricing and selling works, the better off you'll be.

Using a Car-Buying Service

Car-buying services like those offered by Costco (*www.costco.com*) and Autoweb.com (*www.autoweb.com*) negotiate special member-only prices with dealerships all over the country. You can research the cars you're interested in on Costco's Web site, do side-by-side comparisons of different models, set up an appointment at a participating dealership, and automatically get the no-haggle price if you're a Costco member. AutoWeb.com and other car-buying services work in similar ways.

The True Cost of Ownership

Sometimes cars are a good example of being able to afford to *buy* something but not to *own* it. You may be able to eke out enough money each month to pay for that fancy sports car you love, but can you afford routine repairs that cost 50 percent more than repairs on a less sporty vehicle, tires that cost twice as much, the extra gasoline you'll use by hot-rodding around in a big, gas-guzzling car, and the higher insurance?

Try to look at the cost of ownership over a five-year period. Edmunds.com provides information on the true cost of ownership for many models, broken down by depreciation, financing, insurance, taxes and fees, fuel, maintenance, and repairs. Consider how quickly the car depreciates, or declines in value, by looking up the current Kelley Blue Book value of a five-year-old car of the same or similar model.

You may be tempted by the looks of certain cars or trucks, or the affordable price of a particular model, but there's more to consider than appearances and cost when buying a new car. What's the repair record of this make and model? Are there problems with certain components of the car, like the brakes or the transmission? What does it cost for routine repairs and maintenance? What does it cost to insure? How is its safety record? These are all things you should know before you visit the dealership, especially if costs are important to you.

You can buy a new car for $10,000, but if it's not well made or doesn't have a good repair record, you are likely to end up pumping money into repairs. If, on the other hand, you buy a more expensive car with a good repair record, you may save money over the life of the car. *Consumer Reports* does extensive research on the repair records of many makes and models, so if you do your homework before you buy, you may avoid a costly mistake.

Mileage Costs

The mileage a car gets has a big impact on your pocketbook. If you drove 20,000 miles a year in your Ford SUV that averages sixteen miles to the gallon, gasoline at $1.55 per gallon would cost you $1,937 per year, or $161 per month. Compare that to a Toyota Corolla, for example, that averages thirty-six miles to the gallon, which would cost $861 per year, or $72 per month, for the same 20,000 miles, a savings of $1,076 per year. According to Edmunds.com, the true cost to own the Ford SUV for five years is $48,234 and the true cost to own the Toyota Corolla for five years is $23,105, or $25,129 less than the Ford SUV! That's a difference of $5,025 per year.

FACT

Even the color of your car can affect your insurance rates. For instance, red sports cars cost more to insure because insurance companies assume drivers of red sports cars will drive at excessive speeds and therefore get in more accidents.

Auto Insurance

You may not have given much thought to how auto insurance rates are calculated, but the make and model of the car you buy can have a significant impact on the cost of your auto insurance. Some models are much more expensive to repair than others if they're damaged in an accident. Some models are more likely to be stolen. Insurance companies factor these things into their calculations in addition to such things as the city and state the car will be used in, how much mileage you expect to put on it each year, your driving record, and your claim history.

Extended Warranties

When you buy a new car you'll be offered an auto service contract to help protect you against the expense of major repairs. If the dealer tells you that your lender requires you to purchase an auto service contract to qualify for financing, call the lender directly to verify this. Prices on service plans vary greatly and you'll almost always pay much more if you buy it through the dealer. Read the contract carefully and make sure you're not duplicating coverage that's already offered by the manufacturer. Most new cars come with at least a one-year, 12,000-mile warranty, and some come with a three-year or 36,000-mile warranty. Any service plan you buy should kick in after the manufacturer's warranty runs out, or "wrap around" the manufacturer's warranty. Otherwise you're paying for duplicate coverage.

You'll need to know what repairs are covered (some plans explicitly disallow certain items or repairs), how long the contract lasts, whether repairs must be made by a certain company, and whether parts and labor are included. Most dealer plans are mechanical breakdown plans, not wear-and-tear plans. They cover only things that actually break, so something like piston rings that need to be replaced wouldn't be covered. You want a plan that includes both breakdowns and wear and tear.

Two Good Options

You should check out the company providing the service contract because if they go belly up, you're out of luck unless they've put aside funds to insure your contract. Two reputable companies that provide service protection plans are Warranty Direct and 1SourceAuto Warranty.com. *Forbes* magazine named Warranty Direct one of the Top 200 Small Public Companies. Their plans are nearly half the price you'd pay through the dealer and you're buying directly from the source with no middleman markup. Before you visit the dealership to buy a new car, get an instant online quote on the service plan from Warranty Direct by visiting their Web site at *www.warrantydirect.com*. 1SourceAuto Warranty.com (*www.1sourceautowarranty.com*) offers similar plans.

Both these companies have been rated A or better by A.M. Best (🖘 *www.ambest.com*), the company that rates insurance companies based on their financial strength. With both Warranty Direct and 1SourceAutoWarranty.com service plans, you can take the car to any ASE-licensed repair facility you choose, whether it's an auto dealership, repair shop, or private mechanic. The warranty company will pay the repair shop directly.

Buying Credit Life Insurance

When you finance a car through a dealership, you'll almost certainly be asked if you want to buy credit life insurance. Sometimes it's even added in without you being told, so be sure to look at every line on the financing sheet to make sure there's nothing there that you didn't ask for. Credit life insurance pays off the balance of your loan if you die. Remember that the finance manager who does your paperwork gets paid a commission on the insurance and warranty products she sells, so she's not an objective source of information if you're trying to decide whether credit life insurance is a good thing. In most cases, the answer is no. If you want this type of protection, you should buy term life insurance, which is much cheaper and provides more protection for your family.

The beneficiary of your credit life insurance policy is your lender, not your loved ones. With term insurance, your family or other designated beneficiaries receive the proceeds from the policy directly and can use them as their needs dictate. There's no law that you have to buy credit life insurance when you're financing a car.

ALERT!

Consumers are overcharged more than $400 million a year for credit life insurance, according to the Consumer Federation of America, which warns that credit life insurance is grossly overpriced and is therefore "a rip-off." Most consumers are better off not buying this coverage.

You'll probably also be encouraged to buy credit disability insurance, which would make your car payment for you if you became disabled and couldn't work. You may be able to buy disability insurance through your employer much less expensively that will pay a portion of your salary if you're disabled. The credit disability through the lender only covers your car payment. If you can't get life or disability insurance any other way because of a medical condition or previous disability, you might consider credit life or credit disability if you're concerned about your family's ability to make the car payment if you die or become disabled. Ⓔ

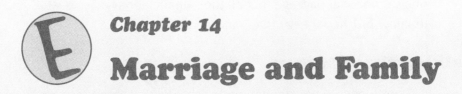

Chapter 14

Marriage and Family

You're tying the knot, and there are decisions to make about merging your finances. Later, you may find yourself planning for a baby, deciding if you can afford to be a stay-at-home parent, and trying to raise financially savvy kids. And although you probably don't want to consider the possibility, you may need to know how to protect yourself if your marriage ends in divorce.

Tying the Financial Knot

For your marriage to succeed, you have to agree about the role money will play in your marriage. Open communication about money is key. Once you've decided to tie the knot, discussions about money shouldn't be far behind. When you get married, you take on not only all your loved one's emotional baggage, but all their financial baggage as well. You need to know just how heavy that baggage is.

Talking about Money

Some people are very uncomfortable talking about money, so you may want to start out gradually by discussing how your parents handled money and how you feel about its role in your life. For some people, money symbolizes love or security; for others, it symbolizes power or control. It can be something to be spent freely with no thought for tomorrow, or hoarded and saved for the future. Explore your feelings about money together.

Dr. Kathleen Gurney, psychologist and author of *Your Money Personality: What It Is and How You Can Profit from It*, offers insight and advice about money to couples on her Web site about the psychology of money at ✑*www.kathleengurney.com.* Her advice could save your marriage.

Once you're married, your partner's finances will be your finances, for better or for worse. After you've had a few initial discussions about money in general, initiate a discussion about your respective financial situations. Figure out whether either of you have any of the following:

- Large debts
- Student loans
- Credit card debt
- Child support or alimony obligations
- A bad credit record

- Past bankruptcy
- Investments
- An inheritance
- A trust fund

Get copies of your credit reports and go over them together. If your fiancé won't talk about money, consider counseling. How can you work toward common goals if one of you can't or won't talk about money? Yet money is considered by many to be a subject more taboo than sex.

What Does Money Mean to You?

It's also important to understand what money means to your future spouse, and vice versa, because your beliefs about money and your emotional attachments to it strongly influence the way you spend.

Every couple needs common goals to work toward together, whether it's buying a house or planning for an early retirement, but it's important to realize that each of you will probably have goals that the other doesn't share. Acknowledge that they're important too, and try to find a way to work toward these individual goals as well as those you have in common.

FACT

There are a number of good books about money and relationships, including *Money Harmony: Resolving Money Conflicts in Your Life and Your Relationships*, by Olivia Mellan, and *Couples and Money: A Couples' Guide Updated for the New Millennium*, by Victoria Collins, Ph.D., and Suzanne B. Brown.

Money may become a metaphor for how you communicate with your spouse. Those arguments about money may not be about money at all. Money may just be the stage upon which you play out your relationship dramas. The real issue is often something else: trust, responsibility, or need for love or attention. If you and your spouse don't talk about what money means to you and you don't explore your reactions and emotions surrounding the subject of money, you may never realize that many of your arguments are not really about money at all.

Coping with a Spender versus a Saver

Tension can develop to the breaking point in a marriage when one person wants to spend and the other wants to save. Spenders often marry savers, so this is a common issue. If you're a saver and you open the credit card statement to find that your spouse has bought several hundred dollars' worth of hunting gear when you were planning to use that money for some much needed auto repairs, an argument is almost inevitable. If your spouse constantly nags at you and blames the constant drip of your ATM habits for the huge leak in the budget by month's end, another argument is on its way. When there's a saver and a spender in a relationship, you have to come to a compromise you can both live with if you want to avoid constant arguments or unspoken resentments over money.

Who Will Do What?

The mechanics of managing your finances may be easier to deal with than the emotional issues surrounding money. How will you handle your banking? Will you keep separate bank accounts and split the bills between you? Will you share a joint account that all of your income goes into and all of your bills are paid from? It's very difficult to keep track of the transactions that two people make to a single bank account and this can lead to bounced checks and frequent arguments. Many couples find that a joint account for household expenses and individual accounts for each spouse's personal spending works very well. It allows each of you to have discretionary money for expenditures that you don't have to explain or justify to each other.

ALERT!

If one person in a relationship controls the other's spending, it gives the controlling person a parental type of power that's not healthy in a marriage, and can cause resentment to build in the spouse who has no financial power in the relationship.

Often there's one person in a marriage who is more interested, motivated, or adept at paying the bills, balancing the checkbooks, tracking expenses and investments, and maintaining a budget. Talk about it. The person who handles the money should be detail-oriented. You may both quickly agree on the obvious choice for these tasks or you may decide to share the responsibility. Regardless of who does what, sit down at least once a month and review your finances together. What progress have you made toward your joint budgeting and savings goals? Are there any cash shortfalls or large expenditures looming? How are your investments performing?

Maintaining Credit in Your Own Name

Virtually all financial experts agree that after marriage you should maintain credit in your own name. Keep a credit card in your name only, and use it occasionally, but always pay off the balance each month. If you find yourself on your own through death or divorce, you'll have immediate credit available. It can be difficult to obtain credit for even the most basic needs, let alone a large purchase like a car or house, if you don't have a credit history that doesn't include your spouse.

Do We Need a Prenuptial Agreement?

Prenuptial agreements may have a negative connotation, but nearly everybody could benefit from one. These agreements designate how your assets and liabilities will be handled in the event of a divorce, but can also be used to protect the interests of children from a previous marriage or spell out other important issues. If you plan to have children of your own, your agreement may contain arrangements for child support, education, or even religious upbringing.

Anybody who owns a business or professional practice, has received valuable gifts or inheritances, has a trust fund, owns a home, has a retirement plan, has substantial savings or investments, or wants to protect the inheritance of children from a previous marriage should draw up a prenuptial agreement.

If one of you expects to inherit money or other assets, you may want to keep your inheritance separate, but most states will consider it marital property to be divided at divorce, unless you have a nuptial agreement. These agreements can be written after marriage, but are much easier to work out ahead of time.

For a prenuptial agreement to be legally binding, each of you has to be represented by your own independent lawyer and must fully disclose all of your assets and liabilities. Prenuptial agreements shouldn't be viewed as planning for a marriage to fail or in any other negative light. They're just good common sense and can save a lot of headaches and heartaches later.

FACT

If this is your spouse's second marriage, a prenuptial agreement might give you the lifetime use of a residence that your spouse owned prior to your marriage, which will then go to a child from the previous marriage upon your death.

Planning an Affordable Wedding

According to *Bride's Magazine*, the average wedding in the United States costs around $19,000. Unless someone else is paying for it and money is no object, you'll probably want to keep it well under that amount and use the money you save for a down payment on a house or to pay off debts.

The Wedding Budget

How can you keep your wedding costs under control? First of all, do a budget. Make a list of everything you can think of that you'll need for the ceremony, rehearsal dinner, and reception and your estimate of what each item will cost. Refine your budget as you get price quotes, and identify the things that are most important to you. Small compromises can often add up to big savings.

The biggest factor influencing your costs is the number of guests that attend. If your average cost per person for food, drink, linens, cutlery, china, and other things you have to rent by the person is $50, knocking twenty people off your guest list will save you $1,000 plus tips. Inviting just the people who really matter can save you thousands of dollars.

Consider a buffet or hearty hors d'oeuvres instead of a sit-down dinner. A good caterer can offer fancy finger foods that your guests will be talking about for long after the wedding, and it will cost you much less. Bar costs can be higher than food costs, and the mark-up on alcohol provided by your caterer is significant. It's cheaper to do it yourself but you'll have to assume the liquor liability. Talk to your insurance agent to see if your homeowner's policy will cover it. One option for limiting bar costs is to provide chits for each guest that they can turn in for drinks. If they want more alcohol after using their chits, they pay cash. To limit your costs even more, you can have a cash bar where everyone pays for their own drinks.

The busiest wedding season is May through October and the most popular day for weddings is Saturday. Reception sites are usually less expensive if you book a wedding in the off-season (November through April) or on any day other than Saturday. Entertainers and photographers may also charge less during the off-season. Think about the things you're going to remember most about your wedding and spend money on those things: the ring, which you'll wear for many years; the wedding gown, which you'll see in photographs; and the photographer, who will capture the memories on film. Everything else can take a backseat.

Tipping is often an overlooked wedding expense that could bust your budget. Don't forget to plan for tipping caterers, limo drivers, parking attendants, and musicians 10 to 20 percent if you're happy with their services.

Rings and Things

Although the rings are important, don't spend more money on them than you can reasonably afford. It's ludicrous to spend $10,000 on a diamond ring when you don't have the money for a down payment on a house. It's the symbolism of the ring that matters, not the monetary value. You can buy a beautiful ring for a fraction of the cost that "experts" recommend you spend.

Preparing for the Marriage Tax Penalty

Your wedding present from Uncle Sam is higher taxes, known as the marriage tax penalty. There are two factors. First, the standard deduction you're allowed to take from your taxable income when you're married filing jointly is less than the amount the two of you could deduct when you were single. The standard deduction for 2002 was $4,700, so if you were still single, the standard deduction would total $9,400 for the two of you. It's only $7,850 for a married couple filing jointly—$1,550 less than you could deduct between you when you were single.

The problem doesn't stop there. The 15 percent tax bracket for singles ends at $27,950 of taxable income; so two single people would be taxed at 15 percent up to a combined total of $55,900. The 15 percent tax bracket for married couples filing jointly ends at $46,700, a difference of $9,200 ($55,900 – $46,700). As a married couple you'd pay 27 percent instead of 15 percent, for a total additional tax bite of $1,104 ($9,200 times the additional 12 percent difference between the 15 percent bracket and the 27 percent bracket).

ALERT!

If you have a complicated financial situation or a large net worth, consult an attorney about separate wills to protect your estate from higher taxes if one of you dies. See Chapter 20 for a more detailed discussion of wills.

Besides higher taxes, you could get a rude jolt when you prepare your income tax return. If you both checked "married" on your new W-4 at work, your payroll departments will calculate withholding based on the standard deduction of $7,850 for married individuals. You'll have taxes withheld as though you were entitled to twice the standard deduction and your taxes will be significantly underwithheld. To prevent this from happening, after you get married you should file new W-4s with your respective employers with one of you checking the married status and the other checking the single status. This will help correct your withholding so you're not hit with a huge tax bill in April.

Beneficiaries, Name Changes, and Wills

After the wedding, there are several financial issues you should take care of right away. Go through the documentation for your retirement plans, life insurance policies, bank accounts, and investment accounts. If you want your spouse to be the beneficiary, file change-of-beneficiary forms. Also look for accounts you want to add your spouse's name to as joint owner, or where you need to change the name of the person to notify in an emergency. If one of you owns property, decide whether you want to change the deed to include both your names.

If you change your name when you get married, apply for a new social security card, vehicle title, and driver's license in your new name. Notify banks, insurance companies, brokerages, and others about your name change. Be aware that if you add your name to your spouse's existing credit card, you'll be equally responsible for the debt that he or she brought into the marriage.

Have a will drawn up, or if you already have one, have it updated or rewritten. If one of you has children from a previous relationship, it's especially important to spell out guardianship and custody issues.

Planning for a Baby

Your home is not the biggest investment you'll ever make—your kids are. You probably won't use cost as a determining factor in whether you decide to raise a family, but you can still benefit financially from some advance planning.

Insurance Issues

The most immediate issue when you're thinking of adding a new member to your family is health insurance. Estimate how much you can expect to pay out of your own pocket, based on the coverage provided by your health insurance policy. If you're covered under an HMO, you'll probably have a copay for each doctor visit (usually $10 to $25) and a copay for the hospital admission for the delivery (usually a minimum of $250 to $500). Check your policy to see what other costs you might incur. Be sure your doctor and the hospital are in your HMO network or you could be faced with some very large medical bills.

If you have an indemnity plan instead of an HMO, you probably have a deductible (usually $200 to $1,000) that you have to pay out of your pocket before the insurance kicks in. After the deductible, a typical plan will pay 80 percent of all other allowed charges, and you'll pay 20 percent, up to a maximum out-of-pocket expense (usually $1,000 to $3,000). After you've satisfied the out-of-pocket maximum, the insurance will pay 100 percent of usual and customary charges. Sometimes charges are only partially paid by insurance because they exceed the usual and customary cost for that service or procedure in your area, but if you ask, doctors will sometimes write off the excess.

Find out how much it will cost to add your new family member to your group medical insurance policy as a dependent. If you and your spouse have separate insurance policies, figure out if it makes sense for one of you to transfer to the other's policy. Dependent coverage may be cheaper if you're all on one policy, especially if one spouse has a cafeteria (section 125) plan and pays premiums with pretax dollars.

The FSA Option

If you or your spouse has an option of contributing to a flexible-spending account (FSA) at work, you could come out ahead by doing so. You contribute your pretax money to an FSA and request reimbursement when you have uncovered medical costs (like your deductibles or co-insurance). You could save as much as 50 percent, depending on your tax bracket, because the amount you contribute doesn't show up as income on your W-2.

FACT

The U.S. Department of Agriculture estimates that one child will cost you between $124,800 (if your annual income is under $39,000) and $249,180 (if your annual income is higher than $65,800) from birth to the age of eighteen, not including any provision for private school or college costs.

Income and Expense Issues

Once you have your bases covered on insurance, think about how you'll manage on one income during maternity leave and possibly reduced income during the pregnancy. Are you covered by short-term disability insurance? If so, you'll receive between 60 percent and 70 percent of your regular income for approximately six weeks following delivery, or sooner if you're deemed medically unable to work during your pregnancy.

Arrange child care well in advance. It takes time to interview potential providers and check them out with other parents who have used them. Child care is a huge expense, so figure the costs into your budget ahead of time and come up with ways to make cuts elsewhere if necessary. Child care expenses are tax-deductible (within limits), as long as your provider is licensed and you provide her social security number to the IRS.

As soon as you have your first thought about having a baby, start a baby fund to cover unexpected costs, and contribute to it monthly. Shop for bargains on baby equipment and supplies, but don't skimp on items that affect safety, like high-quality car seats. Don't go overboard on toys and baby accessories that will be quickly outgrown and that the baby is too young to appreciate. These add up to big bucks.

Can You Afford to Stay Home?

How much money does it cost you to work? Before you jump to the conclusion that you can't afford to live on one salary so you or your spouse can stay home and raise your own kids, you should calculate how much mileage you're really getting out of that second income. Consider the cost of working:

- Day care, after-school care, day camps, babysitters
- Work clothes and shoes, dry cleaning, uniforms, special gear
- Additional wear and tear and more frequent maintenance on your car, plus gas and auto insurance
- Transportation costs like bus fares, parking, and toll fees

- Coffee and vending machine snacks or sodas at work, office gift pools, lunches out
- Professional fees like licenses or certificates, continuing education courses, dues or subscriptions

Estimate all of these costs, add them up, and deduct the total from your net pay (after taxes). This is how much the second income is contributing to your household budget. For an eye-opener, figure out your real hourly rate by dividing the number of hours you work in a typical pay period into the amount you net in a pay period after taxes after deducting the costs of working that you just calculated.

The Average Family's Guide to Financial Freedom, by Bill and Mary Toohey isn't about staying home with your kids, but it shows how an average family, with kids, in debt, and on a modest income, can take control of their finances and sock away a small fortune. The advice is pertinent to anybody trying to live on one income.

For an example: Assume you earn $15 an hour and work thirty hours a week, for a gross weekly pay of $450. Taxes deducted are between $123 and $182, depending on your tax bracket, leaving you a net pay of $327 to $268. Child care is likely to be between $125 and $187 per week, and costs are growing at double the rate of inflation. Subtract the average of these two child care figures, $156, from your net after taxes, leaving you with $112 to $171 per week. Now subtract an estimate of all your other work-related expenses as previously listed. That's what you're really getting out of that second income, before we even calculate the marriage tax penalty, where the second income pushes you into a higher tax bracket and both incomes are taxed at a higher rate.

You may find you're working for minimum wage or worse after your costs of working are deducted from your net pay. If you can't make ends meet without the extra money, however little it is, try going back to your budget and see where you can make cuts. Read up about how other parents have done it. *You Can Afford to Stay Home with Your Kids*, by Malia McCawley Wyckoff and Mary Snyder is a step-by-step guide to the most effective cost-cutting strategies that make it possible to live on one income. The book walks you through the financial planning process necessary to make staying at home possible and is filled with practical advice about the personal and professional issues of being a stay-at-home parent.

Raising Financially Savvy Kids

Kids don't learn about money and personal finance from their parents by osmosis, and they don't learn about it in school. You need to take an organized approach to teaching them sound financial principles and personal-finance skills if you don't want them to grow up to live from paycheck to paycheck, be financially dependent on you, get deeply into debt, develop destructive attitudes about money, or be unable to make wise financial decisions.

You can start with teaching your kids about the basics of spending, banking, and saving when they are around the age of five. Let them make their own bank deposits and withdrawals, make purchases, and decide what to spend their money on (within reason). Give advice, but don't control. It's important for them to be allowed to make mistakes so they can learn about consequences and choices.

Kids should receive an allowance by the time they're in school. The purpose of the allowance is to teach them about managing money. Help them decide how much of each week's allowance they'll put in the bank. They'll quickly learn that if they spend it now, they won't have it when something they really want comes along. An allowance helps them learn to save and to prioritize. Teach your kids with practical everyday examples when the opportunities arise. Real life examples will sink in much more readily than abstract lectures with no immediate practical application.

As your kids get older, adapt your teaching to their age and ability to understand. Read some books about teaching kids about money, or check out some of the excellent Web sites on the subject. Teach older kids how to invest by using the Internet to research stocks or mutual funds and set up a mock stock portfolio so they can track their stocks' performance.

Teach your teenagers how to balance a checkbook and how to track their earnings and expenditures.

Teach Good Consumer Habits

One of the most important things you can teach your kids is how advertising can influence their buying decisions, and how they can resist giving in to the advertiser's message that buying its product makes kids look cool or makes them feel good. Look at print and television ads together and talk about how the ad makes your kids feel or what the ad makes them want. Help them realize that brand-name jeans, for example, are identical to other jeans, except for the label, but cost a lot more. When buying clothing, agree to pay the cost of good nonbrand-name clothes and have your teenager chip in the difference if he or she insists on the brand-name version. This will teach teens about tradeoffs and the cost of image.

Smart-Money Moves for Kids, by Judith Briles helps parents teach their kids about the value and proper use of money. *Allowances: Dollars and Sense*, by Paul Lermitte presents a proven system for teaching kids about money. It's easy to read and includes exercises, worksheets, and checklists.

The Financial Impact of Divorce

You've probably heard that 50 percent of all marriages end in divorce. If yours is one of them, it helps to be aware of some of the financial issues. For example, if you and your spouse agree to a division of your debt, be sure to make this a formal arrangement by contacting each creditor and asking them to legally transfer the debt to you or your spouse and release the other from liability. If you're going to be responsible for a debt, your spouse's name shouldn't be listed as an authorized user (for example, on a credit card) and he or she shouldn't be held responsible if you fail to pay it off—and vice versa. Some couples obtain individual consolidation loans and pay off their portion of the joint debts so the accounts can be closed. This is ideal for a clean split, but if it's not possible and your spouse incurs large amounts of debt, inform the lender in writing that you're no longer responsible for any new charges.

Good references on divorce include *Divorce and Money: How to Make the Best Financial Decisions During Divorce* by Violet Woodhouse and Dale Fetherling, and *Using Divorce Mediation* by Katherine E. Stoner, a complete manual on how to mediate your divorce and avoid prolonged court battles and huge legal expenses that you'll spend years paying off.

Be sure to consider how divorce will impact your health insurance. If you're covered under your spouse's policy and he or she works for a company with more than twenty employees, you're eligible to continue under the same plan for up to thirty-six months by electing COBRA coverage. You'll have to pay the amount the coverage costs the employer plus an administrative fee of 2 percent. If you don't notify your spouse's employer of the divorce within sixty days, you lose your right to coverage, so don't rely on your spouse to do this—call the employer's human resources department yourself and follow up with a written notification. They will then send you the legally required COBRA notifications and forms.

FACT

Certified divorce planners are professionals who give financial advice that lawyers aren't qualified to give, like the short- and long-term financial impact of a proposed divorce settlement, tax consequences, dividing retirement plans, and stock option or insurance issues. They serve as your advocate in achieving a financially equitable divorce settlement.

Child Support

If your marriage is headed for divorce and you're the custodial parent, file for child support as soon as you and your spouse separate. Despite the obvious moral obligation, your spouse has no legal obligation to pay child support unless there's a court order from a divorce, marriage dissolution, establishment of paternity, or legal separation. An attorney or your local child support agency can help you get a court order. Child support judgments are issued as of the date of filing and are not retroactive.

Unfortunately, having a court order is not always enough. The Association for the Enforcement of Child Support (ACES) estimates that there's $41 billion in unpaid child support for over 30 million children in the United States. If your ex-spouse is delinquent in child support, the Child Support Enforcement Agency (CSEA) in your state is required to help you collect payment by serving your ex-spouse with papers requiring him or her to meet with the district attorney and arrange a payment schedule. If your ex-spouse refuses, he or she could serve jail time. The CSEA will provide you with a free attorney if necessary.

Other measures include taking the parent's tax refund, garnishing wages, taking unemployment insurance proceeds, seizing assets, suspending a professional or business license, and in some states, revoking a driver's license. The government can even take your lottery winnings if you owe back child support.

If you're not the custodial parent, remember that you can break the bond of marriage but you can never break the bond of parenthood. Your responsibility to your children continues even after your marriage ends. Child support payments should be one of your highest financial priorities.

If your spouse lives out of state, there are methods of locating him or her and having the courts in the two states work together to enforce the child support judgment. Despite all these efforts, you may not be able to collect the child support due you, but child support is a liability that never goes away, so don't ever give up. Ⓔ

Chapter 15

Unwed but Not Unwise

Millions of couples live together without the benefits of marriage, many unaware of the legal and financial consequences of their arrangement. If you're living with your partner, you should consider the issues involved with mingling your assets and sharing your expenses and take steps to protect yourself in case your relationship ends.

Moving in Together

Whether you're getting married or just moving in together, it's a good time to talk about your finances. Inform your partner of any skeletons in your financial closet, such as bad credit, a past bankruptcy, a lien on your house, unpaid child support, or a tax lien. Since you'll be mingling finances to some extent, it's only fair to be up-front about these things and start your time together on the right foot. It's likely your partner will find out about any financial issues once you're living together anyway, and may feel that your failure to share this information earlier reflects badly on your relationship. You can always change the way you do things after you've lived together for a while, but don't wait until then to discuss how you're going to handle the money issues that affect you both, from spending habits to investments and financial goals.

Debt Counselors of America offers a brochure called "Living Together: A Financial Contract for Unmarried Couples." It's available from their Web site at ✍ *www.dca.org/pubs.htm* for $2.50 or by mail for $5.00 by writing to ✉ DCA Publications, P.O. Box 8587, Gaithersburg, MD 20898.

Nonmarital Agreements

We take for granted the legal rights afforded to married couples. If one of the couple dies, the other inherits their joint property and may receive social security or retirement benefits. If the couple divorces, their assets are divided between them. Unfortunately, these same rights don't apply to unmarried couples, so financial planning may actually be more critical for them than for those who have tied the knot.

Why Do I Need a Nonmarital Agreement?

It may not sound romantic, but it's wise to have a written agreement that spells out how property, other assets, and shared expenses will be handled if your relationship ends. The best legal protection for unmarried couples living together is a nonmarital agreement, also referred to as a cohabitation, relationship, or "living together" agreement. It's a written contract that gives each of you legal control over your property and finances if the relationship ends, and it can save you attorney's fees and court costs if there's any disagreement about who gets what.

FACT

Regardless of how many years you and your partner live together unmarried, when you split up, you're legally entitled only to property that is in your own name or was specifically designated yours by written contract.

There are obvious financial benefits to living together, like sharing rent and utilities, but there are also dangers involved, especially if you already own assets. Remember that 50 percent of marriages end in divorce, and an even larger percentage of unwed couples eventually go their separate ways. If you're in your twenties and haven't accumulated many assets yet, a nonmarital agreement may seem totally unnecessary. If your relationship is likely to be short-term, you may be right. But if you're in a committed relationship that you expect to be long-term, a nonmarital agreement is important.

A failed relationship often causes problems with debt when the relationship ends. You may get stuck with the bills for things you bought together. If the apartment or house you share with your partner was leased in your name based on your joint income, you may find you can't afford the rent after you and your partner split. You may have lent your partner money or cosigned on a loan, only to be left holding the bag. If you buy a house together, you could be the one out on the street but still responsible for paying the mortgage. By taking a few precautions, you can protect yourself against these and other potential problems. You're never too young to make wise legal and financial choices, especially if you earn a good salary and are accumulating assets such as cars, real estate, and investments.

ALERT!

You should be aware that if one of you is still legally married to someone else, you might not be protected legally regardless of what you do. Some states won't enforce agreements or promises you make to your live-in partner if one of you is still legally married.

What's Covered in a Nonmarital Agreement?

Nonmarital agreements can cover a wide range of issues but are especially critical if you're buying a house together, purchasing other large assets with joint funds, coming into the relationship with previously owned property or assets, or if one of you has a lot of debt. If your partner has large debts, you should protect yourself against creditors who may seize joint property if your partner falls behind in the payments.

The agreement can accomplish the following:

- Address how property you own and what you accumulate together will be handled if you no longer live together.
- Cover how gifts or inheritances will be dealt with.
- Include provisions for support after separation or death, or an agreement to waive the right to palimony.
- Spell out who's responsible for the mortgage and who gets to take the tax deduction for interest.
- Stipulate that property be kept separate.
- Indicate who gets to keep a rental apartment if you split up.
- Discuss how credit cards and other debt will be handled.
- Cover a myriad of other issues tailored to your personal situation.

It's a good idea to include a clause stating that mediation will be used for resolving any disputes and that if you still can't come to an agreement after mediation you'll go to formal and binding arbitration. This will save you from the expense and hassle of a messy lawsuit.

Timing Is Everything

You may feel uncomfortable planning for what will happen if your relationship ends, but you can save yourself a lot of potential stress, expense, and grief if you make these plans while your relationship is good and you can communicate effectively. If one of you owns significantly more assets than the other, an agreement of this type may make that partner feel more comfortable about merging them into one household. It can take considerable pressure off your relationship to have this addressed early on and not have to deal with niggling doubts and concerns.

What Happens Without a Nonmarital Agreement?

If you can't settle issues at the end of your relationship regarding who owns what, you may end up in court. In most states the court will first ask if there's a written contract, and if there isn't, will try to determine if there was an oral agreement (difficult to prove). If not, the court will examine your actions to try to determine if there was an implied contract. If there's proof that you've shared expenses and assets equally, for instance, or that you shared a bank account, the court could rule that there's an implied contract and enforce it as such. One of you may end up paying a settlement or support payments to the other, even in the absence of a written or oral agreement.

This is a general overview of nonmarital agreements and is not offered as legal advice. Sometimes laws in a particular state will override anything you write in an agreement, so you may think you're protected when in fact you may not be. If, after reading this material, you decide you want a nonmarital agreement, contact an attorney.

Common-Law Marriages

Common-law marriages between heterosexuals are recognized to some extent by fourteen states and the District of Columbia. Several of those states only recognize common-law marriages that began before a certain year. In a common-law marriage, you're considered married even though you've never gone through the formalities. There are four requirements.

1. You have to live together.
2. You have to present yourself as a married couple, for instance by using the same last name or referring to your partner as your husband or wife.
3. You must intend to be married.
4. You must live together for a significant number of years.

The number of years it takes before you're considered married by common law is not clearly defined in any of the fourteen states that recognize common-law marriages. There's also no simple way to determine if you're married by common law, and it usually only comes up if you have to go to court for a legal matter related to your relationship. Common-law marriage is not something you should rely on to give you any kind of legal protection.

If you become married by common law and later decide you want to end your relationship, you have to go through a regular legal divorce. This could be tricky if you don't realize you've met the requirements for a common-law marriage and you decide to marry someone else. That marriage could be legally null and void. To avoid becoming common-law married when it's not your intention, if you live in a state that recognizes common-law marriages, you and your live-in partner may want to sign a statement saying it's not your intention to be married.

FACT

There's a common misperception that if you live together for seven years you're married by common law. No states specify a minimum number of years. The states that recognize common-law marriages fully are Alabama, Colorado, Iowa, Kansas, Montana, Oklahoma, Pennsylvania, Rhode Island, South Carolina, Texas, and Utah, as well as the District of Columbia.

Mingling Your Assets

If it's important to discuss the mingling of your assets and finances when you're planning to get married, it's even more important if you're moving in together without the legal benefits of marriage. If either or both of you own assets that you'll be sharing, like vehicles, furniture, art, collectibles, or anything else of value, it's critical. Even if you don't think it's necessary when you first move in together, if you find that you're accumulating joint property, consider clarifying who owns what in a legal document.

Making Joint Purchases

Some couples use a joint purchase agreement when they buy large items together, if they don't have a nonmarital contract that covers how these purchases will be handled. Joint purchase agreements spell out what will happen to an item purchased with joint funds if the relationship ends for any reason, without addressing the broader issues usually included in a nonmarital agreement.

If you don't have a written agreement about how assets purchased together will be dealt with if your relationship ends, you should document your contribution for these assets. When you buy an asset together, get a receipt as evidence that you contributed toward ownership of the asset. Better yet, pay your portion by check and make a notation on the check itself, such as "50 percent of the jointly owned bedroom furniture."

ALERT!

Never purchase a major asset jointly that doesn't have your name on the title or deed. The person whose name is on those papers is the person who legally owns the property, and you could end up losing whatever money you've put in to it.

Buying a House Together

If the two of you decide to buy a house together, in addition to making sure that both of your names are on the deed, you should make sure the deed also indicates your preferred method of jointly holding property. Specify either "joint ownership with rights of survivorship" or "tenants in common."

Joint Ownership with Rights of Survivorship

The simplest method of transferring property is joint ownership with rights of survivorship, which means that if one of you dies, the other automatically inherits the property. You avoid inheritance tax because the house isn't considered part of the estate. The downside is that you don't have the option of selling your share or leaving it to someone other than your partner, and joint ownership provisions in the deed will override any bequest in your will.

Tenants in Common

Tenants in common means that each of you owns half of the house. If you die, your share will go to the person or persons indicated in your will (if you have one), or else to your next of kin. This method of ownership allows for owners with unequal equity. For example, you may own 75 percent of the house and your partner may own 25 percent. Each of you can sell or give away your share or leave it to one or more individuals of your choice, such as kids from a previous relationship. Having a will is critical if you own property as tenants in common.

Who Gets the House If You Break Up?

Your nonmarital agreement should spell out what will happen if both of you want to keep the house when you break up. How will you decide who goes and who stays? Does the person who gets the house buy out the person who's leaving? How is the buyout price calculated? Is it half the equity in the house, or is an amount deducted equal to the Realtor fees that would have been paid if the house had been sold? These issues are fodder for heated arguments if you don't spell them out ahead of time.

If one of you contributed more to the purchase of the house than the other, your nonmarital agreement should spell out how this will be compensated if you break up. Even if you each contributed 50 percent, you may want to allow for one person to build equity or offset contributions to the household fund by doing repairs or improvements on the house.

Sharing Expenses

Although many of the issues faced by unmarried couples living together are very different from those that married couples face, the issues surrounding the sharing of expenses is common to both.

While the actual method you decide on for sharing expenses may be unimportant, to avoid disagreements later you should discuss up-front how you want to handle this issue. Will you divide housing costs and day-to-day expenses equally or contribute to a household fund in proportion to your income? The latter may be the fairest method if one of you earns significantly more than the other. For example, let's say one of you makes $40,000 per year and the other makes $20,000. The one that makes twice as much will contribute $2 for every $1 the other contributes to the joint household fund.

FACT

The number of unmarried couples cohabitating in the United States increased 72 percent from 1990 to 2000, to over 5.5 million couples, according to the U.S. Census Bureau. It's estimated that less than half of cohabitating unmarried couples will get married. Of those that do, about half will later get divorced.

What will your banking arrangements be? Will you share a checking account, deposit both your checks into it, and pay all your household bills from it, or will you maintain separate accounts and settle up with each other as bills come in? If you choose to maintain separate accounts, it's a good idea to document your intention to share expenses by paying your portion of bills directly rather than paying your partner your share in cash or by check. This documents the implied contract (mentioned previously) and could protect you if your relationship ends in court. If you decide to have a joint bank account, be aware that either of you could legally take all the money out of the account. Many people have ended a live-in relationship by walking away with the cash and leaving their partner high and dry. It's safer to keep separate bank accounts, especially in the early years of your relationship.

Taxes for Unmarried Couples

Unlike married couples, unmarried couples can't file joint returns. There's actually one benefit to this: You won't be subject to the marriage tax penalty (see Chapter 14). However, this also means that you can't claim your partner as a dependent.

> For a comprehensive guide to the legal and financial implications of living together, see *Living Together: A Legal Guide for Unmarried Couples* by attorneys Ralph Warner, Toni Ihara, and Frederick Hertz, available from Nolo.com (*www.nolo.com*). Click on "Search" and type in the keywords "Living Together Guide."

Home Mortgage Interest Deduction

When you own a house together, the issue of who will get to claim the mortgage interest and property tax deductions for federal income tax return purposes has to be addressed. You could split the deductions in half, but you might not benefit as much from this method if one of you makes significantly more than the other, because the deductions will create more tax savings for the person with the higher tax rate. It might make more sense to let that person claim the entire deduction and compensate the other person in some monetary way.

Head of Household and Earned Income Tax Credit

If a dependent child lives with you and your unmarried partner at least six months a year, and you provide more than 50 percent of the cost of maintaining the household, you can claim head of household status on your income tax return. This allows you to take the child and dependent care credits to reduce your taxes. See IRS Publication 17, Chapter 33, for detailed information on the "head of household" status and a checklist to see if you're qualified to claim it.

If your income is below the limit, you can also take the earned income tax credit, which offsets your income tax liability and can sometimes supplement your income by allowing you to get back more than you actually paid. If you have a dependent child living with you, you may want to consult a tax accountant before filing your income tax returns.

Other Issues

Other issues that unmarried couples face include wills, trusts, and advance directives. While the latter is not directly related to finances, it's definitely related to your relationship should one of you die while you're together.

Wills

Dying intestate means dying without a written will. Each state has laws that designate the method of distributing your property if you die intestate, and there's a good chance your property won't go to the individuals you'd want to receive it. That's why a will is important even if you're single. If you have kids, it's absolutely critical, because your will is the instrument for indicating who you'd want to take guardianship, something that is much too important to leave to chance or the courts.

If you're married, in most states your spouse and children automatically inherit your property if you die intestate. If you're unmarried and die intestate, your property will be divided among your parents, sisters and brothers, and other relatives. Your partner will not receive anything. Without a written nonmarital contract the only way to leave property to your partner if you die is through a will. If you have neither a contract nor a will, the chances of your partner getting anything are slim. See Chapter 20 for more information about wills and advance directives.

ALERT!

Dying is not something you usually think much about in your twenties and thirties, but it happens to people of all ages, so think about taking steps to protect your loved one, especially if he or she develops a serious illness.

Advance Directives

An advance directive is a legal document identifying the treatments and lifesaving measures you want if you become ill and there's no reasonable hope of recovery. There are two basic types of advance directives: a living will and a durable power of attorney for health care. In a living will, you state the kind of health care you want under certain circumstances and the kind you don't want. For example, if you're terminally ill, you may not want to be resuscitated if you stop breathing. In a durable power of attorney for health care, also called a health care proxy, you designate somebody close to you to make decisions about your health care if you're unable to make them for yourself.

It's a good idea to have both types of advance directives. If you want your partner to be the person making health care decisions for you if you're unable to, a durable power of attorney for health care is a must. ⒠

Chapter 16

Minimizing Income Taxes

Filling out the forms properly is not even half the battle when it comes to taxes. You also want to avoid penalties and keep as much of your money as possible by taking advantage of every tax-saving strategy available to you. That requires a basic understanding of how taxes work and an awareness of significant tax-reduction opportunities.

Federal Income Taxes—the Basics

By having income taxes withheld from your paycheck each pay period, you're really prepaying an estimate of the taxes you'll owe for the year. You settle up your bill with Uncle Sam when you prepare your tax return after the end of the year.

The W-4 Form

The amount you have withheld is calculated based on your filing status (married or single) and the number of withholding allowances you claim on the W-4 form you file with your employer. You should file a new W-4 with your employer if you:

- Got a big refund last year
- Owed over $100 last year when you filed your tax return
- Got married or divorced
- Had a child
- Can no longer claim a dependent that you claimed last year

Most people have too much tax withheld and let the IRS borrow their money interest-free all year. You could be earning interest on that money or saving between 12 and 20 percent in interest charges by using the extra money to pay down credit card debt.

ALERT!

The only time it makes sense to have more withheld than you're going to owe is if you find it impossible to save money on a regular basis. You could accomplish the same thing by having a fixed amount automatically deducted from your check each month and deposited in a savings account.

Exemptions

An exemption is a gift from the IRS, a fixed amount you deduct from your taxable income for yourself, your spouse if you're married, and each eligible dependent you claim on your income tax return. In 2002, each exemption was worth $3,000, so if you're married but have no kids, you can claim $6,000 if you file jointly. The exemption phases out at certain income levels but unless you're single with income over $137,300 or married with combined income over $206,000, you'll be able to take the full deduction. You have to pass five tests for each dependent in order to claim them on your income tax return. See Section 3, Part One, of IRS Publication 17 for details.

Marginal and Effective Tax Rates

Your income is taxed based on taxable income brackets, ranging from 10 percent to 38.6 percent, as shown in the tax bracket table in this chapter. The higher your income, the more tax brackets you'll cross, with the income that falls within each bracket being taxed at the rate for that bracket.

	2002 Tax Bracket Limits				
Filing Status	**10 percent**	**15 percent**	**27 percent**	**30 percent**	**35 percent***
Single	$6,000	$27,950	$67,700	$141,250	$307,050
Married filing jointly	$12,000	$46,700	$112,850	$171,950	$307,050
Married filing separately	$6,000	$23,350	$56,425	$85,975	$153,525
Head of household	$10,000	$37,450	$96,700	$156,600	$307,050
Qualifying widow(er)	$12,000	$46,700	$112,850	$171,950	$307,050

*Income in excess of these amounts is taxed at 38.6 percent

For example, if you're single and your adjusted gross income (AGI) is $40,000, your tax would be calculated as follows:

The first $6,000 at 10 percent = $600.
The next $21,950 (the difference between $27,950 and $6,000) at 15 percent = $3,292.50.

The next $12,050 (the difference between your AGI of $40,000 and $27,950) at 27 percent = $3,253.50.

That means your total tax burden would be $600.00 + $3,292.50 + $3,253.50 = $7,146.00.

Your effective tax rate is the tax rate you actually pay on your total income, considering that part of your income isn't taxed at all due to exemptions and the standard deduction or itemized deductions, and part of your income may fall in different tax brackets. To calculate your effective federal tax rate, divide your total federal income taxes for the year (from your latest tax return) by your total income. If your marginal rate is 27 percent, your effective tax rate may be between 15 and 17 percent.

FACT

If all this talk about marginal tax rates seems confusing, just remember that if your marginal rate is 27 percent, then 27 percent of any additional earnings will go to the IRS, and additional tax-free or tax-deferred deductions will produce savings of 27 percent. This is important information for tax planning.

Your marginal tax rate is the rate you pay on your highest dollars of income. Look up your total income (including capital gains, interest income, and so on) in the tax bracket table. Your marginal rate is the percentage shown in the column that your total income falls into. For example, if your income is $40,000, your marginal tax rate in 2002 is 27 percent. Your marginal tax rate tells you two important things: how much you'll gain by reducing your taxable income, and the true cost of a tax-deductible expense.

For example, if you want to increase your tax-deferred contributions to your employer's 401(k) plan by $100, you could quickly calculate your real out-of-pocket expense by using your marginal tax rate of 27 percent and your state tax rate, which we'll assume is 6 percent for purposes of the example. Since 401(k) contributions aren't subject to federal or (in most states) state taxes, the $100 could go into your account with only $67 coming out of your pocket (savings of 27 percent + 6 percent = 33 percent; $100 × 33 percent = $67). You'd save $33 in federal and state income tax by reducing your income $100. You don't find deals like this every day.

You can also quickly calculate the real value of additional income, such as overtime, bonuses, or a second job, which will be taxed at your marginal tax rate. If your marginal federal tax rate is 27 percent, $1,000.00 in extra income will net you around $593.50 (7.65 percent for social security taxes, 27 percent for federal income taxes, and 6 percent for state income taxes for purposes of our example, for a total tax rate of 40.65 percent; $1,000.00 × 40.65 percent = $406.50 in taxes; $1,000.00 – $406.50 = $593.50 net pay).

Standard and Itemized Deductions

When it comes to deductions, you have two choices. You can take the standard deduction, which is a fixed dollar amount that you deduct from your taxable income, or you can itemize deductions. For 2002 the standard deduction is $4,700 if you're filing single, $7,850 for married filing jointly, $3,925 for married filing separately, and $6,900 for head of household.

If your actual allowable deductions total more than the standard deduction, you'll save money by itemizing. To see if you qualify, use a copy of Schedule A from Form 1040 to list the amounts of each of the deductions that apply to you, such as home mortgage interest, real-estate taxes, state income taxes, and personal-property taxes. If the total is more than the standard deduction, itemize.

ALERT!

So many deductions have disappeared over the years that if you have no mortgage interest or very low mortgage interest, you probably won't be able to itemize unless you have extremely large medical expenses or charitable contributions.

Preparing Your Tax Return

Just the thought of preparing your own tax return may make you shudder, but the average person is more than capable of completing Form 1040EZ and Form 1040A (the short form). Form 1040 (the long form) is definitely more challenging but is much less so thanks to the availability of robust tax preparation software programs for your personal computer. The biggest requirement is time.

Types of Federal Tax Return Forms

There are four versions of the U.S. Individual Income Tax Return Form 1040:

- **Form 1040EZ:** The simplest form, for those under age sixty-five with no dependents, no itemized deductions, no more than $1,500 of taxable interest income, no advance earned income tax credit (EITC), and taxable income from line six of less than $50,000. There are a few other little caveats so be sure to read the instructions with the form to make sure you qualify to use it.
- **Form 1040A:** Only slightly more difficult to complete than the 1040EZ. You can use this form if you don't itemize deductions, your taxable income on line 27 is less than $50,000, you claim only certain tax credits (see the form instructions for a list), and you had income only from the following sources: wages, salaries, and tips; interest and ordinary dividends; capital gains; taxable scholarship and fellowship grants; pensions, annuities, and IRAs; unemployment compensation; taxable social security; Alaska permanent fund dividends.
- **Form 1040** (the long form): If you don't qualify to use Form 1040A, you're stuck with Form 1040 but you're in good company. Nearly three-quarters of all taxpayers use this form. There are a number of special circumstances that require you to use the long form, so be sure to read the instructions.
- **Form 1040PC:** A special version of your tax return that can be generated by income tax preparation software like TurboTax. It will look like hieroglyphics to you, but the IRS computers will translate it into meaningful information, and it's much shorter than a regular 1040.

Using Tax Software on Your PC

Doing your own taxes is easy using tax software like TurboTax by Intuit or TaxCut by H&R Block. You can buy the software from office supply stores like Staples or download them online for around $30 for the basic version. They handle both simple and complex returns with ease, although it does take a bit of time. The program walks you through an interview process by asking you questions, does all the calculations, and produces your finished tax return and any necessary schedules, plus worksheets to keep in your file as backup. You can either print the return and mail it or file it electronically. Both federal and state versions are available.

Using Web-Based Software

If you don't want to buy new tax software every year, you can use Web-based software. It's no longer significantly cheaper than buying your own, so the main advantage now to Web-based software is that you don't have to be on your own PC to work on your return. You can do so from any computer that has access to the Internet. You don't have to complete your return in one sitting; you can come back to it as often as you want until you're ready to hit the "send" button.

ALERT!

There are a few instances where you can't file electronically. If your return includes one of several schedules that require another person's signature—for instance, noncustodial parents claiming exemptions for their kids—you'll have to file a paper copy.

Using Paper and Pen

For techno-phobes or those with the simplest of tax returns, there's nothing more satisfying than preparing tax returns with pen and paper. However, one of the disadvantages is that it takes much longer to get your refund. If you file electronically, you can get your money in half the time—in nine to sixteen days if you have your refund automatically deposited to your bank account. If you file a paper return, expect it to take at least twice that time, depending on when you file.

Hiring a Tax Accountant or Service

Approximately half of Americans use a tax preparation service of some type. Three-quarters of a million of them pay a tax preparer to complete the very simple Form 1040EZ. Many others use a preparer for the 1040 form, even though the average person is more than capable of doing it alone. Some people say they simply don't want to deal with the hassle of doing it themselves. While it pays to use expert help if you have a complex tax situation, you can save yourself $100 to $200 or more by preparing your own return if you use the short form. Having a very complex return done professionally could cost $1,000 or more. The more organized your records are and the more information you can give the preparer about your personal situation, the less it will cost.

There are times when it's almost certainly a good idea to seek professional tax assistance, for instance if you exercised incentive stock options, had complex investments, have a home-based business, own rental property, or had a major life transition such as marriage, divorce, having a baby, or starting your own business. The qualifications of tax preparers vary immensely, and you'll pay more if you choose someone who is overqualified to handle the complexity level of your return. You could hire a tax attorney to do it, but is it really necessary? Certified public accountants, tax attorneys, and enrolled agents (certified by the Treasury Department) are the only professionals who can represent you in an audit if that ever becomes necessary, but you can also use other trained preparers suited to your needs.

You can search for tax professionals near you by visiting the National Association of Tax Professionals Web site at ✍ *www.taxprofessionals.com* and using the "U.S. Search" feature. Members' names, addresses, telephone numbers, and e-mail addresses are provided.

Finding a Reputable and Skilled Preparer

Start by asking friends, family, coworkers, and other professionals, like bankers, for recommendations. If you can't come up with a recommendation this way, try contacting the local chapter of a professional association like the American Institute of Certified Public Accountants (AICPA). Once you've identified someone you'd like to use, talk to him or her on the phone and ask about qualifications, background, and fees. Find out whether this person works full-time or part-time doing tax consulting, number of years of experience, and participation in continuing professional education. The latter is important because tax preparers need to keep up with yearly changes in tax laws. When you've made a decision, make an appointment well in advance of the filing deadline. Most tax professionals become totally booked up for the tax season early in the year.

Making Tax-Wise Financial Decisions

Think about how much of your income goes toward taxes. If you're in the higher tax brackets, you may be handing nearly half of every dollar you earn to Uncle Sam, but there are things you can do to keep more of your hard-earned money. Good tax planning is a year-round activity. Decisions you make during the year about spending, borrowing, and investing impact your taxes at the end of the year, so it's a good idea to get in the habit of considering the tax consequences whenever you make any financial decision.

Reducing Your Taxes

One of the easiest ways to reduce your taxes is to take advantage of tax-free or tax-deferred employer-provided fringe benefits, such as:

- Benefits provided under cafeteria plans and flexible-spending accounts that allow you to take benefits in lieu of cash (tax-free)
- Medical and accident insurance paid by your employer (tax-free)
- Educational assistance programs (tax-free)
- Retirement plans like 401(k) and 403(b) that allow you to make contributions (tax-deferred)
- Incentive stock options (tax-deferred)
- Employee stock purchase plans (tax-deferred)

- Group term health insurance up to $50,000 (tax-free)
- Free parking up to $175 per month (tax-free)
- Employer-provided meals and lodging under certain circumstances (tax-free)

Owning a home is another one of the best tax shelters available. Not only do you get to deduct your mortgage interest from your taxable income, you also get to keep up to $250,000 ($500,000 for married couples) of profit when you sell, without paying any taxes on the gain.

Another way to reduce taxes is to be sure you take all the credits and other tax-reductions you're entitled to, such as the child credit (in addition to claiming the child as a dependent), filing as head of household, or taking the earned income tax credit if you qualify.

Taking Advantage of Tax-Saving Strategies

You can save money by taking advantage of a few tax-saving strategies and making sure you take all the deductions you're entitled to. Bunching and accelerating deductions are two time-honored approaches to cutting taxes. Both require an awareness of what your tax situation is before the end of the year. If you're close to being able to itemize, bunching your deductions may put you over the threshold. Bunching is a strategy that involves timing your payments of deductible expenses by pushing as many deductions as possible into one year. When you bunch, you fatten up your deductions for one year and slim them down the next year, or vice versa. If you're close to having enough medical expenses to meet the 7.5 percent of income requirement, and there's a medical procedure you're planning, having it before the end of the year could put you over the limit and reduce your taxes.

Accelerating deductions is similar to bunching, but you increase your deductions in the current year by paying tax-deductible bills that aren't actually due until the following year. For example, pay your property taxes before the end of the year instead of waiting until they're due in the following year, to push the deductions into the year you'll be able to take advantage of them.

Keeping Good Tax Records

You should keep detailed and organized records as though you expect to be audited. Then if you ever have to prove your income or deductions you won't be scrambling to find receipts and other documents, and facing possible disallowances from the IRS.

Records to Keep

What types of records should you keep? Hang onto any documents that identify your sources of income (W-2s, 1099s), help determine the value of assets (brokerage and mutual fund statements), and prove your deductions (receipts or invoices *and* canceled checks, property tax statements, mortgage interest statements, and proof of any business expenses if you file Schedule C). Checks alone may not prove the deductibility of an expense. The best proof is an itemized invoice accompanied by a canceled check proving that you paid it.

Keep your tax records in a separate file for each year. After six years you can throw the backup documents away if storage space is an issue, but keep your income tax returns, retirement account statements, home purchase or sale documents, and stock or other investment documents indefinitely.

Home Ownership Records

Even though profits (up to $250,000 for singles and up to $500,000 for married couples) on the sale of your primary residence are no longer taxable, you should keep all records related to the sale and purchase of your home(s), including settlement papers and documentation for improvements or additions to your home. To calculate whether you can claim exemption from taxes if you make a gain on the sale of your house, you have to be able to accurately document its cost basis. If you bought or built your home, the original basis is the price you paid, plus any closing costs. Improvements you make to your home increase your basis as long as they pass the IRS requirements of adding to the value of the house, extending its useful life, or adapting it to a new use. You must differentiate between improvements and repairs. Repairs can't be added to the basis of your home. If you hire contractors to do improvements, the entire cost can be used to increase your basis; if you do the work yourself, you can only add the cost of supplies.

Surviving an Audit

Nobody likes to have the taxman come knocking on the door. There are a few simple steps you can take to reduce your chances of being audited, but if you're one of the 0.5 percent who get chosen randomly for the experience, don't panic. Being prepared is more than half the battle.

The most basic thing you can do to reduce your chances of being audited is to make sure there are no math errors on your return. Too many math errors will red flag your return for review. Make sure social security numbers for you and your dependents are accurate. If you won't be able to file your return by the April 15 deadline, file for an extension before the deadline. Attach an explanation for anything that's not obvious. For example, if you report an amount that differs from the amounts on your W-2 or 1099s, explain the reason. Be sure to sign your return.

ALERT!

Some steps, such as filing Schedule C for self-employed individuals or claiming the home office deduction, will increase your chances of being audited. But as long as you reported everything accurately and have documentation to prove it, you have nothing to worry about.

How Are Returns Chosen for Audit?

The IRS uses something called the discriminant function system (DIF), which assigns a score to key elements on your return. If the total score for your entire return is greater than the IRS guidelines, the computer will kick your return out for review by an IRS agent. If the agent feels your return should be audited after reviewing it, you'll be contacted. A very small percentage of returns are chosen completely by random. There's nothing you can do to reduce your chances except to file close to the filing deadline rather than early. There's some evidence that people who file early may have a greater chance of being randomly selected for audit.

For everything you always wanted to know about federal income taxes but were afraid to ask, see the IRS's surprisingly user-friendly Web site (*www.irs.gov*). View and print any form or publication using Adobe Acrobat Reader (it's a free download if you don't already have it on your computer).

What to Do If You're Audited

During an audit you'll be asked to substantiate certain items by producing receipts or other proof. You may be able to do this by mail. If a face-to-face audit is requested, you have the right to have a representative (your accountant or tax preparer) attend with you or in your place. If you attend, keep your emotions under control, don't volunteer any information, and don't act defensive. Treat the agent respectfully. Have all of the requested documents with you and organized in a logical manner. It may be best to let your representative answer all questions or meet with the IRS agent without you. If your representative can't answer a question, he or she will ask you later and get back to the agent. This prevents you from making comments that can get you in hot water and gives you time to think about your answers.

When You Can't Pay Your Taxes

It's a disturbing moment when you finish your tax return and realize you owe additional tax and don't have the money to pay it. Don't panic. First of all, don't compound the problem by filing your tax return late. File by the due date or file for an extension even if you can't pay the tax due. Penalties for late filing can add up to 25 percent to your tax bill.

You have a number of options for coming up with the cash later. Try to take out a bank loan for the amount you owe. The interest rate will be lower than the rate charged by the IRS. If that doesn't work, consider using your credit card or applying for a new card with a low introductory rate and paying the balance off before the rate goes up.

If you can show the IRS that you can't sell assets or borrow money to pay the taxes without causing undue hardship, consider requesting an extension of time to pay by filing Form 1127 at the time the taxes are due. You'll have to provide a list of your assets and liabilities (debts) and three months' worth of your incoming and outgoing cash.

Another option is to request an installment agreement with the IRS by completing Form 9465, Installment Agreement Request, and attaching it to your return. State the amount you can pay monthly toward your tax debt. If your request is approved, you'll have to pay interest at ½ percent per month, but you won't incur any penalties.

Be Prepared in the Future

To ensure that this doesn't happen to you again, review your withholding every year and make sure you're having enough taken out to cover your income. If you receive income that taxes weren't withheld from, make quarterly estimated tax payments or increase the amount of your withholding at work to compensate.

You can avoid incurring tax penalties for underpaying taxes by estimating your tax liability before the end of the year to allow time to catch up if you've been underwithheld. If your tax status has changed during the year (for example, you've gotten married or divorced or added a dependent), do a projection of your taxes using your new status as soon as possible after the change takes place. To avoid penalties, you must pay at least 90 percent of your tax for the current year before December 31, or at least as much as your total tax liability for the prior year.

FACT

Tax Freedom Day illustrates how much of the average American's budget goes toward paying for government services. It's the day by which you will have worked enough to pay your tax obligations for the year, starting from January 1. According to the Tax Foundation, in 2003 Tax Freedom Day was April 19.

If it looks like you may not have had enough tax withheld, change your withholding by filing a new W-4 with your employer to have additional tax taken out each pay period through the end of the year. After the start of the new year, complete another W-4 to adjust your withholding back to a more normal amount. The withholding calculator on the IRS Web site will help you determine what your withholding should be and is more accurate than the worksheets used on the W-4 form. On the IRS site, enter the keywords "Withholding Calculator" in the search box.

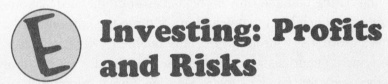

Chapter 17

Investing: Profits and Risks

Let's dispel the two biggest myths that keep people from investing: You don't need to be a financial guru, and you don't need to have a lot of money. To be a successful investor, you need to understand the basics about stocks, bonds, mutual funds, and cash equivalents. It takes effort, but it's not voodoo or rocket science.

The Big Picture

Before you even think about investing, you should have some basics in place. If you have credit card debt, get rid of it before diverting money to investments. Why put your money into an investment with a low or uncertain return when you can immediately earn 15 percent to 20 percent by paying off the balance on your high-interest credit card? If you don't have an emergency fund that would cover three to six months of basic expenses if you lost your job or became unable to work, establish one before tying up your cash in investments. If you're not taking advantage of your employer's 401(k) plan, you're ignoring a great opportunity. You're never too young to start saving for retirement, and a 401(k) is the best way to do it. Not only do you postpone taxes on your earnings, your employer probably matches some portion of your contribution.

FACT

When you're young, you have the greatest investment tool of all—time. Not only can you take advantage of the power of compounding, you can also afford to take intelligent risks because you know there's time to recover from downturns in the market.

If You're Ready

Once you have these three basics taken care of, you're ready to start investing. If you allow yourself to be intimidated by the complexities of the stock market, you'll miss out on the benefits of one of the best investments available. Forget about gold, futures, options, puts and calls, and all those confusing terms you hear bantered about by news analysts. The average investor never deals with them. You're probably not going to be making a living as a stock picker or day-trader, either, and hopefully you won't be throwing your hard-earned money into high-risk investments.

Keep the Goal in Sight

Your overall investment objective is to create wealth. If you've read Chapter 1, you've already thought about the specific things you'd like to do with your money. You may want to save for a down payment on your first house, finance your kids' college educations, go on a luxury vacation, provide for a comfortable retirement, or achieve any number of other objectives.

Each of your financial goals has a time frame that will influence your decision regarding the types of investments you choose. The shorter the time frame, the more conservative the investment should be. The longer the time frame, the more aggressive the investment can be. That's why the bulk of your 401(k) plan or other retirement funds should be in stocks or mutual funds when you're young and won't need the money for several decades. If you're saving for a down payment on a house that you hope to buy in three years, your money should be in much more conservative investments, like CDs and other places to stash your short-term cash. These investments are discussed in Chapter 4.

QUESTION?

Where's the best place to invest my long-term savings?
If you don't need the money for at least five years, the stock market is the best option. You can buy individual stocks and bonds or you can lower your risk by buying mutual funds, which invest in the stocks and bonds of many different companies.

Risk Tolerance and Asset Allocation

Before you can begin investing intelligently, you need to assess your risk tolerance. This is your ability to watch your investments decline in value in the short term because you believe they'll increase in the long term. The higher the risk, the greater the potential reward, and vice versa. You may risk only the impact of inflation if you put your money in an interest-bearing savings account at an FDIC-insured bank, but there's no chance that you're going to make more than the prevailing interest rate. You risk everything if you put your money into junk bonds or highly speculative stocks, but there's a small chance that you could strike it rich. The key is to strive for a balance between risk and return without losing sleep worrying about your choices.

What's Your Risk Level?

If you can tolerate fluctuations in market value by focusing on the long-term, consider investing in aggressive assets, like stocks. If you become nervous and uncomfortable when your investments suffer even a small decline in value, then conservative, low-risk choices are probably more your style. Even if you have a high tolerance for risk, don't gamble with your money by following hot tips or investing in companies you don't really understand.

How do you know what risk level you'd be comfortable with? High-risk investors are willing to take major risks in exchange for the possibility of substantial returns. They can still sleep at night even if they lose large amounts of money. Moderate-risk investors are willing to take low to medium risk to increase their chances of investment growth. Conservative investors are uncomfortable at the thought of losing even a small part of their investments and will give up the chance of high returns for the stability and safety of conservative investments with predictable income.

Low-risk investors face a greater risk: not having enough money for retirement. If you don't invest in stocks, you miss out on the most financially rewarding investment. Historically, the stock market has always out-performed other investments over time.

The highest-risk investments are futures, commodities, limited partnerships, collectibles, real-estate investment trusts (REITs), penny stocks (stocks that cost under $1 per share), speculative stocks (such as stock in new companies), and high-yield (or "junk") bonds. Moderate-risk investments include growth stocks (companies that reinvest most of their profits to grow the business), corporate bonds with low ratings, balanced mutual funds, aggressive mutual funds, rental real estate, annuities, and international stocks. Limited-risk investments are corporate and municipal bonds with high ratings, index mutual funds, and blue-chip stocks. The lowest-risk investments are treasury bills, U.S. savings bonds, bank CDs, and money market funds.

Practicing Wise Asset Allocation

Asset allocation uses a formula to divide your portfolio among the three main types of investments: stocks, bonds, and cash equivalents. An aggressive asset allocation might include 80 percent stocks, 20 percent bonds, and 10 percent cash. A conservative asset allocation might include 40 percent stocks, 40 percent bonds, and 20 percent cash. Because different types of investments grow at different rates, it's a good idea to reallocate your investments once a year. For instance, after you've been investing for a while, you might have a conservative portfolio of 40 percent stocks, 40 percent bonds, and 20 percent cash. If your stocks have a banner year and bonds are sluggish, the value of your portfolio might change to 60 percent stocks, 20 percent bonds, and 20 percent cash. This could cause your portfolio to change from conservative to aggressive without you even realizing it, so you may want to realign it by making some changes in your investments.

Choosing what percentage to invest in each category depends on a number of factors, including your risk tolerance, your age or how much time you have to invest before you need the money, the current state of the market, and what direction interest rates are headed. Most experts recommend that you invest as much as 80 percent of your portfolio in stocks or stock mutual funds if you're in your twenties or thirties.

ALERT!

It's not a good idea to buy bonds when interest rates are expected to rise soon, because you'll be stuck with a lower than market interest rate and will be earning less than you would have if you'd waited a short time.

Diversify, Diversify, Diversify!

Diversification means not putting all your eggs in one basket. The more you spread out your investments between different kinds of securities and different sectors of the industry (financial services, biomedical, technology), the lower the risk of substantial losses.

A well-diversified portfolio includes cash or cash equivalents (Treasury bills, CDs, etc.), stocks, bonds, and mutual funds. The latter should be divided between small-cap, mid-cap, and large-cap (more on this to follow). Usually when one sector or type of investment has low returns, another has high returns, so diversifying evens out some of the ups and downs of the market.

Investing in Stocks

Publicly owned companies sell shares of stock to raise money for operations or business expansion, invest in new technology or equipment, or meet other financial needs. When you own stock, you actually own part of that company, and the value of your share rises and falls as the company's value changes.

When stock prices go down, you don't actually lose anything unless you sell while the price is low. A loss that is only on paper can be recouped the next time the stock rebounds, but selling locks in your loss and makes it final. This is one of the reasons it's important to "buy and hold," which means you pick solid stocks or funds and hang on to them through thick and thin unless there's an underlying flaw that affects the stock's ability to recover. Of course, not all stocks that decline in value recover. Another school of thought recommends setting a lower and upper level for the price of the stock and selling when either threshold is reached. For example, you buy a stock at $30.00 per share and at the time of purchase you set a price range of $25.50 to $34.50 (15 percent below and above your purchase price, respectively). If the stock falls to your lower threshold, you sell. If the stock rises to the upper threshold, you sell. This way you can limit your losses and take advantage of gains.

Stock Price

It's important to understand that a stock's price has more to do with investors' perceptions than it does with the actual financial standing of the company. Internet stocks are a prime example. Yahoo!, Amazon, and other Internet stocks were inflated far beyond their real value because investors were enamored of the concept and the demand for the stocks kept pushing up the prices. When the bottom fell out of the technology market, some of these stocks lost most of their value. Yahoo, for instance, was once at $250 per share and is currently at $16 per share.

When a stock price gets so high that investors are reluctant to buy, the company may declare a stock split. With a two-for-one split, you receive a free share of stock for every share you own, and the price per share is cut in half. The value of your investment doesn't change, but the lower price may make it more attractive to investors and demand for the stock may eventually push the price up. Since you have more shares, your investment is worth more than it would have been without the split. Stock splits don't always result in higher prices, though.

Risk Level of Stocks

Stocks don't offer a guaranteed return, which is why it's important to choose them carefully instead of acting on some hot tip you heard in an elevator or from your uncle's business partner's cousin. Don't ever invest in something you don't understand. Do your homework. Making an informed decision to assume risk creates an opportunity for a greater return on your investment. Jumping into investments you know nothing about, or that you hope will create a quick profit, puts your money at risk.

FACT

In fifty-two weeks, General Electric's stock price fell from $41.83 to $21.41, losing nearly half its value. A $20,000 investment in GE would be worth only $10,236 at the end of that year. An investment of $20,000 in an indexed stock mutual fund for the same period would be worth around $16,000.

Stock Indexes

A stock index reports changes in prices for the market that it tracks. There are many U.S. and international stock indexes, but the best known in the world is the Dow Jones Industrial Average (DJIA), which tracks thirty U.S. blue-chip stocks. Blue chips are the stocks of very large, well-established companies.

Other U.S. indexes include the Russell 2000, which measures the overall performance of small- to mid-cap companies, the S & P 500, an index of the 500 largest companies in America, and the Wilshire 5000, which tracks the entire stock market. It's helpful to compare the performance of your stock or mutual fund to the applicable index. If you have a small-cap mutual fund, compare its return to the Russell 2000. If the fund consistently underperforms the index, consider selling your shares and putting the money in a fund with better performance.

How to Buy Stocks

You can buy stocks through a full-service brokerage or a discount brokerage by calling a stockbroker and placing an order, or you can use a discount Internet broker like E-Trade (✑ *www.etrade.com*) to execute your own orders. Make sure you understand all of the terms on the online form before finalizing your purchase. You don't need a full-service broker unless you want advice regarding which stocks you should buy. Since brokers are paid on commission, they stand to gain financially from their recommendation, so you should make up your own mind about what to buy or sell. You can still get advice from a broker if you're more comfortable doing so, but don't buy on a broker's recommendation alone. Do your own research and your own thinking.

Another way to buy stocks is through dividend reinvestment plans (DRIPs) offered by many corporations. Corporations often pay out part of their earnings as dividends to shareholders, usually quarterly. The dividend can be paid in cash or stock. With a DRIP, you can reinvest the dividends in additional shares of stock, often without paying a commission. When the stock price goes up, so does the value of your reinvested shares. If you take your dividends in cash instead of stock, you lose the opportunity for them to increase in value as the price of the stock goes up.

The best way to invest is to do your research, choose a good stock or mutual fund, and stick with it for the long haul. There will no doubt be dips and rises, but historically the stock market has outperformed all other investments. You don't need to "churn" your stocks, buying and selling constantly and trying to anticipate ups and downs in the market.

You can't afford to ignore changes in the financial condition of the companies you're invested in, but you shouldn't have to review their status more than quarterly. If something fundamental about a company has changed and you believe the stock won't regain its value, think about selling it.

Investing in Bonds

Bonds are known as fixed-income securities because their income is fixed at the time the issuer sells them. When you buy a bond, you're lending the bond issuer money in return for a fixed rate of return. This interest is usually paid quarterly but is sometimes paid at the maturity date, when the issuer repays the principal it borrowed from you. Corporations, states, cities, and the federal government all issue bonds for the same reason companies issue stock: to raise money for operations, expansion, or other financial needs.

Bonds are rated for safety by bond-rating companies and given a grade between A (low risk) and C (high risk) to indicate the likelihood that the issuer will pay the interest and principal as promised. Look up ratings at A.M. Best (✐*www.ambest.com*), Moody's (✐*www.moodys.com*) and Standard & Poor's (✐*www.standardandpoors.com*).

Risk Level of Bonds

Bonds issued by the federal government are extremely safe. Some corporate bonds are safe and others are high-risk. High-yield bonds pay a higher interest rate, but their nickname of "junk bonds" should give you fair warning of their risk. One of the risks associated with bonds is related to interest rates. If you lock in your money for a number of years at a fixed interest rate, you could be stuck if market rates go up. You may not be able to sell the bond for full price if other bonds are paying higher interest rates.

Municipal bonds are issued by states and cities to fund projects such as road repairs, bridge building, prison renovations, and any number of other projects requiring large amounts of money. These bonds aren't guaranteed, but defaults are rare. Earnings are exempt from federal income tax, which makes them attractive to people in a high tax bracket.

How to Buy Bonds

You can buy federal government bonds, including U.S. savings bonds, directly from the U.S. Treasury, and both government and corporate bonds through a stockbroker. If you don't want to buy individual bonds, you can buy shares in a bond fund, which invests in a number of different bonds. You'll incur fund expenses that will eat at your return, so bond funds are best if you'd rather pay a fee for broad diversification and professional management instead of choosing the bonds yourself.

Series EE U.S. Savings Bonds

U.S. savings bonds aren't the most exciting investment in the world, but they may have their place in your portfolio. Their appeal is that they're fully backed by the U.S. government, they're free of state and local income taxes, and they're federal income tax-deferred. You won't get rich buying U.S. savings bonds, but neither will you lose your shirt. You can buy them at banks and financial institutions, through many employers' payroll-deduction programs, through automatic debits from your checking or savings account using the EasySaver program, or directly from the U.S. Treasury online at ✒ *www.savingsbond.gov.*

FACT

Series EE bonds are guaranteed to mature in no more than seventeen years and will continue to pay interest for thirty years. You can buy up to $15,000 of EE bonds per year.

There are several different types of U.S. savings bonds. You purchase Series EE bonds at one half the face value (a $50 bond costs $25) in denominations of $50, $75, $100, $200, $500, $1,000, $5,000, or $10,000.

The interest rate changes every six months and is based on the yield on five-year U.S. Treasury securities. The higher the interest rate, the faster the bonds mature.

Series I and HH U.S. Bonds

I bonds are similar to EE bonds but are issued at face value (a $100 bond costs $100) and the interest is paid when the bond is redeemed. You can purchase up to $30,000 of I bonds in a year. The interest rate is based on a fixed rate adjusted for inflation and there are no guaranteed minimum earnings.

Like the I Bonds, HH Bonds are issued at face value, but interest is paid every six months instead of when the bond is redeemed, so you receive current income. You can't buy HH bonds; you can only get them in exchange for Series EE/E bonds or if you reinvest the proceeds of matured Series H bonds. You can trade Series EE/E bonds for HH bonds in denominations of $500, $1,000, $5,000, or $10,000.

At the U.S. Treasury Web site at ✎*www.publicdebt.treas.gov* you can download the Savings Bond Wizard, a program that allows you to maintain an inventory of your U.S. savings bonds and determine the current redemption value and interest earned to date.

U.S. Treasury Securities

Unlike U.S. savings bonds, U.S. Treasury securities (bills, notes, and bonds) can be transferred from one person to another, so you can buy and sell them in the securities market. They provide steady income, flexibility, and security. Treasury bills (or T-bills) mature ninety days to one year from their issue date. You buy them for less than their face value, and you receive full face value when they mature. Treasury notes pay a fixed rate of interest every six months until maturity, which is from one to ten years.

Don't Go Overboard

U.S. savings bonds and Treasury securities have a place in your portfolio, but are too conservative to get the lion's share of your investment money. Use them for your cash savings. You'll earn more interest than you would on savings accounts. Once you've built your portfolio, you can also use them for long-term investments to balance more aggressive and riskier investments, like stocks. Another attractive feature is that you can cash them in any time after six months from the issue date and receive what you paid for them plus any earned interest.

FACT

U.S. Treasury bonds aren't currently available, since the Treasury Department decided in October 2001 to suspend issuance of the thirty-year bond indefinitely. Federal budget surpluses have reduced the government's need to borrow.

Mutual Funds

Mutual funds are a way for investors to pool their money so they can invest in many different stocks. Each investor is charged a percentage of his or her investment as a fee to pay for the expenses of having a professional fund manager and all the costs associated with researching, buying, and selling stocks. Mutual funds are the best alternative for most people for several reasons:

- They automatically diversify your portfolio among a larger number of stocks than you could achieve by purchasing individual stocks.
- Some funds invest in stocks, bonds, and cash equivalents, which gives you even greater diversification.
- They require only a small amount of money to get started, sometimes as little as $50.

Like stocks, some mutual funds are riskier than others, so be sure to read the fund's objectives and know what it invests in. Will your money be buying stocks in blue-chip companies or in the corporations of developing countries? Although past performance is no guarantee of the future, look at how the fund has done over the last several years and compare it to an applicable index to see if it kept pace with its competitors. Also consider the expense ratio. The lower it is, the more of your return you get to pocket.

Risk Level of Mutual Funds

Mutual funds tend to be less risky than individual stocks because their investment in any one stock is relatively small compared to their entire holdings. If one company takes a nosedive, the effect on the fund is usually minimal, or at least diluted. When entire sectors, such as technology stocks, head downhill, the impact can be great if the fund is heavily invested in technology stocks.

Income versus Growth

Different funds have different investing objectives. Funds whose objective is current income invest heavily in bonds because of the steady interest income they generate. These funds appeal to retirees and those on a fixed income. Funds whose objective is long-term growth invest in stock, stock mutual funds, and real estate because those investments usually increase in value over time. Growth and income funds are a hybrid of these two types and invest in both kinds of securities.

Load and No-Load Funds

Load is a sales fee or commission charged by some mutual funds, and is usually stated as a percentage of the amount purchased or sold. Front-end loads are fees charged up-front when you buy the fund. Back-end loads are fees you pay when you sell the fund. If the load is 6 percent and you invest $2,000, the load will be $120. Funds that don't charge front-end or back-end loads are called no-load funds. When choosing a mutual fund, consider the load, if any, and the annual expense ratio. These eat into your return. If you buy a fund with a 6 percent load and a 2 percent expense ratio, you have to earn an 8 percent return the first year before you break even.

Index Funds

If you don't want to spend a lot of time keeping up with the financial status of the companies you're invested in, and you don't want to pay a manager to pick stocks, a stock index mutual fund is the best choice. Interestingly, most professionally managed funds underperform the stock market in general, which is why some financial advisors recommend that their clients buy index stock funds. An index fund's objective is to match the return of a specified index by buying shares in each stock in that index.

FACT

The best-known index is the Standard & Poor 500, which invests in the top 500 U.S. stocks. The largest and best-known index stock fund is Vanguard's S & P 500 fund. Over the last decade it has outperformed 90 percent of all other mutual funds, while having one of the lowest expense ratios in the market.

Market Capitalization

Mutual funds are classified based on the market capitalization of the companies they invest in because cap is one of the criteria investors look at when choosing funds. A company's cap is calculated by multiplying the current stock price times the number of outstanding shares of stock. The categories are:

- **Large-cap funds:** Companies with market capitalization over five billion dollars.
- **Mid-cap stock funds:** Companies with market capitalization of one to five billion dollars.
- **Small-cap funds:** Companies with market capitalization of $250 million to one billion.
- **Micro-cap funds:** Companies with market capitalization of less than $250 million.

The large-cap funds, like Vanguard's S & P Index 500, are considered the least volatile and the smaller funds are considered the most volatile.

How to Buy Mutual Funds

You can use full-service or discount brokers to buy mutual funds, or you can buy directly from a family of mutual funds, like Vanguard (✍*www.vanguard.com*) or Fidelity (✍*www.fidelity.com*). Call the company's toll-free number or request an investor's kit online, fill out the forms, and send them in with your check. You can initiate this procedure on the mutual fund's Web site, but you'll still have to send in your check—unless you want to transfer the money electronically.

Using the Internet for Investment Research

The Internet has made what was once a time-consuming process of researching investments as easy as a few clicks of your mouse. Vast amounts of information about investing, individual stocks and mutual funds, and performance ratings and reviews is available online. Most of the work has been done for you. You should still review the fund's prospectus, which explains the fund's objective, a description of how the fund operates (its investing philosophy), a summary of investments, and information about its management. Prospectuses are dry reading, but the more easily digestible information from reputable Internet sites helps interpret the information in the prospectus.

Morningstar.com features Quick Take reports, which tell you everything you need to know about the fund in one easy-to-read report complete with graphs. You can also search for mutual funds that meet the criteria you set, whether it's a certain return over the past five years, low expenses, or minimum required contribution to open an account.

Whenever you use the Internet for research or advice, keep in mind that anybody can post anything on the World Wide Web. Just because you see it in writing doesn't mean the information is legitimate or the advice is wise. Try to stick with sites you know by name and reputation.

See Appendix B for a list of reputable sites by topic. For mutual fund research, it's difficult to find a better site than Morningstar.com (*www.morningstar.com*), which tracks thousands of mutual funds and presents a great amount of information free on its Web site.

Using a Financial Planner

You may want to see a financial planner to help you chart a course for the future, or you may want to consult with a planner at a big turning point in your life (such as a marriage, divorce, or birth of a child). If you use a financial planner to help you choose investments, be aware that even the best-laid plans can go awry. Using expert advice is not a guarantee that your investments will make money. Millions of people who used financial planners have lost large amounts of money in the stock market, insurance, and other types of investments. If you have the time and interest to do your own research and educate yourself, you probably don't need a financial planner for choosing investments, unless you have a complex situation. Consider developing your own written financial plans, but meet every few years with a financial planner to make sure there are no glaring issues or gaps in the course you've charted for yourself.

Don't ever rely totally on another person to make investment decisions for you. If you use a professional, educate yourself about the recommended investments and be involved in the buying and selling decisions he or she executes on your behalf. Many financial planners earn commissions from the companies they deal with, so they may not be entirely objective when making recommendations. You can avoid this problem by choosing a fee-only planner who is paid by the hour and doesn't benefit from recommending one investment over another.

To locate a fee-only financial planner near you, use an online search form provided by the National Association of Personal Financial Advisors (NAPFA) at *www.napfa.org*. You can also order two free booklets: *Financial Planner Interview* and *How to Choose a Financial Planner*, as well as NAPFA's brochure, *Why Select a Fee-Only Financial Advisor?*

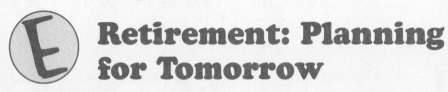

Chapter 18

Retirement: Planning for Tomorrow

You're never too young to start investing for retirement. Compounding of earnings is so powerful that if you start investing in your twenties, you can amass a large nest egg with little effort by the time you are in your sixties or seventies. All that's required is a basic understanding of retirement plans and the commitment to start now.

The Younger, the Better

If you're in your twenties or thirties, you may feel like you have all the time in the world to invest for retirement. Don't find out the hard way that you can't start in your forties and expect to catch up to those who started in their twenties. The younger you are when you start, the less you'll need to invest, thanks to the power of compounding and the length of time until retirement.

It's difficult to think ahead to your retirement when you're young. There are so many things you want to do and so little money at your disposal. Yet investing a relatively small amount of money in your twenties can save you from having to invest much more when you're in your forties and fifties in order to be able to live comfortably in retirement.

To illustrate, if you start contributing $750 a year (less than $15 a week) at the age of twenty-one and you earn 8 percent a year, at the age of sixty-five you'll have amassed $289,129. If you invest the same amount starting at age thirty, you'll have $139,577; and if you wait until age forty, you'll have only $59,216.

You can't rely on social security as your sole source of retirement income, but fortunately there are a growing number of alternatives. Employers sponsor some of them; others are the do-it-yourself variety. Most employer-sponsored plans fall into one of three categories: defined benefit, defined contribution, and profit-sharing plans.

Defined-Benefit Plans

Employee-sponsored defined-benefit plans, also known as pensions, provide a guaranteed income for the rest of your life after you retire. The amount varies depending on your years of service with the company, your salary, and your age at retirement. Your employer uses an actuarial formula to arrive at the amount to put into the fund each year to ensure there's enough to meet the future retirement needs of its employees. All funds are mingled in one account managed by your employer.

ALERT!

By the time you reach retirement age, traditional pension plans may be a thing of the past. They're already being replaced or supplemented in large numbers by defined-contribution plans, which put more of the responsibility for retirement savings on you and less on your employer.

Defined-Contribution Plans

Unlike defined-benefit plans, employee-sponsored defined-contribution plans don't guarantee a specific dollar amount at retirement. How much you receive depends on how much you and your employer contributed and how well your investments performed over the years. Your contributions, as well as your employers' (if any), are always kept in an individual account in your name.

With defined-contribution plans, you're in the driver's seat when it comes to deciding how your money will be invested. You'll choose from a variety of stock or bond mutual funds, guaranteed funds, annuities, cash equivalents like money market accounts, or your company's stock. Your plan will stipulate how frequently you can change your investment choices. Many plans allow you to manage your account online and make investment changes as often as you like.

One of the attractive features of defined-contribution plans is that they're portable. If you change jobs, you can take your money with you. The following are the most common defined-contribution plans:

- 401(k) plans, offered by private companies
- 403(b) plans, offered by nonprofit, tax-exempt employers, such as schools and colleges, hospitals, museums, and foundations
- 457 plans, offered by federal, state, and local government agencies and nonprofit organizations

Other defined-contribution plans include ESOPs, money purchase plans, profit-sharing plans, simplified employee pension (SEP) plans, savings incentive match plans (SIMPLEs), and thrift or savings plans (TSAs). These plans all have one important thing in common: You pay no taxes on your contributions or your earnings until you withdraw the money.

401(k) Plans

One of the best things Congress ever did was create the 401(k) plan, an employer-sponsored retirement plan that gives a special tax break to employees saving for retirement. Here's how the tax break works: If you contribute $2,000 a year and you're in the 28 percent federal tax bracket, you'll save $560 because the $2,000 is deducted from your pay before your taxes are calculated. If you live in one of the states where 401(k) contributions are tax-deferred, and you're in a 6 percent state income tax bracket, you'll save another $120 in state taxes, for a total savings of $680.

FACT

According to the Profit Sharing/401(k) Council of America, pretax 401(k) contributions in 2001 averaged 5.3 percent of pay for lower-paid employees and 6.4 percent of pay for higher-paid employees. The average dollar amount contributed by those participating in 401(k) plans in 2001 was $3,514.

The bottom line is that you add $2,000 to your investment account but only $1,320 comes out of your pocket ($2,000 – $680 = $1,320). It's like getting a raise. You don't pay taxes on your earnings until you withdraw them, presumably at retirement, so your investments grow faster as your untaxed earnings benefit from compounding.

Employer Match

To sweeten the pot even more, many employers match a certain percentage of your contributions. The amounts vary but a typical match is between fifty cents and $1 for every dollar you contribute, up to

6 percent of your salary. Even if your employer doesn't contribute, 401(k) plans are great, but if a match is offered and you don't participate, it's like walking past money lying on the sidewalk and not picking it up. Where else are you going to find a guaranteed 100 percent return on your money (assuming your employer matches dollar for dollar)? Actually, the return is greater than 100 percent when you factor in your tax savings.

Contribution Limits

The IRS sets limits, adjusted annually for inflation, on how much you can contribute to a 401(k) plan each year. For 2002, you can contribute up to $11,000 as long as it doesn't exceed 25 percent of your combined wages and your employer's contributions. At this time, the contribution limit is set to increase $1,000 a year from now until 2006, when it reaches $15,000. The total of all contributions, including yours and your employer's, cannot exceed 100 percent of your compensation for the year, or $40,000, whichever is less.

Your employer is subject to strict IRS regulations to ensure that your 401(k) plan doesn't discriminate against lower-paid employees. If you're a highly compensated employee, your contributions will be limited by how much the less highly compensated employees contribute. Highly compensated employees are defined as those who made $90,000 or more in the prior year or owned 5 percent or more of the company. Your employer may have adopted a safe-harbor provision that does away with the limits for highly compensated employees by making a certain level of matching contributions or nonelective employer contributions for all eligible employees.

ALERT!

If you earn $30,000 and your employer matches 100 percent of your 401(k) contributions up to 6 percent of your salary, you'd have to contribute $1,800 per year ($30,000 × 0.06 = $1,800) to take full advantage of the employer match. Any less than that and you'd be leaving money on the table.

401(k) Vesting

You're always 100 percent vested in your own contributions to the plan. The employer match is often subject to vesting, which means you earn the right to it gradually, over a number of years of employment with the company. There are two types of vesting schedules. About half of all 401(k) plans have cliff vesting, where you don't own any of the matching contributions until you've worked for the company for a certain amount of time. The Tax Relief Act of 2001 shortened the maximum vesting schedule for cliff vesting to no more than three years. The other type of vesting schedule is graded vesting, where you own an increasing percentage of the employer match over several years. Under the Tax Relief Act of 2001, vesting must take place in no more than 6 years. A typical vesting schedule will now be 20 percent after the second year, 40 percent after the third year, 60 percent after the fourth year, 80 percent after the fifth year, and 100 percent after the sixth year.

It's important to consider the impact on your 401(k) when you're thinking of changing jobs. If your plan has cliff vesting, and you leave before working the required number of years, you walk away from everything your employer has contributed as matching funds, which could be a substantial amount. You could possibly earn thousands of additional dollars in company matching funds by staying in your current job for a few more months or years. Let's assume you had matching contributions of $6,000 and a vesting schedule of 20 percent per year for five years. If you left for a new job after three years, you'd take $3,600 ($6,000 × 60 percent = $3,600) of matching funds with you, plus all the contributions you made from your salary and any associated earnings.

Good deal, right? Yes, but it could be better if you stayed longer. You'd forfeit $2,400 ($6,000 × 40 percent = $2,400) plus any earnings that money has accumulated. You could miss a whole year's worth of vesting by leaving a month or week before your vesting date. Congress is considering changes to the law that would shorten vesting periods, making it easier for you to take matching funds with you when you change employers.

Switching Jobs

The portability of 401(k) plans is a great feature, but what do you do with your money when you change jobs? You have three choices:

1. If you have over $5,000 in your account, you have the option of leaving your funds in your employer's plan.
2. You may be able to roll your balance over into your new employer's plan.
3. You can set up an individual IRA at a bank, through a broker, or directly with a mutual fund.

401(k) Loans

If your 401(k) plan allows loans, you can borrow up to 50 percent of your vested balance, not to exceed $50,000. Loans typically have to be repaid over no more than five years unless the funds are used to buy a first home. Interest rates are typically low—between one and three points above the prime rate. Because you pay yourself back instead of paying a creditor, 401(k) loans are touted as a great deal. Even the interest you pay goes back into your 401(k).

FACT

According to the Employee Benefit Research Institute (EBRI) and the Investment Company Institute (ICI), at the end of 2000 the average 401(k) account balance, net of loans, was $49,024. Total 401(k) plan assets totaled an estimated $1.75 trillion at the end of 2001.

But it's not as simple as it sounds. The first reason you should avoid borrowing from your 401(k) if possible is the tax consequences. Your repayments are not tax-sheltered. They're made with after-tax money. If your monthly payment is $200 and you're in the 28 percent federal tax bracket and a 6 percent state tax bracket, you'd have to make $303 to net enough to make the payment. Worse, when you retire and take withdrawals, you pay taxes on that money again. The second reason you shouldn't borrow from your 401(k) is the opportunity costs. The money that you borrow could be earning interest or appreciating if you left it in your plan. Over time, the impact on your 401(k) could be substantial.

If you have a loan balance when you leave your job, you'll be required to repay the loan immediately. If you don't, you'll owe federal and state income taxes on the amount you borrowed, plus a 10 percent early withdrawal penalty. Think carefully before borrowing your retirement funds, and do so only if you need the money for something important, like a down payment on a house, and you have no other alternatives. Never borrow from your 401(k) for something like a vacation or a new car.

403(b) and 457 Plans

403(b) plans are defined-contribution plans used by nonprofit organizations. They work very much like 401(k) plans. Your contributions are tax-deductible and your earnings are tax-deferred until you take the money out at retirement. Like 401(k) plans, the amounts that you and your employer can contribute are limited by law.

Section 457 plans are defined-contribution plans established by government agencies. Like 401(k) and 403(b) plans, they allow you to make tax-deductible contributions and your earnings grow tax-deferred until retirement. One important difference is that your account is funded solely by your own contributions. Your employer doesn't contribute a dime. These plans are still a great benefit because of their tax-deferred feature, but not as great as a 401(k), 403(b), or other plans that include an employer match.

Individual Retirement Accounts

Individual retirement accounts or IRAs have evolved in the more than twenty years since they were established and now include such variations as SEP IRAs, Roth IRAs, SIMPLE IRAs, and more. IRAs provide the same tax-deferred benefits as 401(k) and similar employer-sponsored plans and allow you to decide how your funds will be invested.

If you have employment income, you can contribute up to 10 percent of your income each year, not to exceed $3,000 in 2002, to an IRA. The limit is set to increase to $4,000 in 2005 and $5,000 in 2008. You can set up an IRA through most banks and financial institutions, or through a mutual fund company or broker. You can start making withdrawals at age fifty-nine and a half, and you must start doing so by age seventy and a half. Like 401(k) plans, a 10 percent penalty is placed on any funds you take out early unless you retire, need the money to pay medical expenses, or are disabled.

Contributing to an IRA doesn't make sense unless you're maximizing your contributions to your 401(k) or 403(b) plan by contributing the IRS limit. Take full advantage of these employer-sponsored defined-contribution plans first and if you have money left to invest for retirement, consider IRAs. If you don't have access to an employer-sponsored plan, then by all means, invest as much as possible in IRAs.

You can use the online calculators at FinanCenter.com (✍ *www.financenter.com*) to help you determine which IRA you're eligible for and whether you should convert your IRA to a Roth IRA. The site also offers other IRA-related tools.

Traditional IRAs

Depending on your income and whether you have a qualified retirement plan at work, your IRA contributions may not be fully tax-deductible. If you (and your spouse) don't participate in an employer-provided retirement plan, you can each deduct your entire contribution, up to $3,000 in 2002. If you (and your spouse) do participate in an employer's retirement plan (see if the pension box on your W-2 is checked), you'll be able to take the full deduction if your adjusted gross income (AGI) is below $34,000. If your AGI is between $34,000 and $44,000 (for singles), and between $54,000 and $64,000 (for married couples), you'll only be able to take a partial deduction. You have until April 15 to make an IRA contribution for the previous year, but make sure you do it before filing your income taxes. The IRS will check to make sure your contribution was made within the deadline.

Roth IRAs

There are several important distinctions between traditional IRAs and Roth IRAs. Traditional IRA contributions are tax-deductible. Roth IRA contributions are not. Traditional IRAs grow tax-deferred until you withdraw the funds at retirement, and then they're taxed at your regular income tax rate. Roth IRA earnings are never taxed. You're required to withdraw a minimum amount each year from your traditional IRAs once you reach the age of seventy and a half. There are no such requirements for Roth IRAs.

The income limits for Roth IRAs are much more liberal and you can contribute even if you participate in an employer-provided retirement plan. To make the full $3,000 contribution, your income must be $150,000 or less if you're married filing jointly and $95,000 or less if you're single. You can make a partial contribution if your income is between $95,000 and $110,000 if you're single and between $150,000 and $160,000 if you're married. If your income exceeds these limits, you can't contribute at all.

FACT

According to the Investment Company Institute, at the end of 2001 IRA investments were comprised of $2.41 trillion, representing 22 percent of the $10.9 trillion U.S. retirement market. An estimated 43 percent of U.S. households own IRAs.

SIMPLE IRAs and SEPs

The Savings Incentive Match Plan for Employees (SIMPLE) IRA is a plan offered by businesses with no other retirement plans and with fewer than 100 employees. As in 401(k) plans, your contributions and earnings are tax-deferred. You can contribute up to $7,000 a year, and your employer must either match 100 percent of your contributions, up to 3 percent of your salary, or contribute 2 percent of compensation (up to $3,200) for each eligible employee, even those who don't contribute to the plan.

A Simplified Employee Pension (SEP) IRA is similar to a SIMPLE IRA, except that only your employer can contribute. The disadvantage of this plan is that you have no control over how much goes into your plan because you can't contribute any of your own money. The limit on employer contributions is 15 percent of your compensation up to a maximum of $40,000. With both the SIMPLE IRAs and the SEP IRAs, you can still invest in a traditional or Roth IRA.

Choosing the Best IRA for You

It can be difficult to determine whether you'd come out ahead in the long run with a traditional or a Roth IRA. It depends on a number of factors, such as how long before you retire, when you plan to start taking money out, and your tax bracket now and at retirement. There are benefits to Roth IRAs besides tax-free earnings. In some cases you can withdraw your contributions before retirement without owing taxes or penalties, although you may have to pay taxes on the withdrawal. You can withdraw up to $10,000 in earnings without penalty to buy your first home if the money has been in the Roth IRA for at least five tax years, pay medical expenses exceeding 7.5 percent of your gross income, pay college expenses for certain family members, or if you're unable to work because of disability. Any other withdrawals before the age of fifty-nine and a half will be subject to the penalty.

If your income exceeds the limits for a traditional IRA, you can still contribute but it won't be tax-deductible. Since tax-deductibility is the biggest advantage of a traditional IRA, if you don't qualify for the tax deduction, then a Roth IRA is probably the best choice.

Keogh Plans

Keoghs are tax-deferred retirement plans for people who have self-employment income. The IRS no longer uses the term "Keogh plan," but two types of defined-contribution plans are still referred to as Keoghs by most people: profit sharing and money-purchase plans. Money-purchase Keoghs require the same contribution each year even if you don't make a profit. Contributions are limited to the lesser of $40,000 or 25 percent of your self-employment income. Contributions to profit-sharing Keoghs can be 0 to 25 percent of self-employment income up to $40,000 and can change each year. These are complex plans and their setup requires the use of an accountant or other professional.

Choosing the Right Investments

If you have a traditional pension plan, your employer makes all the investment decisions for you. With most of the other retirement plans discussed in this chapter, you're in the driver's seat. Some people find that intimidating, but it doesn't have to be. If you've read Chapter 17, you have a basic understanding of the investment options that are probably available in your retirement plan: stocks, bonds, mutual funds, cash equivalents, and maybe your employers' stock. Putting all your funds in one type of investment increases your risk of loss if that investment doesn't perform well, so spread your funds out over several types of investments.

Stocks, Bonds, and Mutual Funds

With retirement investing, it's important to think long-term. Because retirement earnings grow tax-deferred and you have many years before you'll make withdrawals, retirement plans are best suited for your most aggressive investing, which means stocks and mutual funds. Don't make the mistake of putting all your money in money market funds or guaranteed investment contracts (GICS). Diversify your portfolio to balance risk and reward and you should come out far ahead in the long-term. This doesn't mean you shouldn't choose your investments carefully. If 80 percent of your retirement funds are in stock mutual funds, most of it should be in well-established funds with a history of solid performance. If you want to get aggressive with some of your money, you can place a small percentage of your stock investments in higher-risk funds.

ESOPs

Chapter 9 briefly mentioned ESOPs, which give you an opportunity to own stock in the company that employs you. These plans can be a great benefit, but there's one very important caveat: Don't put all your eggs in one basket. Thousands of employees who did so have lost their entire retirement funds when their employer's stock lost value due to corruption or shaky accounting practices that hid serious financial problems. If company stock is the only option available to you in your 401(k) plan, look at other investment vehicles for some of your retirement savings.

Annuities

When you buy an annuity, you sign a contract with an insurance company that stipulates the amount of your investment, whether you choose a fixed or variable rate for interest, the method of payment, and any fees. Fixed-rate annuities guarantee a specific interest rate for the life of the annuity. Interest rates on variable-rate annuities fluctuate with the ups and downs of the financial markets. You can invest with one lump-sum payment or build it gradually over time.

Your earnings grow tax-deferred, but the money you put in is not tax-deductible, so this is an investment best suited for someone who has taken full advantage of all the tax-deductible plans available and still has money left over to invest. It's unlikely that the average person in her or his twenties or thirties would choose this investment vehicle, but you should be aware of it in case an insurance agent attempts to sell you one.

QUESTION?

Will social security still be around when I retire?
By 2037 the taxes collected will pay only 72 percent of benefits owed. While there's no reason to fear that the system will be bankrupt, it's clear that you shouldn't rely on social security for more than half of your retirement income.

A Word on Social Security

Social security is a benefit plan that's been around since 1935. In addition to retirement, social security includes several other programs, including Medicare (the health care plan for people over sixty-five), disability benefits, and survivor benefits for spouses or dependents.

These programs are funded by mandatory taxes deducted from your pay and matching taxes paid by your employer. The current tax rate is the same for both: 7.65 percent of wages under $84,900 and 1.45 percent of wages over that amount.

Social Security Benefits Statement

When you reach retirement age, you'll receive benefits based on a complex calculation using the number of years you worked, the income you earned during those years, and your age at retirement. You can request a Social Security Benefits Statement that will include a record of your earnings history by year as reported on your W-2s and the amount you and your employers paid in social security taxes. It also includes an estimate of the benefits you can expect to receive at retirement.

Counting on Social Security

There was a time when many retirees relied on social security to get them through their golden years. Today social security is considered a supplement to your retirement income, not the main source.

ESSENTIAL

You can compute estimates of your future social security benefits and get information about the factors that influence your benefit amount by visiting the planner and calculator section of the Social Security Administration's Web site at *www.ssa.gov*.

There's been much discussion about whether social security is going broke. It appears that the system will be able to meet all benefit payment requirements for the next thirty years, but that may not be the case when you retire. Sixty-five million baby boomers will put a strain on the system when they start collecting benefits, but some experts project that even then they'll be able to pay 75 percent of the benefits that workers have earned. This will probably equate to no more than 40 percent of your preretirement income and will fall far short of what you'll need for even the simplest lifestyle.

Chapter 19

Insurance: Buying Security

The purpose of insurance is to protect your assets against catastrophic losses that could damage your financial future. Whether that asset is a house, a car, or your income-earning ability, insurance protects you from financial disaster. Decide how much risk you can assume and insure the rest.

Life Insurance

You may or may not need life insurance, depending on your personal situation. If you don't need it, don't buy it. It may give you a false sense of security but you'll be wasting your money. To figure out whether or not you need life insurance, consider its purpose, which is to replace income in the event of the policyholder's death. If you're single and have no dependents, nobody is relying on the income you bring in, so you don't need life insurance.

If you're a stay-at-home parent and aren't making a significant contribution to the household income, you probably don't need life insurance. The money could best be invested or used elsewhere. On the other hand, if your salary is important to supporting your family, paying the mortgage, or sending your kids to college, life insurance can ensure that these financial obligations are covered in the event of your death.

QUESTION?

Should I buy life insurance policies on my kids?
Although insurance companies use advertising that pulls on your heartstrings to encourage parents to buy life insurance on their kids, it's unnecessary. Your kids don't produce income and therefore their lives don't need to be insured. You'd be better off putting the money you'd spend into a savings account.

How Much Insurance Do I Need?

The amount you need depends on your other sources of income, the number of dependents you have, your debts, and your lifestyle. There's no hard and fast rule of thumb, but the general guideline is between five and ten times your annual salary.

To estimate your need, list your family's annual expenses, such as the mortgage, day care expenses, debt payments, and educational costs. Multiply the total by the number of years you need the insurance to cover. For example, if you have a child who has four years of high school ahead, you need coverage for at least four years. Add the costs of the funeral and burial of the insured person. If you can afford the premiums, consider adding in the total balance of your mortgage so your family can pay it off after your death, as well as the cost of sending your kids to college.

The cost of pure life insurance is based on actuarial tables that project your life expectancy. If you're considered a high risk, if you're for instance overweight or a smoker, have a preexisting health condition, or a dangerous hobby or occupation (flying, for example), you'll pay higher rates. It's not a good idea to lie about any of these factors on your application. The insurance company could end up refusing to pay your beneficiaries if they find that you didn't tell the truth, the whole truth, and nothing but the truth.

Your employer may provide a basic amount of life insurance at no cost (one or two times your salary) and allow you to purchase additional coverage at group rates, which are often lower than you could find on your own.

Term Life

Term insurance is "pure" insurance that offers a predetermined death benefit if you die within the term covered, but doesn't build up a cash value during your lifetime. (By comparison, whole life insurance offers both a death benefit and a cash value, but is much more expensive.)

The life insurance that many employers offer to their employees is generally term insurance that is in force only during your period of employment with the company. If you die during that time, your beneficiary receives the life insurance proceeds. If you leave the company your policy terminates, unless you convert it to an individual policy.

If your employer doesn't offer term life insurance, you can buy a policy through an insurance agent. The cost will depend in part on your age, your health, and whether you smoke. A healthy thirty-year-old man could expect to pay approximately $300 a year for $300,000 of term life insurance. To buy the same amount of whole life insurance would cost over $3,000.

Whole Life

Whole life is part life insurance and part investment. A portion of your premiums goes toward the insurance coverage, a portion goes toward administrative fees, and a portion goes toward the cash value or investment. You have no control over how the insurance company invests the cash value. Unlike term insurance, whole life covers you for your entire life. The premiums remain fixed. You can borrow against the cash value or cash the policy in, but it takes a number of years to build up any real cash value because large commissions and fees eat up most of your premium in the early years. Some experts say you lose money if you cash in a whole life policy within the first twenty years.

FACT

The Wall Street Journal has reported that half of all cash value policies are surrendered or cashed in within the first seven years. This makes the coverage very expensive because it doesn't allow enough time for the cash value to build up enough to cover the initial commissions and fees.

Variable and Universal Life

The difference between regular whole life insurance and variable life insurance is that variable life policies allow you some choice in what your cash value will be invested in. You can usually put it only in investments your insurance company manages. With variable life, the amount of your life insurance coverage fluctuates depending on how well the investment portion is doing.

Universal life insurance differs from variable life in one important aspect. In universal life policies, the pure insurance part of the policy is kept separate from the investment part of the policy. The insurance premium costs are paid out of the proceeds of the investment part of the policy. Universal life offers more flexibility in the death benefit and the annual premium. In years when the investment portion does well, you may choose to put more of the money into building up the cash value. In years when the investment doesn't do as well, you may elect to reduce premiums or let the entire premium for the year be deducted from the investment account. You pay for this flexibility in higher administrative fees.

Which Type of Insurance Is Best?

Many financial experts recommend that you keep your life insurance and your investments separate. If you need life insurance, buy term life. If you want to invest money, do it yourself. Why pay thousands of dollars in commissions and administrative fees? If you're convinced that you want a whole life policy, consider consulting with a fee-only insurance advisor who, for a fixed fee, will research the various policies available to you and recommend the one that best suits your needs. Make sure the advisor isn't affiliated with any particular insurance company and receives no commissions so you can be sure you're getting objective advice.

Health Insurance

If you have health insurance, you're most likely covered under a group plan provided by your employer or your spouse's employer. Some people who don't have the benefit of a group plan through work purchase their own individual policies or are covered under COBRA (more on that a little later). Others have no coverage at all.

No matter how old (or young) you are, you need health insurance to protect yourself against financial disaster if you become seriously ill or have an accident. These things happen to people of all ages. It's extremely foolhardy to go without some type of health insurance at any age. If you simply can't afford the premiums, buy a policy with a very high deductible ($5,000 for example) to limit your exposure.

Indemnity or Fee-for-Service Plans

Whether you're eligible for health insurance under an employer's plan or buying your own individual policy, you'll probably be offered a number of choices, including HMOs, PPOs, and point of service or indemnity plans. Indemnity plans, also referred to as fee-for-service plans, are traditional plans that allow you to go to any doctor you choose. These plans provide the most flexibility, but due to spiraling health care costs and higher premiums, fewer employers are offering them. Employers are attempting to control costs by shifting more of the cost to employees who choose these plans instead of HMOs and PPOs. Often indemnity plans require you to pay up-front and submit a claim to your insurance company for reimbursement.

ALERT!

If your health history makes you uninsurable, you may be able to buy health insurance through your state's risk pool. A list of states with risk pools can be found at *www.cainc.org*.

The biggest advantage of indemnity plans is that you can get your medical care anywhere you want without getting referrals or approvals from your primary-care physician. You don't have to go to doctors that belong to a specific network. Because this freedom of choice results in higher costs, insurance companies shift more of the costs to you, making indemnity plans the most expensive type of coverage.

Health Maintenance Organizations (HMOs)

An HMO is an association of health care professionals and medical facilities that sell a fixed package of health care services for a fixed price. Each patient has a primary-care physician, who is often referred to as a gatekeeper because services provided by a specialist are not covered unless the gatekeeper determines that the specialist is necessary.

The advantages of HMOs are lower and more predictable out-of-pocket costs and no claim forms. The major disadvantage is that services provided by health care professionals outside the network of your HMO aren't covered. If your network is small, your choices of doctors and other health professionals will be very limited, and services provided by specialists will be dependent on a referral from your primary physician. In HMOs, it's possible that you might not receive the medical care you need due to incentives paid to HMO doctors by the insurance company that reward doctors who limit tests and referrals to specialists.

Preferred Provider Organizations (PPOs)

PPOs combine the managed care aspects of an HMO with the flexibility of a fee-for-service plan. When you use doctors in your approved network, more of your medical costs are covered, but you can go outside the network of health care professionals and facilities to any health care provider of your choice when you feel it's necessary. The main advantage of a PPO is the flexibility and a wide choice of doctors and facilities. The only disadvantage is that it's more difficult to predict your out-of-pocket costs and you'll pay more for your health care if you go out of network.

If group health coverage isn't available to you, buy an individual policy, but be prepared to pay dearly for it. Research your options and compare benefits and costs. If you're in good health, consider buying a policy with a higher deductible to cover you in the event of a serious illness. You'll pay less for it but you could incur out-of-pocket costs up to the deductible amount.

What about COBRA?

Under the Consolidated Omnibus Reconciliation Act (COBRA) of 1986, employees who lose medical and dental insurance for certain reasons can often buy group coverage for themselves and their dependents for a specified period of time at group rates. The law applies to group health plans maintained by private sector and state and local government employers with twenty or more full- and part-time employees in the prior year. It doesn't apply to plans maintained by the federal government or church organizations.

To be eligible, you must experience a "qualifying event." These events as applied to the employees, as well as their spouses and dependents, is outlined in the COBRA Insurance Continuation chart.

COBRA Insurance Continuation		
Qualifying Event	**Beneficiary**	**Coverage Period**
Termination of employment; reduced hours	Employee, spouse, dependent child	18 months
Employee entitled to Medicare; divorce or legal separation; death of covered employee	Spouse, dependent child	36 months
Loss of dependent child status	Dependent child	36 months

The Process of Electing COBRA

It's your responsibility to notify your employer or your spouse's employer within sixty days of a qualifying event that the plan administrator might not know about, such as legal separation, divorce, or a child reaching the maximum age to be a covered dependent. Your failure to do so can cause you to forfeit your COBRA rights. Your plan administrator has fourteen days after the qualifying event (or after being notified by you of a qualifying event) to provide you and any other covered person with written notice of your rights under COBRA. You have an election period of sixty days from the date of the qualifying event or the date the notice was sent to choose whether to continue your coverage under the employer's group health plan.

Once you elect coverage, you're required to pay premiums retroactive to the date of the qualifying event, which will provide you with continuous health insurance with no lapse in coverage. Your cost for COBRA coverage is the employer's actual cost plus a 2 percent administrative fee. You have the same grace period that the employer is given by the insurance company, usually thirty days. If you don't pay the premium within the grace period, your coverage will be terminated. Each qualified beneficiary may elect COBRA coverage independently of any other qualified beneficiary. Coverage ends at the end of the maximum coverage period (eighteen or thirty-six months) or sooner, if one of the following occurs:

- You fail to pay your premium within the grace period.
- The employer no longer maintains any group health plan.

- You obtain coverage under another employer group plan that doesn't limit coverage for any pre-existing condition.
- You become entitled to Medicare benefits.

You may be eligible to convert your group health coverage into an individual policy at the end of the maximum COBRA continuation period. Check with your plan administrator.

ALERT!

It's very important for you to familiarize yourself with your rights related to health care and other benefits. Employers are required to provide a Summary Plan Description and plan booklets that spell out the coverage, your rights, and your responsibilities. Read this material and ask questions about anything you don't understand.

Should You Elect COBRA?

Nobody should be without health insurance coverage. If you lose coverage and are eligible to elect COBRA, you should do so unless you have other options that provide at least basic coverage at a reasonable cost. Even if you pick up coverage with a new employer, you may want to elect COBRA during the period that you'd be subject to a pre-existing condition if you've had recent serious health problems. Be aware, however, that under the Health Insurance Portability and Accountability Act of 1996 (HIPPA), if you've been continuously covered by insurance for at least twelve months, a new plan can't limit coverage for a pre-existing condition that was covered under the previous plan. When you lose coverage, your employer or spouse's employer should give you a notice stating that you were continuously covered for twelve months so you can prove this to a new insurance company if necessary.

You may want to consider COBRA if your new employer doesn't offer a health plan or you've had recent health problems, are taking expensive prescriptions, have been declined for private health insurance, have had an accident within the election period, or are pregnant.

Disability Insurance

Have you thought about how you would pay your bills if you were physically unable to work? Short- and long-term disability insurance protects your income-producing ability when you're unable to work due to illness or injury.

Many employers provide group disability insurance as a benefit at little or no cost to employees. If there's a cost for the coverage, it's usually paid with pretax dollars and is much less than you'd pay for an individual policy. When you have both coverages through your employer, the policies often dovetail so that your long-term coverage would pick up as soon as your short-term coverage expired (if your disability lasted that long).

FACT

According to the Social Security Administration, the average twenty-year-old worker has a 30 percent chance of becoming disabled before retirement. For a thirty-year-old, disability is 4.1 times more likely than death, yet many people in their twenties and thirties insure their lives but not their income-producing ability.

The Purpose of Disability Insurance

Ironically, although the likelihood of becoming disabled is greater than the likelihood of dying during any given period of time, more people buy life insurance than disability insurance. Your greatest asset is your ability to generate income. Shouldn't you insure it? Don't make the mistake of thinking that you're too young or healthy to require disability insurance. While it's true that your chances of experiencing a period of disability are greater as you get older, illness and accidents can happen to you at any age. You could suffer a sports injury, a back injury, or an injury caused by a car accident. You could come down with mono and be out of commission for a few weeks or months.

Before purchasing an individual disability policy, be sure you understand the terms used and read the policy carefully to make sure you know what benefits you're getting. Find out if there are any exclusions, what the elimination period is, what the benefit period is, and the definition of total disability.

ALERT!

Make sure the insurance company you purchase a policy from has the financial strength to pay your claims. Check the company's rating at *www.moodys.com*, *www.standardandpoors.com*, or *www.ambest.com*. You should stick to insurance companies that are rated A by one or more of these rating companies.

Elimination and Benefit Periods

With both types of disability insurance, there's an elimination period, which is the period of time after you become unable to work before you can begin receiving benefits under the policy. A short-term disability policy may have an elimination period of one to two weeks for illness or a shorter time for accidents. Long-term disability elimination periods are typically at least thirty days and more commonly ninety days.

If you become disabled, you'll receive benefits until you recover or reach the maximum benefit provided by your policy. Short-term disability policies pay benefits for a shorter period of time, from six weeks to two years. Long-term disability policies pay benefits for several years or until the age of sixty-five (or longer). The shorter the elimination period and the longer the benefit period, the higher the premium will be. Most policies replace only 60 percent of your income, up to a maximum of $5,000 to $10,000 per month.

Definition of Disability

The best policies will have a definition of disability that includes the inability to perform the major duties of your own occupation. Under these policies, if you're unable to perform your major duties, you can go to work in a different occupation that you *are* able to perform and still collect your disability pay. Less expensive or lower-quality policies won't pay benefits unless you're unable to do any work you're reasonably suited to do, or they'll offset your monthly benefit check against any income you're earning elsewhere. Read the fine print! There are three types of long-term disability policies.

1. **Non-cancelable and guaranteed renewable:** The insurance company guarantees that you'll be able to renew the policy for as long as you wish at the same premium and for the same monthly benefits, regardless of any changes in your occupation or income.
2. **Guaranteed renewable:** The insurance company can't drop you but it can raise prices.
3. **Conditionally renewable:** The company can decide not to renew your policy, perhaps when you most need it, or it can raise prices and add conditions at any time.

Obviously, noncancelable and guaranteed renewable is the best type but will also be the most expensive. Avoid conditionally renewable policies. You want to have the assurance that your coverage will be there when you need it. Buy residual disability benefits. This means if you aren't totally disabled but can't work full-time, you'll be paid partial benefits. Expect to pay between 1 and 3 percent of your annual income for a long-term disability policy, so if you're earning $30,000, a policy will probably cost you between $300 and $900 a year. Your cost will depend on your age and the policy features you choose. The average period of disability is about three years.

FACT

One out of every seven workers will suffer a five-year or longer period of disability before age sixty-five, and if you're thirty-five now, your chances of experiencing a three-month or longer disability before you reach age sixty-five are 50 percent.

Homeowner's Insurance

Homeowner's insurance protects you if your home and any structures attached to it or other structures on your property are damaged or destroyed. It also covers your home's contents if they're damaged or destroyed, and it helps protect you from liability and medical costs if someone is hurt on your property. (For information on renter's insurance, see Chapter 10.)

If you own a home, no matter how modest, you can't afford to be without this coverage. If you want to keep costs down, choose a higher deductible, but don't forgo the insurance altogether. If your house were destroyed, you'd still be responsible for paying the mortgage, and you'd have to pay for housing elsewhere.

There are several basic types of homeowner's policies. They vary by the types of perils, or potential damages, covered and by the extent of coverage. For example, some policies reimburse you only for the depreciated value of your belongings. You'd have to come up with a chunk of change of your own to replace the items that were destroyed. Replacement coverage, on the other hand, reimburses you for the cost to replace those items at their current prices. You should always choose replacement coverage.

The part of the insurance that covers the house itself, or the dwelling, is based on what it would cost to rebuild the house if it were completely destroyed. Again, be sure to have guaranteed replacement coverage so the insurance company will pay whatever it costs to rebuild even if it costs more than the limits in your policy. It's important that you increase the limits as the costs of homebuilding increase. You can do this by buying an inflation rider, which increases your coverage annually at the rate of inflation, but you may end up overpaying if the value of your home decreases. It's best to review your policy every year and make sure you don't have more or less coverage than you need. Homeowner's insurance doesn't cover land, so when you are deciding how much insurance you need, exclude its value.

Prepare Ahead

If you had to file a claim under your homeowner's insurance, think about how you'd prove what you lost in a fire or other damage to your home. You'd never be able to remember every item you owned. It's a good idea to take an inventory of your household belongings by going through every room and writing down each item, and to the best of your memory, when you bought it, where you bought it, and how much you paid for it. Photos are helpful for expensive or unique items. Some people use a video camera to take their inventory. Regardless of how you do it, keep a copy of the inventory someplace other than in your home so you'd have access to it if your home were damaged.

Auto Insurance

Most states require you to have bodily injury liability insurance on your vehicle, which pays your medical bills and lost wages, the medical bills of others hurt in an accident you caused, and property damage, up to the limits you've chosen. The limits are shown in thousands of dollars as bodily injury for one person/bodily injury for more than one person/ property damage. For example, 20/40/10 would mean $20,000 of coverage for one person, $40,000 of coverage for more than one person, and $10,000 of coverage for property damage. Personal injury protection or medical coverage pays your own medical costs if you're injured in an accident. It's required in approximately one-third of all states. Some states also require you to buy additional coverage that will cover your medical costs and lost wages if you're injured in an accident caused by an uninsured motorist.

The legally required minimums for liability coverage are so low that they're not adequate if you own a house or other assets that an injured person could come after if your insurance wasn't enough to cover his or her medical expenses. Unless you have no assets to speak of, you should elect limits of at least 100/300 for bodily injury.

Collision coverage pays for repairing your car if you hit something, whether it's another car, a building, or any other object. Comprehensive coverage covers other types of damage such as theft, broken windshield, fire, flood, falling objects, and so on. If you drive an old beater, you may not need either of these coverages. Cars with a Blue Book value of $2,000 or less are probably not worth insuring for collision coverage and you'll save a lot of money by dropping it. If you have a good driving record, consider raising your deductible to $500 or $1,000 to significantly lower your collision premiums.

Ask your insurance company about discounts. Many offer reduced premiums if you have more than one car insured with them, if you also have your homeowner's insurance with the same company, if your car has certain safety features like antilock brakes or air bags, or you have a good driving record. Some cars cost more to insure than others. If your car is expensive to repair or is a favorite with thieves, be prepared to pay higher insurance rates.

Other Types of Insurance

If you finance a new car or other large purchase, you'll probably be offered credit life insurance. Do you need it? Probably not. See Chapter 13 for information about credit life insurance. What about contact lens insurance? Air travel insurance? Rental car insurance? No, no, and probably not. Your personal auto insurance usually covers you for rental cars, but call your insurance agent to find out for sure.

> Don't buy travel insurance from your tour operator. If they go out of business, the insurance will do you no good. If you feel you need trip insurance, buy it from an independent company. You can get quotes on trip and other types of insurance online at Insure.com (✐ *www.insure.com*).

Trip insurance may be worthwhile if you're going out of the country and you've prepaid large amounts, but it doesn't come cheap. Expect to pay between 3 and 7 percent of your costs in premium. For example, if your trip costs $6,000, you'll pay between $180 and $420 for trip insurance. Be sure to read the fine print very carefully. You may be surprised at what isn't covered.

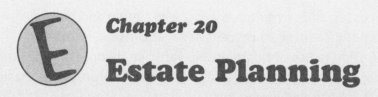

Chapter 20

Estate Planning

In your twenties and thirties estate planning may seem like a low priority, but don't believe the misconception that it's only for the elderly or the wealthy. The terrible events of September 11 made us all acutely aware that tragedy can strike at any age. Planning for the unexpected is best done today, especially if you have a family.

In Your Twenties and Thirties

Some aspects of estate planning are important only if you have a very large estate or are elderly. Those issues won't be covered here. Instead, we'll discuss the issues that may apply to you in your twenties and thirties.

ALERT!

For most people, writing a will is a very simple and inexpensive procedure, yet over 70 percent of Americans die intestate. Addressing issues of guardianship for your children and disposition of your assets in a will is the only way to ensure that these things are handled as you wish.

Aren't I Too Young for Estate Planning?

Planning for how your affairs will be handled if you become incapacitated or die may seem like something your wealthy grandparents should do and it may even make you uncomfortable because it forces you to face your own mortality. However, some issues are important at any age. If you own anything or have kids, for example, you need a will. A durable power of health care and durable power of attorney are important to ensure that your wishes are carried out if you become incapacitated by accident or illness and are unable to make your own health care and financial decisions.

Reviewing Your Plans

Regardless of how simple your estate plan is at this point in your life, review it whenever significant events take place. If you marry, divorce, remarry, or have a child, you may want to make changes to your will. If you move to another state, make sure your will complies with the laws in that state and is still valid. If the value of your assets changes significantly, you may want to review the terms of your will and decide if any changes are in order. If one of your heirs dies, you should change your will to remove that person. If the executor of your will, administrator of your trust, or the guardian you appointed for your kids dies or becomes incapacitated, make changes immediately.

Where There's a Will, There's a Way

A will is a legal document that's used to transfer assets you own to the people or organizations you want to leave them to after your death. In it, you name an executor, who is the person you choose to carry out your wishes, and an alternate in case your first choice is unable to serve. If you have minor children, you use the will to name a guardian to care for them.

FACT

You may not feel that the person you appoint as guardian to raise your kids is the best person to manage their financial affairs. If this is the case, you can use your will to name a trustee, who will work with the guardian in your kids' best financial interests.

Who Needs a Will?

As soon as you acquire your first assets as an adult (car, stocks, bonds, stereo equipment, savings accounts), get married, or have a baby, you should make a will. If you die intestate (without a will) the state will determine who gets what. More importantly, the state will decide who will gain guardianship over your minor children, regardless of what your wishes were and who you expressed them to. Don't operate under the common misconception that if you die intestate, your spouse will inherit all your property. In fact, if you have kids, in most states your spouse will receive between one-third and one-half of your assets and the rest will be split among your kids, no matter how young they are.

If you're married with no kids, in most states your spouse will get one-third of your assets and your parents will get the rest. If your parents aren't alive, your siblings will inherit. In some states, your children from a previous marriage or relationship could be disinherited and your entire estate could go to your new spouse. If you're unmarried and childless, the state will divide your estate among your relatives as it sees fit.

If you're in your twenties, single, and don't own much, you may feel that a will is unnecessary. Still, you probably own things that don't have any great monetary value but do have sentimental value and that you'd like a particular person to have. There may be other things you'd rather didn't end up in someone else's hands.

What to Include in Your Will

The first step in estate planning is getting a handle on what you own so you can decide whom to leave it to. If you've followed the advice in Chapter 1, you've already prepared a Net Worth Statement and have a good grasp on the value of your assets and belongings. To this list, add those items that have meaning to you but may not have a significant monetary value, like family photo albums, personal journals, book or record collections, and pets.

Decide how you want your assets distributed if you die. For your primary beneficiaries, use percentages, not fixed dollar amounts, so that your will remains up-to-date as your assets increase or decrease. You can use fixed dollar amounts for secondary beneficiaries, for instance, if you want to leave money to a niece or nephew that you dote on.

Issues that you might want to address in your will include:

- Whether you want equal or unequal shares to go to your heirs.
- What age you want your kids to be when they inherit.
- How you want to distribute property that can't be divided without being liquidated or sold, such as a house.
- What special arrangements you want made for kids from a previous marriage.
- Whether you should make special provisions for one of your heirs that doesn't handle money wisely.
- What arrangements you want made for a special-needs child who requires special care.

One of the most important functions of your will is to identify who you'd like to raise your kids in the unlikely event that you can't. It will put your mind at rest knowing that if something happens to you and your spouse, your kids will be taken care of by someone you trust. Name one person to act as guardian for each of your kids and one alternate guardian in case the first choice can't serve. If you name coguardians, such as your sister and her husband, and they split up, they could fight for guardianship. If it's your intention for your sister to act as guardian, name her alone. You can name different guardians for each of your kids. For instance, if you have kids by two different spouses, you may want them to be taken care of by two different guardians. Talk to the person you want to name as guardian and make sure he or she is willing and able to do the job.

Is It Necessary to Use a Lawyer?

Unless your estate is very large or you have complex issues to cover, you can draw up your own legal will without paying for an attorney. There are good books available to guide you through the process, but the best way to do it yourself is by using computer software like Quicken Lawyer 2003 Personal, which walks you through the process by asking questions, and then generates a will that is legal in all fifty states.

FACT

Quicken Lawyer replaces the popular WillMaker software program created by Nolo, and adds the ability to generate living wills, financial powers of attorney, and many other legal documents. The software is available at office supply stores or from Nolo.com (✍www.nolo.com) for $49.95.

The Legal Requirements for Signing a Will

For a will to become legal, it should be typed or computer-generated. Handwritten wills are legally binding in only twenty-five states and those states have different requirements about signing the pages and other issues, so it's much safer to have it typewritten. Your will must state that it's your will and it must be signed and dated; at least two (in some states three) people who won't inherit anything under the will must witness your signature and sign their names to the will. The witnesses must watch you sign and you must watch them sign. They don't need to read the will or know what's in it.

Serving as Executor of a Will

Not only must you appoint an executor of your own will, you may find yourself appointed executor of your parents', grandparents', or elderly relative's will. An executor is in charge of settling the estate and is legally obligated to follow the wishes of the deceased, as spelled out in the will.

Your first duty as executor is to initiate probate by filing an application to appear before the probate court. Next, you need to notify all named beneficiaries that you've applied to the court to process the will. You'll also need to notify the Social Security Administration, insurance companies, financial institutions, and other interested parties.

The probate court decides on the authenticity of the will, which is usually a routine matter unless someone challenges it. Once the court rules that the will is valid, you can start to pay taxes and other amounts owed by the estate and distribute the assets to the beneficiaries. When all assets have been distributed and all costs paid, you apply to the court to finalize the estate, providing proof, such as receipts from the beneficiaries, that assets have been distributed.

Among the specific duties of the executor are the following:

- Presenting the will to the probate court.
- Taking an inventory of the deceased person's assets.
- Appraising the worth of the assets.
- Paying income taxes and estate taxes, if any.
- Collecting amounts due to the estate.
- Settling debts.
- Distributing the remaining assets to the beneficiaries.

QUESTION?

What if I'm unwilling or unable to serve as an executor of a will?
You need to file a declination, a document declining your designation as executor, with the court. The alternate executor named in the will then takes on those duties. If no alternate executor is named, the court will appoint one.

Wishes for Your Final Arrangements

Many people are uncomfortable thinking or talking about their own death, but we all go sooner or later, and just in case it's sooner, you should be prepared so that your wishes about your funeral and final arrangements are carried out. Stating your wishes in advance can also ease the burden on your loved ones, who will be left to deal with your personal affairs at a painful time.

Your Funeral and Burial

Your will isn't a good place to state your wishes about your final arrangements because it may not be located and read until long after it's too late to follow your wishes. If you don't leave written instructions, the right to make these decisions will most likely rest with those closest to you, in this order: spouse, child or children, parent or parents, the next of kin, or a public administrator appointed by a court. You can prevent disagreements by putting your wishes in writing. Your instructions may include the following:

- Whether you want to be embalmed.
- Whether you want to be cremated or buried.
- Your preference for the mortuary that will handle your burial or cremation.
- The type of casket or other container your remains will be placed in for burial or cremation.
- Your wishes regarding the funeral.
- Who your pallbearers will be.
- Where you want your remains to be scattered.
- What kind of marker you want where your remains are buried.

Donating Your Organs

Successful tissue and organ transplants have created a great demand for organ donations. If you wish to donate your organs, you should obtain an organ donor card from a local hospital or your state's Department of Motor Vehicles. Most states have a method of indicating on your driver's license that you're an organ donor. Discussing your wishes with family and friends will help increase the likelihood that your organs will actually be used.

Medical Directives or Living Wills

Most people have strong feelings about the type of health care they would or wouldn't want to receive if they were unable to make health care decisions for themselves. An advance medical directive, popularly known as a living will, is a document you create while you're healthy that specifies how you want to be treated if you're terminally ill or incapacitated. By making your wishes known ahead of time, you'll receive the care you want and save your loved ones some of the anguish of making difficult decisions on your behalf. Your living will can cover issues such as organ donation, funeral arrangements, and hospital or nursing home arrangements, as well as acceptable medical treatments.

Health Care Power of Attorney

The living will requires a health care directive and a health care proxy or health care power of attorney. A health care directive is the written statement spelling out how you want to be treated, in as much detail as possible. Some states have mandated forms that must be used in that state, but thirty-four states and the District of Columbia recognize a questionnaire called "Five Wishes" as a legal advance directive. This questionnaire guides you through the decisions you need to make about the health care you want at the end of your life and is very easy to complete. Every adult, regardless of age, should have advance directives.

Order the Five Wishes questionnaire, which can serve as an advance directive for health care, by visiting the Web site of Aging with Dignity at ✑*www.agingwithdignity.org*. Check the listing on the site to make sure you live in a state that recognizes it as a legal document.

A health care proxy is the person you designate to make sure the health care decisions you included in your living will are carried out if you're incapacitated or unable to communicate on your own behalf. Usually, a health care proxy is a family member or close friend. Regardless of who it is, you should discuss your wishes with him or her in detail.

You should also discuss this with your primary care physician and make sure your physician has a copy in your file. Other copies should go to the person you designate as your health care proxy and your attorney, and a copy should be kept in your personal files. You must sign the document in the presence of two adult witnesses who are not the person you've appointed as your proxy.

FACT

A will and all of its associated documents, including a list of all of your assets and debts and what you left to whom, become public when your will goes through probate. The terms of a living trust, however, can be kept private.

Durable Power of Attorney for Finances

A durable power of attorney (a form that must be signed in front of a notary public) allows you to appoint a trusted agent to manage your financial affairs if you become unable to do so yourself due to physical disability or mental incapacity. The power of attorney lasts until your death, unless you revoke it. The person you give power of attorney to can enter into contracts, negotiate, pay bills, buy and sell property, and handle your other financial affairs on your behalf if you're not able to.

These documents are important for elderly people who may suffer from Alzheimer's disease or senile dementia, but they have to be created and signed while the person still has their mental faculties. You may become acquainted with durable power of attorney long before you need one yourself because your parents or an older relative may ask you to become their durable power of attorney.

Probate and Trusts

Probate is the legal process that validates your will and oversees the transfer of assets from your estate to your beneficiaries after your death. Trusts are legal instruments used to take the transfer of some types of assets out of the probate process.

Probate

Probate takes place in the probate court of the city or county where the legal residence of the deceased was located. Wills must go through probate in order to be legally validated, a process which can take between six and twelve months. Attorney and court costs usually range between 3 and 5 percent, so if the estate is worth $100,000, the probate process costs between $3,000 and $5,000. Not all assets go through probate, and the fewer that do, the better.

Trusts

Some assets bypass the probate process and go immediately to the beneficiaries. Examples are assets that have named beneficiaries, like life insurance policies and 401(k) accounts, assets you own jointly with another person, like a house you own with your spouse, and assets held in a trust. A trust is a legal arrangement allowing for the transfer of property to a trustee who holds it for the benefit of another person, the beneficiary. You can be the trustee of your own trust and maintain total control, or you can indicate one or more trustees to administer your trust.

After you set up a trust, you have to fund it by transferring property from your name to the trust. There are legal fees associated with setting up a trust and your situation may not warrant the expense. If you do decide to set one up, find a reputable lawyer who specializes in estate planning; don't buy a do-it-yourself kit or fall for high-pressure sales techniques from companies pushing trusts.

Estate Taxes

Your estate consists of everything you own, from real estate to jewelry, stocks and bonds, life insurance policies, bank accounts, a business, 401(k) funds, and other items of value. When you die, everything you leave to your surviving spouse is transferred tax-free. You're allowed to transfer a certain amount to others tax-free during your lifetime as gifts and let your estate use the balance of the credit after your death.

The amount you can transfer without incurring a tax liability is determined by the Federal Unified Tax Credit, which in 2002 allows you to transfer $1,000,000 tax-free. While that seems like a very large amount, more and more people have estates of this size due to the increasing value of their homes, retirement funds, and life insurance policies. The federal taxes on the taxable amount of your estate can be as high as 55 percent. To reduce taxes and leave more to their heirs, many people set up trusts, which can be complex and expensive. In 2001, Congress passed a law that phases out estate taxes over a ten-year period, with total repeal taking place in 2010.

If you want to read more about the tax aspects of estate planning and methods for reducing your estate taxes, visit Nolo.com (✐*www.nolo.com*) or FindLaw.com (✐*www.findlaw.com*) for easy-to-understand discussions.

Appendix A

Glossary of Financial Terms

Personal finance has a language all its own, but it doesn't have to be intimidating. The average person only needs to know the basics, so if you have an understanding of the terms in this glossary, you're off to a good start.

APR: Annual percentage rate; a way of expressing the interest rate on a loan. Because it includes fees that are paid up-front, it gives the borrower a more accurate picture of the true cost of borrowing.

asset: Anything you own that is of monetary value, including cash, **stocks, bonds, mutual funds,** cars, real estate, and other items.

bankruptcy: A court process in which you acknowledge that you are unable to pay your debts and you allow your **assets** to be sold to repay creditors to the extent possible (Chapter 7 or liquidation bankruptcy); or, you work with the court to set up a plan to pay all or some of your debt over a period of several years (Chapter 13 or reorganization bankruptcy).

Blue Book value: The market value of a car after an allowance for depreciation is deducted. This is an estimate of what a seller can expect to receive for the vehicle upon resale, as posted in the Kelley Blue Book.

bonds: Loans from investors to corporations and governments given in exchange for interest payments and timely repayment of the debt. Interest rates are usually fixed.

budget: A forecast of income and expenses by category. Actual expenses and income are compared to the forecast and a plan is developed to reduce or control expenses to provide for savings to meet financial goals.

CD: Certificate of deposit; money lent to banks for a set period of time, usually between one month and five years, in exchange for **compound interest,** usually at a fixed rate.

COBRA: Consolidated Omnibus Reconciliation Act; a federal law that requires most employers to allow terminating employees to continue their health insurance coverage at the employee's expense, for a limited time.

compound interest: If interest earned on an investment is calculated only on the original amount invested, it's known as *simple interest*. If interest earned is calculated on the original amount plus any previously earned interest, it's known as *compound interest*, which makes the investment grow more quickly.

defined-contribution retirement plan: A retirement plan offered by employers that allows employees to contribute to the plan but does not guarantee a predetermined benefit at retirement. **401(k)**, 403(b), 457, and profit-sharing plans are examples.

DRIP: Dividend reinvestment plans allow investors to automatically reinvest their dividends in the company's **stock** rather than receive them in cash. Many companies waive the sales charges for stock purchased under the DRIP.

escrow: Money or other **assets** held by an agent until the terms of a contract or agreement are fulfilled. Many mortgage companies require borrowers to pay prorated property taxes monthly with their mortgage payment. These funds are held in an escrow account until payment is due to the local government.

foreclosure: A legal process that terminates an owner's right to a property, usually because the borrower defaults on payments. Home foreclosures usually result in a forced sale of the property to pay off the mortgage.

head of household: A tax-filing status that provides tax breaks to single parents who maintain a home for one or more eligible dependents.

intestate: Dying without a **will** that specifies who should receive the property and personal belongings of the deceased.

IRA: Individual retirement account; a retirement account that anyone who has earned income can contribute to. Amounts contributed to traditional IRAs are usually tax-deferred. Amounts contributed to Roth IRAs are not deductible but taxes are never due on the earnings.

joint tenancy with right of survivorship: Shared ownership of property by two or more people, giving the surviving owner(s) rights to a deceased owner's share. See also **tenancy in common.**

liability: An amount owed to creditors or others. Common liabilities include mortgage, car payments, student loans, and credit card debt.

lien: A legal claim against an **asset,** usually used to secure a loan.

living will: A legal document used to specify what, if any, life-prolonging measures a person wants if he or she becomes terminally ill or incapacitated.

load: A sales charge or commission paid to a broker or other third-party when **mutual funds** are bought or sold. Front-end loads are sometimes incurred when an investor purchases the shares and back-end loads are sometimes incurred when investors sell the shares.

marriage tax penalty: A feature of the U.S. tax system that results in married couples paying more in taxes than they would if they were single.

mutual fund: An investment that allows thousands of investors to pool their money to purchase **stocks, bonds,** or other types of investments, depending on the objectives of the fund.

net worth: The value of all of a person's **assets** (anything owned that has a monetary value) minus all of the person's **liabilities** (amounts owed to others).

nonmarital agreement: A written agreement between two unmarried people living together, spelling out how their finances will be handled.

PMI: Private mortgage insurance; insurance that protects a lender if a borrower defaults on a mortgage. Lenders require PMI if the mortgage exceeds 80 percent of the appraised value of the home.

points: Finance charges paid by a borrower when a loan is initiated. One point is worth 1 percent of the loan amount. Borrowers can "buy down" an interest rate to get a lower rate by paying points up-front.

probate: A court process to determine the validity of a **will** and oversee the distribution of property upon the owner's death.

risk tolerance: An investor's ability to tolerate fluctuations in the value of an investment in the expectation of receiving a higher return.

rollover: Reinvestment of a distribution from a qualified retirement plan into an IRA or another qualified plan in order to retain its tax-deferred status and avoid taxes and penalties for early withdrawal.

Rule of 72: A method of estimating the time it will take for a certain amount of money to double at a given interest rate (72 divided by the interest rate equals roughly the number of years it will take for the money to double).

standard deduction: The fixed amount deducted from adjusted gross income allowed taxpayers who don't itemize deductions.

stock: An ownership share in a corporation, entitling the investor to a pro rata share of the corporation's earnings and **assets.**

tenancy in common: Shared ownership of property by two or more people, giving each owner the legal right to pass on his or her share of the property to any other person in a written **will.** See also **joint tenancy with right of survivorship**.

term life insurance: Life insurance that pays the beneficiary a predetermined amount of money as long as the covered individual dies within a specified period of time (the term of the policy).

whole life insurance: Life insurance that covers an individual for his or her whole life rather than a specified term. Whole life policies contain a savings component that allows cash to accumulate over time.

will: A legal document that specifies how a person's belongings will be disposed of upon his or her death. It can also identify a legal guardian for children.

401(k): A **defined-contribution retirement plan** that allows participants to contribute pretax dollars to various investments.

Appendix B

Internet Resources

In this day and age, one of the greatest resources available to us is the World Wide Web. There are an astounding number of Web sites out there. Some are very helpful, but others may have a hidden agenda or be a scam. The Web sites listed in this appendix are reputable sources of information. Although many of them are there mainly to offer paid services, there are plenty of useful insights that you can get for free.

Banking

Bankrate.com, *www.bankrate.com*
StopATMFees.com, *www.stopatmfees.com*
Federal Trade Commission, *www.ftc.gov*
Federal Deposit Insurance Corporation, *www.fdic.gov*

Budgeting and Saving Money

Financial Planning at About.com, *http://financialplan.about.com*
Personal Budgeting and Money Saving Tips,
www.personal-budget-planning-saving-money.com
The Dollar Stretcher, *www.stretcher.com*
Frugal Living at About.com, *www.frugalliving.about.com*

Cars

Autos at MSN, *http://autos.msn.com*
Autobytel, *www.autobytel.com*
CarBuyingTips.com, *www.carbuyingtips.com*
CarInfo.com, *www.carinfo.com*
Consumer Reports, *www.consumerreports.org*
Edmunds, *www.edmunds.com*
IntelliChoice, *www.intellichoice.com*
Kelley Blue Book, *www.kbb.com*
AutoTrader.com, *www.autotrader.com*
LeaseGuide.com, *www.leaseguide.com*
Warranty Direct, *www.warrantydirect.com*
1SourceAutoWarranty.com, *www.1sourceautowarranty.com*

Consumer Information

Consumer World, *www.consumerworld.org*
ConsumerREVIEW, *www.consumerreview.com*
Better Business Bureau, *www.bbb.org*

Credit and Debt

National Foundation for Credit Counseling, *www.nfcc.org*
Consumer Credit Counseling Service, *www.cccsintl.org*
Bankrate.com, *www.bankrate.com*
Myvesta, *www.getoutofdebt.org*

Credit-Reporting Bureaus

Equifax, *www.equifax.com*
Experian, *www.experian.com*
TransUnion, *www.transunion.com*

Employee Ownership

National Center for Employee Ownership, *www.nceo.org*

Financial Advice

The Motley Fool, *www.fool.com*
CNNMoney, *http://money.cnn.com*
Financial Planning at About.com, *http://financialplan.about.com*
AskMen.com, *www.askmen.com*
MSN Money, *moneycentral.msn.com*
Quicken, *www.quicken.com*
MsMoney.com, *www.msmoney.com*
SmartMoney.com, *www.smartmoney.com*
NewlywedFinances.com, *www.newlywedfinances.com*

Financial Calculators

FinanCenter.com, *www.financenter.com*
Java Financial Calculators, *www.dinkytown.net*
Financial Calculators, *www.fincalc.com*

Fraud

The National Fraud Information Center, *www.fraud.org*
The Federal Trade Commission, *www.ftc.gov*
National Association of Attorneys General, *www.naag.org*
Contractor Fraud, *www.contractorfraud.net*

Home Buying

National Association of Realtors, ✐ *www.realtor.com*
Homestore.com, ✐ *www.homestore.com*

Insurance

Northwestern Mutual Financial Network, ✐ *www.lifeinsurance.com*
Insure.com, ✐ *www.insure.com*
Insurance Information Institute, ✐ *www.iii.org*
Health Insurance Association of America, ✐ *www.hiaa.org*

Investing

Morningstar.com, ✐ *www.morningstar.com*
Investing Online Resource Center, ✐ *www.investingonline.org*
Savings Bonds from the Treasury Department, ✐ *www.savingsbond.gov*

Job/Occupational Information

U.S. Bureau of Labor Statistics, ✐ *www.bls.gov*
Monster.com, ✐ *www.monster.com*
Job Search at About.com, ✐ *jobsearch.about.com*

Legal Advice

Nolo, ✐ *www.nolo.com*

Loans and Mortgages

Fair Credit Reporting Act, ✐ *www.ftc.gov/os/statutes/fcrajump.htm*
Mortgage Expo.com, ✐ *www.mortgageexpo.com*
E-Loan, ✐ *www.eloan.com*
HSH Associates, ✐ *www.hsh.com*
Mortgage101.com, ✐ *www.mortgage101.com*

Money and Young People

Kids' Money, ✐ *www.kidsmoney.org*
Young Money, ✐ *www.youngmoney.com*

Moving

National Association of Realtors, ✐ *www.homefair.com*
Fannie Mae, ✐ *www.fanniemae.com*
Moving Center, ✐ *www.movingcenter.com*

Renting

Rentlaw.com, ✐ *www.rentlaw.com*
ApartmentGuide.com, ✐ *www.apartmentguide.com*

Retirement

RetirementPlanner.org, *www.retirementplanner.org*
Social Security Administration, *www.ssa.gov*
American Association of Retired Persons, *www.aarp.org*
Profit Sharing Council of America, *www.401k.org*
Roth IRA, *www.rothira.com*

Student Loans

Northwest Education Loan Association, *www.nela.net*
Sallie Mae, *www.salliemae.com*

Taxes

H&R Block, *www.hrblock.com*
WorldWideWeb Tax, *wwwebtax.com*
Internal Revenue Service (IRS), *www.irs.gov*
TurboTax software, *www.turbotax.com*
National Association of Tax Professionals, *www.taxprofessionals.com*

Index

THE EVERYTHING SERIES!

BUSINESS & PERSONAL FINANCE

Everything® Accounting Book
Everything® Budgeting Book
Everything® Business Planning Book
Everything® Coaching and Mentoring Book
Everything® Fundraising Book
Everything® Get Out of Debt Book
Everything® Grant Writing Book
Everything® Home-Based Business Book, 2nd Ed.
Everything® Homebuying Book, 2nd Ed.
Everything® Homeselling Book, 2nd Ed.
Everything® Investing Book, 2nd Ed.
Everything® Landlording Book
Everything® Leadership Book
Everything® Managing People Book, 2nd Ed.
Everything® Negotiating Book
Everything® Online Auctions Book
Everything® Online Business Book
Everything® Personal Finance Book
Everything® Personal Finance in Your 20s and 30s Book
Everything® Project Management Book
Everything® Real Estate Investing Book
Everything® Robert's Rules Book, $7.95
Everything® Selling Book
Everything® Start Your Own Business Book, 2nd Ed.
Everything® Wills & Estate Planning Book

COOKING

Everything® Barbecue Cookbook
Everything® Bartender's Book, $9.95
Everything® Chinese Cookbook
Everything® Classic Recipes Book
Everything® Cocktail Parties and Drinks Book
Everything® College Cookbook
Everything® Cooking for Baby and Toddler Book
Everything® Cooking for Two Cookbook
Everything® Diabetes Cookbook
Everything® Easy Gourmet Cookbook
Everything® Fondue Cookbook
Everything® Fondue Party Book
Everything® Gluten-Free Cookbook
Everything® Glycemic Index Cookbook
Everything® Grilling Cookbook

Everything® Healthy Meals in Minutes Cookbook
Everything® Holiday Cookbook
Everything® Indian Cookbook
Everything® Italian Cookbook
Everything® Low-Carb Cookbook
Everything® Low-Fat High-Flavor Cookbook
Everything® Low-Salt Cookbook
Everything® Meals for a Month Cookbook
Everything® Mediterranean Cookbook
Everything® Mexican Cookbook
Everything® One-Pot Cookbook
Everything® Quick and Easy 30-Minute, 5-Ingredient Cookbook
Everything® Quick Meals Cookbook
Everything® Slow Cooker Cookbook
Everything® Slow Cooking for a Crowd Cookbook
Everything® Soup Cookbook
Everything® Tex-Mex Cookbook
Everything® Thai Cookbook
Everything® Vegetarian Cookbook
Everything® Wild Game Cookbook
Everything® Wine Book, 2nd Ed.

GAMES

Everything® 15-Minute Sudoku Book, $9.95
Everything® 30-Minute Sudoku Book, $9.95
Everything® Blackjack Strategy Book
Everything® Brain Strain Book, $9.95
Everything® Bridge Book
Everything® Card Games Book
Everything® Card Tricks Book, $9.95
Everything® Casino Gambling Book, 2nd Ed.
Everything® Chess Basics Book
Everything® Craps Strategy Book
Everything® Crossword and Puzzle Book
Everything® Crossword Challenge Book
Everything® Cryptograms Book, $9.95
Everything® Easy Crosswords Book
Everything® Easy Kakuro Book, $9.95
Everything® Games Book, 2nd Ed.
Everything® Giant Sudoku Book, $9.95
Everything® Kakuro Challenge Book, $9.95
Everything® Large-Print Crossword Challenge Book
Everything® Large-Print Crosswords Book
Everything® Lateral Thinking Puzzles Book, $9.95
Everything® Mazes Book

Everything® Pencil Puzzles Book, $9.95
Everything® Poker Strategy Book
Everything® Pool & Billiards Book
Everything® Test Your IQ Book, $9.95
Everything® Texas Hold 'Em Book, $9.95
Everything® Travel Crosswords Book, $9.95
Everything® Word Games Challenge Book
Everything® Word Search Book

HEALTH

Everything® Alzheimer's Book
Everything® Diabetes Book
Everything® Health Guide to Adult Bipolar Disorder
Everything® Health Guide to Controlling Anxiety
Everything® Health Guide to Fibromyalgia
Everything® Health Guide to Thyroid Disease
Everything® Hypnosis Book
Everything® Low Cholesterol Book
Everything® Massage Book
Everything® Menopause Book
Everything® Nutrition Book
Everything® Reflexology Book
Everything® Stress Management Book

HISTORY

Everything® American Government Book
Everything® American History Book
Everything® Civil War Book
Everything® Freemasons Book
Everything® Irish History & Heritage Book
Everything® Middle East Book

HOBBIES

Everything® Candlemaking Book
Everything® Cartooning Book
Everything® Coin Collecting Book
Everything® Drawing Book
Everything® Family Tree Book, 2nd Ed.
Everything® Knitting Book
Everything® Knots Book
Everything® Photography Book
Everything® Quilting Book
Everything® Scrapbooking Book
Everything® Sewing Book
Everything® Woodworking Book

Bolded titles are new additions to the series.
All Everything® books are priced at $12.95 or $14.95, unless otherwise stated. Prices subject to change without notice.

HOME IMPROVEMENT

Everything® Feng Shui Book
Everything® Feng Shui Decluttering Book, $9.95
Everything® Fix-It Book
Everything® Home Decorating Book
Everything® Home Storage Solutions Book
Everything® Homebuilding Book
Everything® Lawn Care Book
Everything® Organize Your Home Book

KIDS' BOOKS

All titles are $7.95

Everything® Kids' Animal Puzzle & Activity Book
Everything® Kids' Baseball Book, 4th Ed.
Everything® Kids' Bible Trivia Book
Everything® Kids' Bugs Book
Everything® Kids' Cars and Trucks Puzzle & Activity Book
Everything® Kids' Christmas Puzzle & Activity Book
Everything® Kids' Cookbook
Everything® Kids' Crazy Puzzles Book
Everything® Kids' Dinosaurs Book
Everything® Kids' First Spanish Puzzle and Activity Book
Everything® Kids' Gross Hidden Pictures Book
Everything® Kids' Gross Jokes Book
Everything® Kids' Gross Mazes Book
Everything® Kids' Gross Puzzle and Activity Book
Everything® Kids' Halloween Puzzle & Activity Book
Everything® Kids' Hidden Pictures Book
Everything® Kids' Horses Book
Everything® Kids' Joke Book
Everything® Kids' Knock Knock Book
Everything® Kids' Learning Spanish Book
Everything® Kids' Math Puzzles Book
Everything® Kids' Mazes Book
Everything® Kids' Money Book
Everything® Kids' Nature Book
Everything® Kids' Pirates Puzzle and Activity Book
Everything® Kids' Princess Puzzle and Activity Book
Everything® Kids' Puzzle Book
Everything® Kids' Riddles & Brain Teasers Book
Everything® Kids' Science Experiments Book
Everything® Kids' Sharks Book
Everything® Kids' Soccer Book
Everything® Kids' Travel Activity Book

KIDS' STORY BOOKS

Everything® Fairy Tales Book

LANGUAGE

Everything® Conversational Chinese Book with CD, $19.95
Everything® Conversational Japanese Book with CD, $19.95
Everything® French Grammar Book
Everything® French Phrase Book, $9.95
Everything® French Verb Book, $9.95
Everything® German Practice Book with CD, $19.95
Everything® Inglés Book
Everything® Learning French Book
Everything® Learning German Book
Everything® Learning Italian Book
Everything® Learning Latin Book
Everything® Learning Spanish Book
Everything® Russian Practice Book with CD, $19.95
Everything® Sign Language Book
Everything® Spanish Grammar Book
Everything® Spanish Phrase Book, $9.95
Everything® Spanish Practice Book with CD, $19.95
Everything® Spanish Verb Book, $9.95

MUSIC

Everything® Drums Book with CD, $19.95
Everything® Guitar Book
Everything® Guitar Chords Book with CD, $19.95
Everything® Home Recording Book
Everything® Music Theory Book with CD, $19.95
Everything® Reading Music Book with CD, $19.95
Everything® Rock & Blues Guitar Book (with CD), $19.95
Everything® Songwriting Book

NEW AGE

Everything® Astrology Book, 2nd Ed.
Everything® Birthday Personology Book
Everything® Dreams Book, 2nd Ed.
Everything® Love Signs Book, $9.95
Everything® Numerology Book
Everything® Paganism Book
Everything® Palmistry Book
Everything® Psychic Book
Everything® Reiki Book
Everything® Sex Signs Book, $9.95
Everything® Tarot Book, 2nd Ed.
Everything® Wicca and Witchcraft Book

PARENTING

Everything® Baby Names Book, 2nd Ed.
Everything® Baby Shower Book
Everything® Baby's First Food Book
Everything® Baby's First Year Book
Everything® Birthing Book
Everything® Breastfeeding Book
Everything® Father-to-Be Book
Everything® Father's First Year Book
Everything® Get Ready for Baby Book
Everything® Get Your Baby to Sleep Book, $9.95
Everything® Getting Pregnant Book
Everything® Guide to Raising a One-Year-Old
Everything® Guide to Raising a Two-Year-Old
Everything® Homeschooling Book
Everything® Mother's First Year Book
Everything® Parent's Guide to Children and Divorce
Everything® Parent's Guide to Children with ADD/ADHD
Everything® Parent's Guide to Children with Asperger's Syndrome
Everything® Parent's Guide to Children with Autism
Everything® Parent's Guide to Children with Bipolar Disorder
Everything® Parent's Guide to Children with Dyslexia
Everything® Parent's Guide to Positive Discipline
Everything® Parent's Guide to Raising a Successful Child
Everything® Parent's Guide to Raising Boys
Everything® Parent's Guide to Raising Siblings
Everything® Parent's Guide to Sensory Integration Disorder
Everything® Parent's Guide to Tantrums
Everything® Parent's Guide to the Overweight Child
Everything® Parent's Guide to the Strong-Willed Child
Everything® Parenting a Teenager Book
Everything® Potty Training Book, $9.95
Everything® Pregnancy Book, 2nd Ed.
Everything® Pregnancy Fitness Book
Everything® Pregnancy Nutrition Book
Everything® Pregnancy Organizer, 2nd Ed., $16.95
Everything® Toddler Activities Book
Everything® Toddler Book
Everything® Tween Book
Everything® Twins, Triplets, and More Book

PETS

Everything® Aquarium Book
Everything® Boxer Book
Everything® Cat Book, 2nd Ed.
Everything® Chihuahua Book
Everything® Dachshund Book
Everything® Dog Book
Everything® Dog Health Book
Everything® Dog Owner's Organizer, $16.95
Everything® Dog Training and Tricks Book
Everything® German Shepherd Book
Everything® Golden Retriever Book
Everything® Horse Book
Everything® Horse Care Book
Everything® Horseback Riding Book
Everything® Labrador Retriever Book
Everything® Poodle Book
Everything® Pug Book
Everything® Puppy Book
Everything® Rottweiler Book
Everything® Small Dogs Book
Everything® Tropical Fish Book
Everything® Yorkshire Terrier Book

REFERENCE

Everything® Blogging Book
Everything® Build Your Vocabulary Book
Everything® Car Care Book
Everything® Classical Mythology Book
Everything® Da Vinci Book
Everything® Divorce Book
Everything® Einstein Book
Everything® Etiquette Book, 2nd Ed.
Everything® Inventions and Patents Book
Everything® Mafia Book
Everything® Philosophy Book
Everything® Psychology Book
Everything® Shakespeare Book

RELIGION

Everything® Angels Book
Everything® Bible Book
Everything® Buddhism Book
Everything® Catholicism Book
Everything® Christianity Book
Everything® History of the Bible Book
Everything® Jesus Book
Everything® Jewish History & Heritage Book
Everything® Judaism Book
Everything® Kabbalah Book
Everything® Koran Book
Everything® Mary Book

Everything® Mary Magdalene Book
Everything® Prayer Book
Everything® Saints Book
Everything® Torah Book
Everything® Understanding Islam Book
Everything® World's Religions Book
Everything® Zen Book

SCHOOL & CAREERS

Everything® Alternative Careers Book
Everything® Career Tests Book
Everything® College Major Test Book
Everything® College Survival Book, 2nd Ed.
Everything® Cover Letter Book, 2nd Ed.
Everything® Filmmaking Book
Everything® Get-a-Job Book
Everything® Guide to Being a Paralegal
Everything® Guide to Being a Real Estate Agent
Everything® Guide to Being a Sales Rep
Everything® Guide to Careers in Health Care
Everything® Guide to Careers in Law Enforcement
Everything® Guide to Government Jobs
Everything® Guide to Starting and Running a Restaurant
Everything® Job Interview Book
Everything® New Nurse Book
Everything® New Teacher Book
Everything® Paying for College Book
Everything® Practice Interview Book
Everything® Resume Book, 2nd Ed.
Everything® Study Book

SELF-HELP

Everything® Dating Book, 2nd Ed.
Everything® Great Sex Book
Everything® Kama Sutra Book
Everything® Self-Esteem Book

SPORTS & FITNESS

Everything® Easy Fitness Book
Everything® Fishing Book
Everything® Golf Instruction Book
Everything® Pilates Book
Everything® Running Book
Everything® Weight Training Book
Everything® Yoga Book

TRAVEL

Everything® Family Guide to Cruise Vacations
Everything® Family Guide to Hawaii

Everything® Family Guide to Las Vegas, 2nd Ed.
Everything® Family Guide to Mexico
Everything® Family Guide to New York City, 2nd Ed.
Everything® Family Guide to RV Travel & Campgrounds
Everything® Family Guide to the Caribbean
Everything® Family Guide to the Walt Disney World Resort®, Universal Studios®, and Greater Orlando, 4th Ed.
Everything® Family Guide to Timeshares
Everything® Family Guide to Washington D.C., 2nd Ed.
Everything® Guide to New England

WEDDINGS

Everything® Bachelorette Party Book, $9.95
Everything® Bridesmaid Book, $9.95
Everything® Destination Wedding Book
Everything® Elopement Book, $9.95
Everything® Father of the Bride Book, $9.95
Everything® Groom Book, $9.95
Everything® Mother of the Bride Book, $9.95
Everything® Outdoor Wedding Book
Everything® Wedding Book, 3rd Ed.
Everything® Wedding Checklist, $9.95
Everything® Wedding Etiquette Book, $9.95
Everything® Wedding Organizer, 2nd Ed., $16.95
Everything® Wedding Shower Book, $9.95
Everything® Wedding Vows Book, $9.95
Everything® Wedding Workout Book
Everything® Weddings on a Budget Book, $9.95

WRITING

Everything® Creative Writing Book
Everything® Get Published Book, 2nd Ed.
Everything® Grammar and Style Book
Everything® Guide to Writing a Book Proposal
Everything® Guide to Writing a Novel
Everything® Guide to Writing Children's Books
Everything® Guide to Writing Research Papers
Everything® Screenwriting Book
Everything® Writing Poetry Book
Everything® Writing Well Book

Available wherever books are sold!
To order, call 800-258-0929, or visit us at *www.everything.com*
Everything® and everything.com® are registered trademarks of F+W Publications, Inc.